In this eye-opening book Jonathan Bernis ⟨...⟩ conflict in the Middle East relate to us today. He helps us u⟨...⟩ significance of the times we live in from a historical, biblical, and Messianic perspective and reminds us that no matter what, God is still on His throne and He is still in control.

—ROBERT MORRIS
FOUNDING SENIOR PASTOR, GATEWAY CHURCH
BEST-SELLING AUTHOR, *THE BLESSED LIFE*, *THE GOD I NEVER KNEW*,
AND *FREQUENCY*

Jonathan Bernis' book is a must-read for anyone who wants to understand the conflict in the Middle East and the fight for the truth about Israel. With his clear analysis written in everyday terms, Jonathan gives a powerful message of God's purpose for Israel in today's world.

—AMBASSADOR DANNY AYALON
ISRAELI AMBASSADOR TO THE UNITED STATES, 2002–2006

Israel is the epicenter of all end-times activity. Every Believer must be on God's side of the fence involving Israel. Only a God-ordained "teacher" and Messianic Jewish rabbi like Jonathan Bernis can make this complex issue simple and easy to understand.

—SID ROTH
HOST, *IT'S SUPERNATURAL!*

In *A Lasting Peace*, Rabbi Jonathan Bernis not only gives you a masterful review of the history and biblical context of modern Israel; he also answers the question "What happens now?" With Iran, Syria, Turkey, and Russia all having active military operations in the Middle East, the asymmetrical war with the Palestinian Authority could quickly turn into a regional conflict with global impact. The news headlines today all point to a future conflict that could threaten Israel's existence. To understand today's headlines, you need to read this book and find the answer to this question: Is lasting peace in the Middle East possible?

—GORDON ROBERTSON
CEO, THE CHRISTIAN BROADCASTING NETWORK

My friend Rabbi Jonathan Bernis has written a new book that I believe every Christian leader and Believer in Jesus Christ should read, *A Lasting Peace*. He masterfully leads the reader to an understanding of world events unfolding before our own eyes in the Middle East, events that are taking place in direct confirmation of end-time prophecy recorded thousands of years ago in Scripture, including the attack on Israel and the persecution of Christians. This makes the message of this book relevant and worthy of our careful attention.

As Christians, we must stay informed of what is happening and comprehend the conflict of various kinds in the Middle East and elsewhere. At times, however, all of this may seem too complex and rather difficult to understand well. Thankfully, Jonathan is anointed by the Holy Spirit of God to write in such a way as to clearly explain these conflicts and world events from a historical and biblical standpoint in light of the revelation of prophecy so the reader will finally be able to both fully understand what is happening and know how to personally respond.

The Word of God is eternally true, and it assures us that God is love and that His will is that none should perish but all should receive salvation and eternal life through the only way, truth, and life: Jesus Christ. The only solution to the conflict between Jews and Arabs, or between any other groups, is Jesus. Therefore, we must watch, pray, and speak out! At its core that is the message of *A Lasting Peace*, a book I wholeheartedly recommend you prayerfully read.

—APOSTLE GUILLERMO MALDONADO
KING JESUS INTERNATIONAL MINISTRY

A LASTING PEACE

JONATHAN BERNIS

CHARISMA
HOUSE

Most CHARISMA HOUSE BOOK GROUP products are available at special quantity discounts for bulk purchase for sales promotions, premiums, fund-raising, and educational needs. For details, write Charisma House Book Group, 600 Rinehart Road, Lake Mary, Florida 32746, or telephone (407) 333-0600.

A LASTING PEACE by Jonathan Bernis
Published by Charisma House
Charisma Media/Charisma House Book Group
600 Rinehart Road
Lake Mary, Florida 32746
www.charismahouse.com

Unless otherwise noted, all Scripture quotations are taken from the Holy Bible, New International Version®, NIV®. Copyright © 1973, 1978, 1984, 2011 by Biblica, Inc.®. Used by permission of Zondervan. All rights reserved worldwide. www.zondervan.com. The "NIV" and "New International Version" are trademarks registered in the United States Patent and Trademark Office by Biblica, Inc.®

Scripture quotations marked TLV are taken from the Tree of Life Translation of the Bible. Copyright © 2015 by The Messianic Jewish Family Bible Society.

Visit the author's website at www.jewishvoice.org.

Library of Congress Cataloging-in-Publication Data:
An application to register this book for cataloging has been submitted to the Library of Congress.

International Standard Book Number: 978-1-62999-586-1 (trade paper);
978-1-62999-588-5 (hardback); 978-1-62999-587-8 (e-book)

While the author has made every effort to provide accurate internet addresses at the time of publication, neither the publisher nor the author assumes any responsibility for errors or for changes that occur after publication. Further, the publisher does not have any control over and does not assume any responsibility for author or third-party websites or their content.

19 20 21 22 23 — 987654321
Printed in the United States of America

CONTENTS

CHAPTER 1

BLOODSHED IN ISRAEL

The Zionist regime will soon be destroyed, and this
generation will be witness to its destruction.
—HOJATOLESLAM ALI SHIRAZI,
SUPREME LEADER AYATOLLAH ALI KHAMENEI'S
REPRESENTATIVE TO THE IRANIAN REVOLUTIONARY GUARD

PEOPLE WHO LIVE in Israel never know when an attack is going to come. They have to be ready all the time.

Since 2001, more than 28,000 rockets have been fired into Israel from Palestinian territory—28,352 of them to be exact.[1] That works out to a little over four rockets every day for seventeen and a half years.

Of course, it would be ridiculous to say that four rockets fall on Israel in an average day. Some days there are dozens, even hundreds of them. Other days there are none at all. Go online to israelhasbeenrocketfreefor .com, and you'll find a digital clock that tells you how long it has been since the last attack on Israel. The clock resets every time a rocket falls.

Many Israelis keep well-stocked first aid kits on hand, full of essential supplies such as bandages and even gas masks. They also know where the nearest bomb shelter is. Bomb shelters may be a thing of the past for most Americans—a relic from the Cold War with the Soviet Union. But many Israeli neighborhoods have them and use them on a regular basis.

Bear in mind that the rockets fired into Israel are not aimed at any specific targets. The Palestinians who fire them don't care what they destroy or whom they kill. If a rocket smashes into an Israeli military base, the Palestinians are delighted. But a school or a hospital would make them just as happy. Their desire is to kill Jews. Any Jew will do.

According to the Israeli government, "Although Israel's Iron Dome Missile Defense system stops some of the attacks, most rockets are capable of reaching Israel's biggest cities. More than half a million Israelis have less than 60 seconds to find shelter after a rocket is launched from Gaza into Israel. Many have only 15 seconds."[2]

As I write these words, I am in Tiberius, Israel, where a rocket attack was just launched from Syria by Iran. My hotel shook from the blasts as Israel's Dome system intercepted and destroyed several of the missiles. Some missiles did make it through and exploded in the Golan Heights just a few miles from here. Fortunately there were no casualties and no significant damage. Tensions on Israel's border with Syria have been intensifying and will continue to do so as long as Iran is free to operate there. Of course, Israeli jets were in the air within minutes and attacked a number of Iranian military bases in response.

But missile attacks are not the only threat Israel faces.

FROM ROCKETS TO KNIVES

According to a December 2015 article in the *Washington Post*, near-daily Palestinian attacks against Israeli civilians and soldiers cause fear and anger in Israeli society. The *Post* reported that a series of deadly attacks did not "fit past patterns,"[3] and Prime Minister Benjamin Netanyahu described these attacks by individuals as "a new kind of terrorism."[4]

The *Post* explained:

> Young Palestinians with kitchen knives are waging a ceaseless campaign of near-suicidal violence....Four attacks occurred in the past 48 hours alone—two stabbings and two vehicular assaults. There have been about 120 attacks and attempted assaults by Palestinians against Israelis since early October, an average of more than one a day. At least 20 Israelis have been killed; more than 80 Palestinians have been shot dead by security forces and armed civilians during the assaults.[5]

One knifing victim was Aharon Banita Bennett, a young father pushing his child's stroller while out walking with his family. In another attack, the four children of Eitam and Naama Henkin watched from the back seat of the family's car as their parents were shot to death in the front seat. A victim in another attack, Nehemia Lavi, was an "activist for Jewish settlements"[6]; another victim was a peace activist named Richard Lakin, "whose Facebook page called for the sides to 'co-exist.'"[7]

The *Washington Post* article reported that teens were responsible for more than fifty attacks at the time,[8] which means that violence is deeply ingrained in the younger generation and so is likely to continue far into the future. What may be even worse is a survey by the Palestinian Center for Policy and Survey Research found that those who "support the knife attacks" and "armed struggle against Israel" are in the majority among Palestinians.[9]

This violence has continued to sweep through Israel. The Israel Ministry of Foreign Affairs states the following about the period between September 2015 and June 2017:

- There were "180 stabbing attacks and 124 attempted stabbings, 150 shootings, 58 vehicular (ramming) attacks and one vehicular (bus) bombing."[10]

- "In 2016, 12 vehicular ramming attacks and 100 stabbing attacks were thwarted by security forces."[11]

- "According to the Foreign Ministry website, since September 2015, 50 people have been killed in terrorist attacks and 759 people (including four Palestinians) injured."[12]

If you are someone who tries to keep abreast of what's going on in this world of ours, I realize that I'm not telling you anything new. You may not have known the extent of the recent bombings and knife attacks in the Middle East, but certainly you were aware that they exist. Anyone who occasionally reads a newspaper or watches a national news broadcast knows that the Middle East has been a boiling cauldron of strife and bloodshed for centuries. The killings have continued nonstop since Israel officially became a country in 1948, and the carnage has increased as human beings have developed more efficient ways to kill one another.

PALESTINIANS ARE VICTIMS TOO

I want to make it clear that my intent is not to point a finger at the Palestinian people or try to make them sound inherently evil. They are human beings created in the image of God, as are the Jews who live in Israel. But for many of them, every ounce of human compassion and conscience has been swept away by a river of unreasoning hatred. And so bloodshed and war go on and on with no end in sight, despite the dozens of attempts and countless millions of dollars that have been invested in the effort to bring a lasting peace to the Middle East.

And while I do not support everything Israel does (Israelis have made plenty of mistakes over the years), I do believe that its leaders have done everything possible to live in peace with its neighbors. Israel has made dozens of concessions in response to their demands. Israel has returned land it won—not through acts of aggression but because it was attacked and fought back.[13]

Tragically very few of its overtures of friendship have improved conditions in the Middle East. So Israel has become adept at the practice of "an eye for an eye, a tooth for a tooth." In other words, "If you hit me, I'll hit you back—and harder."

This Jewish response to continual aggression against Israel is understandable. Current Israeli prime minister Benjamin Netanyahu wrote in his book *A Durable Peace*:

> I am convinced of one thing: The Jewish people will not get another chance. There are only so many miracles that history can provide a people, and the Jews have had more than their share. After unparalleled adversity the Jews came back to life in the modern State of Israel. For better or worse, the Jewish future is centered on the future of that state. Therefore we must be extra careful not to toy with Israel's security or jeopardize its defenses, even as we pursue peace with our neighbors, for what is at stake is the destiny of an entire people.[14]

And so thousands of Palestinians have been injured and killed due to their leaders' insistence on attacking Israel, just as hundreds of thousands of Muslims throughout the Middle East have died at the hands of Islamic extremists.

In *A Durable Peace,* Netanyahu talks about a discussion he had with Zian Zemin, the president of China, in 1999. The president pointed out that the Chinese and Jewish people make up two of the world's oldest civilizations, both stretching back thousands of years. Netanyahu agreed, adding India to the list of long-lived civilizations.[15] Netanyahu recounts their continued exchange, beginning with his remarks to Zemin:

> "But there are one or two differences between us.... For instance, how many Chinese are there?"
>
> "1.2 billion," replied Zian Zemin.
>
> "How many Indians are there?" I pressed on.
>
> "About 1 billion."
>
> "Now how many Jews are there?" I queried.
>
> No answer.
>
> "There are 12 million Jews in the world," I said.
>
> Several Chinese jaws dropped in the room, understandably, given that this number could be contained in an enlarged suburb of Beijing.[16]

When the Chinese president asked why there are so few Jews despite a history that stretches back over four thousand years, Netanyahu replied:

> You, the Chinese, kept China; the Indians kept India; but we Jews lost our land and were dispersed to the four corners of the earth. From this sprang all our calamities, culminating in our greatest catastrophe in the twentieth century. This is why for the last two thousand years we have been trying to retrieve our homeland and re-create our independent state there.[17]

THE ELUSIVE SEARCH FOR PEACE

The history of the Middle East is filled with the remnants of many shattered peace treaties. Over the past one hundred years there have been at least ten attempts to bring peace between Jews and Arabs in the Middle East. They include the following:

- **1919: The Faisal-Weizmann Agreement** following World War I was a very "short-lived agreement for Arab-Jewish cooperation on the development" of Jewish and Palestinian homelands in the Middle East.[18]

- **1949: The Armistice Agreements** were signed at the end of the 1948 Arab-Israeli War and "established armistice lines between Israel and the West Bank, also known as the Green Line." This boundary lasted until the 1967 Six-Day War.[19]

- **1978: The Camp David Accords** were signed by Egyptian President Anwar Sadat and Israeli Prime Minister Menachem Begin after twelve days of secret discussions at Camp David.[20] Sadat was later assassinated.

- **1993: The Oslo Accords** constituted "the first direct, face-to-face agreement between Israel and political representatives of Palestinians" and the first time any "Palestinian factions publicly acknowledged Israel's right to exist."[21]

- **2000: The Camp David Summit** failed to establish a "final status settlement"[22] between Israel and the Palestinians. In attendance were Bill Clinton, Israeli Prime Minister Ehud Barak, and chairman of the Palestinian Authority Yasser Arafat.[23]

- **2002: The Road Map for Peace** consisted of principles "first outlined by US President George W. Bush in a speech on June 24, 2002."[24] As had been done many times before, Bush "called for an independent Palestinian state" that lived beside Israel in peace.[25]

WHAT DOES THE BIBLE SAY?

The ancient Hebrew prophets foresaw many bloody battles in the Middle East, which they described in gory detail. We'll take a brief look at some of these prophecies in later sections of this book. The New Testament Book of Revelation also contains a powerful description of a cataclysmic battle that takes place at the end of the age. Yeshua (Jesus) Himself said that we could expect "wars and rumors of wars" (Matt. 24:6) until His return.

Does this mean that Believers should sit on the sidelines and watch the violence continue? Are we supposed to throw up our hands and say, "Oh well, it's all preordained, so there's nothing we can do about it"?

I don't see it that way, largely because of something else Yeshua said: "Blessed are the peacemakers, for they will be called children of God" (Matt. 5:9). I believe that God wants and expects His people to work for peace, even when war seems inevitable. And He wouldn't expect us to work for peace if it were unachievable.

In other words, what we do can make a difference in Israel and the rest of the Middle East. Our actions can save lives and spare innocent children and families unnecessary pain and suffering. We can put peace in the hearts of people whose lives have been filled with anxiety and fear.

Jews Around the World Are Suffering

As president and CEO of Jewish Voice Ministries, I often travel to Israel and countries where Jews are waiting for a chance to move to Israel and start new lives there, which they call *making Aliyah.*

In Ethiopia, for example, there are thousands of desperately poor Jews called the Beta Israel. Many are suffering and dying due to a lack of basic medicines and access to health care. As a direct result, we at Jewish Voice Ministries go there to provide the treatments they desperately need. Thousands of people, many of them children, are suffering terribly.

Some of these precious people have been beaten or burned out of their homes. They have been blocked from finding decent jobs. They are despised and desperately want to start new lives in Israel. They are accused of having "the Buda" (the "evil eye," which is presumably able to make non-Jews sick when these people look at them), and some say they turn themselves into bloodthirsty hyenas that roam the countryside at night looking for victims.[26]

It breaks my heart to see the way these kind and gentle people are treated by their neighbors. But I have discovered that this type of treatment of Jews is not unique to Ethiopia, nor is it unique to the Beta Israel. Jews all over the world have been treated in similar ways, especially in predominantly Arab countries of the Middle East.

I have listened to them tell their stories. Jewish children have told me about attending public primary schools where they were taught that Jews were monsters who killed children and drank their blood as part of their religious rituals. Others told of how they felt at recess when Muslim children pretended to be mowing down Jews with automatic weapons while teachers looked on approvingly.

I could go on and on about what Jewish people have suffered at the hands of their Arab cousins. I don't want to pretend that no Arabs have suffered at the hands of Jews. But if Arabic children are taught to hate Jews from a very early age and are taught that Jews are monsters who deserve to be killed, then what hope is there for a lasting, just peace?

It is also true that despite what the Jews have endured, the Arabs have somehow succeeded in making most of the world think that Jews are always the aggressors and Arabs are always their victims. The Palestinians fire rocket after rocket into Israel in an attempt to kill and maim as many Jews as possible, and the world blames Israel! Palestinians and other Arabs have waged constant war on Israel since 1948, and the world sees Israel as the aggressor!

One of the most important ways we can work to build a lasting peace in the Middle East is by taking the time to look beyond the propaganda and find out what is really going on there. We can take the time to study and understand the history that has led to the current situation. We can stop blaming the Jews for situations that are not their fault and understand that the Jewish people have the right to defend themselves. We can learn about all the concessions the nation of Israel has made in attempting to achieve a lasting peace with its neighbors and not expect it to continue giving, giving, giving, and getting nothing in return.

Article 11 of the Universal Declaration of Human Rights says, "Everyone charged with a penal offence has the right to be presumed innocent until proved guilty according to law in a public trial at which he has had all the guarantees necessary for his defence."[27] Yet for most of the world the Jews are always presumed guilty, even before the evidence has been heard.

In summary, we can promote peace and stand with the Israelis by giving them the same respect we give all other human beings.

CHAPTER 2

THE GROWING CONFLICT

Islam was never a religion of peace. Islam is the religion of fighting.
—ISIS LEADER ABU BAKR AL-BAGHDADI

I N ORDER TO know how we should respond to the conflict in the Middle East, we have to understand what is really happening there. That's why I am writing this book. What we do is vitally important not only for the future of the Middle East but for the whole world.

The conflict that has its roots in the Middle East has spread around the world and is now claiming casualties in England, France, the United States, and many other countries. Here is a brief look at some of what we have seen over the past few years:

- **November 13, 2015:** A series of coordinated terror attacks in Paris killed 130 people and injured hundreds more. Ninety of those killed were gunned down while watching a rock concert.

- **December 2, 2015:** Fourteen people were shot dead at a company Christmas party in San Bernardino, California. The killers were a married couple who swore allegiance to Islamic State leader Baghdadi.

- **March 22, 2016:** Two suicide attacks killed thirty-two people in Brussels, Belgium.

- **July 14, 2016:** Eighty-six people died after a terrorist drove a truck through a large crowd celebrating Bastille Day in Nice, France.

- **December 19, 2016:** A terrorist with ties to the Islamic State drove a large truck through a Christmas market in central Berlin, killing twelve people and injuring forty-eight others.

- **May 22, 2017:** Twenty-two people were killed, many of them teenagers, when a suicide bomber set off an explosion "outside the main concert area"[1] as Ariana Grande fans left a concert in Manchester, England.

- **June 3, 2017:** Eight people were killed when terrorists drove their car through a crowd of pedestrians on the London Bridge and attacked others with knives.

- **August 17, 2017:** Fourteen people were killed in Barcelona when a driver plowed his van through a huge crowd of pedestrians. In August, Barcelona is full of tourists from around the world, and initial reports were that people from twenty-four countries had been either killed or injured.[2]

- **January 27, 2018:** In Kabul 103 people were killed and more than 230 were injured when an ambulance rigged with explosives detonated in the streets.

And of course no American who was alive on that day will ever forget the terror of September 11, 2001, when terrorist attacks on American soil in New York City killed 2,997 people, injured more than 6,000 more,[3] and caused some $10 billion in property damage.[4]

As we look at these terrible statistics, we wonder whether there could ever be a just, lasting peace in the Middle East. There is only one place to go as we search for the answer to this question: the beginning.

How Did It All Begin?

In the previous chapter we talked about the Jewish people's history, which stretches back nearly four thousand years. In comparison with this, most nations are relative newcomers to the world stage. (For example, it wasn't until the late 1700s that residents of the United States were referred to as Americans. Before that they were known as *colonists*.)

When you read the Tanakh (the Hebrew Scriptures), you will find many references to nations that existed at the same time as the ancient Jews. There are Amalekites, Ammonites, Amorites, Hittites, Jebusites, Midianites, and dozens more "ites," and of course the Philistines, the people group that famously produced a giant named Goliath.

When was the last time you ran into someone who told you that he or she was an Amorite, Jebusite, or Philistine? I'm being facetious, of course. That has never happened, because those people long ago disappeared from the face of the earth.

It is not my intent to bore you with a long, involved history of the Jewish people. This is not a book about anthropology. But in order to understand the current crisis that is burning out of control in the Middle East, it is necessary to have at least a rudimentary understanding of how the whole situation began.

The Jews trace their origins to the existence of a man named Abraham who was born right around 2000 BC. His story is told in the Book of Genesis, beginning in the eleventh chapter. Abraham is also mentioned in the Quran, the Muslim holy book. Why? Because both Jews and Arabs trace their origins back to Abraham—Jews to his son Isaac and Arabs (and therefore Muslims) to Isaac's half brother, Ishmael.

Ishmael, as you may remember, was the child of Hagar, who served as a slave for Abraham's wife, Sarah. When it seemed that despite God's promise of a son Sarah was unable to conceive, she urged her husband to father a child through Hagar.

Thus, Ishmael was born. When he was still a small boy, Sarah became pregnant with Isaac. Unfortunately Isaac's birth was not the beginning of one big happy family, as the Bible shows:

> The child grew and was weaned—Abraham made a big feast on the day Isaac was weaned. But Sarah saw the son of Hagar the Egyptian whom she had born to Abraham—making fun [of Isaac]. So she said to Abraham, "Drive out this female slave and her son, for the son of this female slave will not be an heir with my son—with Isaac."

Now the matter was very displeasing in Abraham's eyes on account of his son. But God said to Abraham, "Do not be displeased about the boy and your slave woman. Whatever Sarah says to you, listen to her voice. For through Isaac shall your seed be called. Yet I will also make the son of the slave woman into a nation, because he is your seed."

—GENESIS 21:8–13, TLV

This marks the first recorded instance of trouble between Arabs and Jews. Sadly, they have been squabbling ever since. It was before all this happened that Abraham became the father of the Jewish nation, as Genesis chapter 12 reports:

Then ADONAI said to Abram, "Get going out from your land, and from your relatives, and from your father's house, to the land that I will show you. My heart's desire is to make you into a great nation, to bless you, to make your name great so that you may be a blessing. My desire is to bless those who bless you, but whoever curses you I will curse, and in you all the families of the earth will be blessed."

—GENESIS 12:1–3, TLV

God not only blessed Abraham but also promised him a certain amount of land that would belong to him and his descendants forever. This includes the land upon which the modern nation of Israel has been built. Genesis 15:18–21 says, "On that day ADONAI cut a covenant with Abram, saying, 'I give this land to your seed, from the river of Egypt to the great river, the Euphrates River'" (TLV).

The promise is repeated to Isaac in the twenty-sixth chapter of Genesis and then again to his grandson Jacob in Genesis 28.

A BRIEF HISTORY OF ISRAEL

For the past four thousand years this land has belonged to the descendants of Abraham and Isaac, and it always will. Yet, tragically, for most of their history the people of Israel have not been able to live on the land God gave them. Instead, they have been scattered throughout the earth by a series of wars and other calamities. Yet no matter where they have gone—America, Russia, Europe, Ethiopia, or any other country—the Jewish people have always carried within their hearts a yearning for their ancestral land.

Some Jewish families have not seen the hills and valleys of Israel for hundreds of years. Yet although they have never seen it with their own eyes, they still think of this Promised Land as the home to which they long to return and build their futures.

Why is this? I believe there is only one reason: it is the fire of God burning in Jewish hearts. We Jews know that He gave us the land and said He would call us back to it in the last days. This is what is supposed to be, and we cannot rest until it becomes a reality.

Strangely enough, Abraham's descendants did not live on the land they were given for very long. Abraham lived and died there, and so did his son Isaac. But during the life of Abraham's grandson, Jacob (who was also known as Israel), a terrible famine chased the family from the land, and they settled in Egypt.

At first they prospered in Egypt. It was there that Jacob's twelve sons grew into a mighty nation of several million people. Because of their great numbers—and probably because they refused to assimilate but instead preserved their customs and belief in one God—the Hebrews came to be seen as a threat and were enslaved.

God sent Moses to free them from slavery, lead them out of Egypt, and take them back to the land God promised to Abraham and his descendants. It was not until about 1400 BC that the Israelites finally reentered the Promised Land under the direction of a great general named Joshua.

The Jews were home at last! For the next several hundred years they remained in the land God had given them. These were the glory days of great kings such as David and Solomon. It was the time when Solomon built the majestic temple dedicated to the worship of the one true God. They were years of prosperity and plenty for the Jewish people, but they would not last.

After the death of Solomon the kingdom was divided between his son, Rehoboam, and a man named Jeroboam, who had been one of Solomon's officials. The ten northern tribes became the kingdom of Israel. The southern kingdom, known as the kingdom of Judah, consisted of members of the tribes of Judah and Benjamin and some of the priestly tribe of Levi.

In 722 BC the nation of Israel was officially conquered by the Assyrians. The native people were uprooted from their lands and dispersed throughout the empire. After that they simply disappeared from history. You have probably heard them referred to as the Lost Tribes of Israel.

The kingdom of Judah continued for another 136 years, until 586 BC, when it fell to the Babylonians. The invaders destroyed the temple built by Solomon and carried most of the people off to Babylon. However, in 516 they returned home, rebuilt the city of Jerusalem (which had lain in ruins for seventy years), and also built a new temple, which is known as the Second Temple.

For the next five centuries the Jewish people lived in the land but were never in control of their own destiny. When Alexander the Great defeated the Persians, control of Judah passed to the Greeks. Then, through battles, control passed to the Seleucids and, after that, to Rome.

The period of Roman rule was marked by a series of increasingly violent revolts and uprisings. The Jewish people despised the Romans for meddling in their religion, even selecting rotating high priests.

Shortly before He was arrested and put to death, Yeshua prophesied that the day was coming when the temple would be torn down and no stone would be left unturned. (See Mark 13:1–2.) This dire prophecy was fulfilled in AD 70, when the Roman army utterly destroyed the temple and the city of Jerusalem. The Jewish historian Josephus estimated that more than one million Jews were slaughtered by the Romans, many of them burned alive. He vividly describes the horror that took place in Jerusalem that day:

> As they [Roman soldiers] neared the Sanctuary they pretended not even to hear Caesar's commands and urged the men in front to throw in more firebrands. The partisans were no longer in a position to help; everywhere was slaughter and flight. Most of the victims were peaceful citizens, weak and unarmed, butchered wherever they were caught. Round the Altar the heap of corpses grew higher and higher, while down the Sanctuary steps poured a river of blood and the bodies of those killed at the top slithered to the bottom.[5]

Even that bloody catastrophe was not the last Jewish attempt to regain control of their land from the hated Romans. That came in the form of the Bar Kokhba revolt, which was crushed by the Romans in AD 135. The Jews, once again dispersed throughout the empire and even forbidden to enter Jerusalem, became a wandering people, separated from their homeland.[6]

A LEGACY OF PERSECUTION

Since that time persecution has followed the Jews wherever they go. They have been blamed for causing plagues, falsely accused of using the blood of Christian babies to celebrate the Passover,[7] and often referred to as "Christ-killers."

Jews have been expelled from their homes and countries, had their lands and properties confiscated, and been imprisoned and killed. Hitler was not the first to try to destroy the Jews, although he was by far the most brutal and savage, murdering an estimated six million men, women, and children.

Yet throughout all those years of suffering, the Jewish people never lost hope that one day they would return to their Promised Land. "Next year in Jerusalem" has always been their hearts' cry. And throughout history there have been Jews in Jerusalem.

In her best-selling book *From Time Immemorial* author Joan Peters quotes a letter written from Jerusalem in 1491:

> There are not many Christians but there are many Jews, and these the Moslems persecute in various ways. Christians and Jews go about in Jerusalem in clothes considered fit only for wandering beggars.
>
> The Moslems know that the Jews think and even say that this is the Holy Land which has been promised to them and that those Jews who dwell there are regarded as holy by Jews elsewhere, because, in spite of all the troubles and sorrows inflicted on them by the Moslems, they refuse to leave the Land.[8]

Daily life was harsh and humiliating for Jews who lived in Jerusalem in the fifteenth century, but many felt it was worth the price they paid to live in the land of promise. For example, if a Jew came across a Muslim (then referred to as Moslem) while walking through the city, the Jew had to pass on the left, which was considered to be the side of Satan. They also had to step off the pavement to allow Muslims to pass, being sure not to touch them in the process.

Jews were humiliated in a number of similar ways. Peters reports that in the sixteenth century, six hundred out of seven hundred Jewish widows living in Palestine died from hunger-related causes.[9]

Yet despite the terrible hardships they faced, Jews have always desired to live in the land that was promised to their ancestor Abraham.

Jews Have Always Lived in Jerusalem

Once again, there has never been a time when there were no Jews living in Jerusalem. In 1864 a census found that there were only eighteen thousand people residing in the city of Jerusalem. Over half of these were Jews, a little over five thousand were Muslims, and the rest were Christians.[10] It is a myth to say that Jerusalem has been a Muslim city for centuries.

It wasn't until the late 1800s that thousands of Jewish people began returning to Israel, which was then under the control of the Turkish Ottoman Empire. These Jews came primarily from Eastern Europe and settled in the land as farmers.[11] Known as the First Aliyah, these settlers struggled to survive in a hostile environment. Early leaders such as Eliezer Ben-Yehuda, who revived the use of Hebrew as a language,[12] helped to prepare the way for other Jews to return. He even created a Hebrew dictionary to give the new arrivals a common language.[13]

Much of the major funding for Jews to return to Israel and buy land there came from the wealthy Rothschild banking family, particularly Walter Rothschild of England and Edmond de Rothschild of France.[14] The family gave large sums of money to provide the means necessary to establish the beginnings of the modern State of Israel.

Without the Rothschilds' help it would not have been possible for the early settlers to survive. Mitchell G. Bard, executive director of the nonprofit American-Israeli Cooperative Enterprise, writes about the difficult land they entered:

> For many centuries, Palestine was a sparsely populated, poorly cultivated, and widely neglected expanse of eroded hills, sandy

deserts, and malarial marshes.... The Report of the Palestine Royal Commission quotes an account of the Maritime Plain in 1913:

> The road leading from Gaza to the north was only a summer track suitable for transport by camels and carts...no orange groves, orchards or vineyards were to be seen until one reached [the Jewish village of] Yabna.... Houses were all of mud. No windows were anywhere to be seen. The ploughs used were of wood.... The yields were very poor.... The sanitary conditions in the village were horrible. Schools did not exist.... The western part, towards the sea, was almost a desert.... The villages in this area were few and thinly populated. Many ruins of villages were scattered over the area, as owing to the prevalence of malaria, many villages were deserted by their inhabitants.[15]

The Jews were not coming to steal Arab land. They were, instead, coming to build a future on land that had been neglected and abandoned for centuries. Although their arrival was not welcomed by all, some were glad to see them come, including people such as Dawood Barakat, editor of the Egyptian paper *Al-Ahram*, who wrote: "The Zionists are necessary for the country; the capital which they will bring, their knowledge and intelligence, and the industriousness which characterises them, will contribute without doubt to the regeneration of the country."[16]

CHAPTER 3

THE BIRTH OF ZIONISM

The Jews who will it shall achieve their state. We shall live at last as free men on our own soil.... The world will be liberated by our freedom, enriched by our wealth, magnified by our greatness. And whatever we attempt there for our own benefit will redound mightily and beneficially to the good of all mankind.

—THEODOR HERZL, FOUNDER OF ZIONISM

S WE HAVE already seen, the Jewish people have been fleeing from persecution and rejection for much of their history. They have not been welcomed anywhere. Time after time their neighbors have risen up against them, confiscated their property, and driven them from their land. No other race of people has faced such discrimination and hatred. This is one important reason the Jews have always longed to have a nation of their own on their ancestral homeland. This desire led to the birth of Zionism in the late 1890s and the return of thousands of Jews to Palestine.

Very few people are ambivalent about the Jews. Most have very strong feelings. Some people love and cherish the Jews as God's chosen people, the ones who preserved the Scriptures and clung to faith in the one true God, creator of heaven and earth. (As a Jew myself, I thank God for such people.) Others despise the Jews with a passion and would love to see them wiped off the face of the earth.

This hatred has been boiling for centuries, and it makes no sense. Why have the Jews been singled out for such contempt? I believe there are several reasons for this animosity, all of which come into play in the Middle East today.

Jews are hated because they are "different." Jews have not been easily absorbed into the nations where they have settled. They have sought to maintain their own customs and traditions and are fiercely loyal to their heritage and their religion. Thus, people have come to view them as secretive outsiders—people who must have something sinister to hide. People often need a scapegoat, someone to blame for their troubles, and the Jews make an obvious and easy target.

Jews are hated because they are seen as having rejected Jesus as their Messiah. Those who hate Jews for this reason forget that Jesus Himself was a Jew, as were the apostles Paul, Peter, John, and James, and all the other apostles who turned the world upside down for the sake of the gospel. Many Christian leaders, such as Augustine and Martin Luther, seem to have turned against the Jews over time because of their resistance to the proclamation of the gospel. Surely this is no reason to hate anyone.

Jews are hated by many Arabs because of the animosity that stretches back thousands of years to the time of Ishmael and Isaac. With God's help this chain of sorrow and conflict can be broken, but *only* with God's help.

Jews are hated by Satan because he knows they are God's chosen people and wants to see them destroyed. Once, Satan wanted to destroy the Jews because he knew the Messiah was to come into the world through them. Now he wants to destroy the Jews because they play such an important role in the Messiah's return at the end of the age. He also wants to destroy the Jews because they are God's people, and he hates God.

THE DAWN OF ZIONISM

The modern Zionist movement was born in 1896, when a man named Theodor Herzl wrote a book called *The Jewish State.* Herzl's book was born out of his experiences as a journalist, specifically his coverage of a famous trial that came to be known as the Dreyfus Affair.

> A French Army officer named Alfred Dreyfus was falsely accused
> of selling military secrets to the Germans. Dreyfus was a Jew, and

because of this he could not get a fair trial. Evidence that could have proved his innocence was suppressed, and fake evidence was introduced to help convict him. Dreyfus spent several years in prison at Devil's Island before being pardoned by the French government and, eventually, completely exonerated. Herzl was horrified by the anti-Semitism that emerged in Dreyfus's trial and saw the frightening implications for all Jews in France and throughout Europe. From that point on, he devoted his life to the creation of a Jewish homeland, becoming known as "the visionary of Zionism."[1]

In 1897 Herzl organized the World Zionist Organization, which held its first international conference in Basel, Switzerland. He later stated, "In Basel, I founded the Jewish state."[2] "Unfortunately, he did not live long enough to see his dreams become reality. He died in 1904, at the age of forty-four. In 1949, after the establishment of Israel, his remains were moved from Vienna to Mount Herzl in Jerusalem."[3]

Thirteen years after Herzl died, "British Foreign Secretary Arthur Balfour wrote the famous Balfour Declaration, a milestone leading to the formation of the modern State of Israel. In a letter to Baron Walter Rothschild intended to be transmitted to the Zionist Federation of Great Britain and Ireland, Balfour wrote" the following:[4]

> His Majesty's government view[s] with favour the establishment in Palestine of a national home for the Jewish people, and will use their best endeavors to facilitate the achievement of this object, it being clearly understood that nothing shall be done which may prejudice the civil and religious rights of existing non-Jewish communities in Palestine, or the rights and political status enjoyed by Jews in any other country.[5]

The letter also stated that the British government was acting in sympathy with "Jewish Zionist aspirations."[6]

Misconceptions about the Jews returning to Israel are common. One is the misconception that was sparked by the horrors of the Holocaust, which began more than twenty years after the Balfour Declaration was issued. The truth is that Jews began returning to Palestine in large numbers during the latter nineteenth and early twentieth centuries.

These days some people consider Zionism to be something of a dirty word—a code for Jewish colonization of the Middle East. This idea has come about largely through the efforts of some Arab groups and their sympathizers to discredit the Jews, and it is not true. In the early days of the movement it seemed that much of the world was in favor of Zionism and welcomed the return of the Jews to Palestine. In the United States both houses of Congress voted in favor of it. Zionism was highly regarded throughout Europe.[7] Many Arabs welcomed the return of the Jews to the land because they felt Jewish money would benefit their kingdoms and bring much-needed improvements to the region.[8]

Another misconception is that the Jews were taking land away from Arabs who were already living in the region, or were trampling on the rights of Arabs in other ways. In fact, as the Balfour Declaration shows, the rights of Arabs and others who were living in the Middle East were being considered and upheld.

Yes, there were more Arabs than Jews living in Palestine in the nineteenth century, but there weren't very many of either group living there. By 1875 the population of the entire country was only four hundred thousand, less than 4 percent of what it is today.[9] When Kaiser Wilhelm II visited Palestine in 1898, he told Herzl, "The settlements I have seen, the German as well as those of your own people, may serve as samples of what may be done with the country. There is room here for everyone."[10]

A Swiss scholar named Felix Bovet visited Palestine in 1858 and wrote:

> The Christians who had conquered the Holy Land were not able to keep it; to them it never was anything but a field of battle and a cemetery. The Saracens [i.e., Arabs] who took it from them saw it in turn taken from them by the Ottoman Turks. These latter...have made it into a desert, in which they hardly dare to set foot without fear. The Arabs themselves, who are its inhabitants, can only be considered as encamped in the country; they have pitched their tents in its pastures, or contrived for themselves a place of shelter in the ruins of its towns; they have founded nothing in them; strangers to the soil, they never

became wedded to it; the wind of the desert which brought them there may one day carry them away again, without their leaving behind them the slightest trace of their passage through it.[11]

In 1937 a British Royal Commission reported, "In the twelve centuries and more that had passed since the Arab conquest Palestine had virtually dropped out of history....In economics as in politics Palestine lay outside the main stream of the world's life. In the realm of thought, in science or in letters, it made no contribution to modern civilization."[12]

Some British officials were caught off guard by the Arabs' violent reaction against their plans to carve out a Jewish homeland in the Middle East. They felt that they had always taken the needs of the Arab people into consideration and that they had been more than fair—especially considering that most Arabs had fought against the Allies in World War I.

Lloyd George, who served as British prime minister from 1916 to 1922, said:

> No race has done better out of the fidelity with which the Allies redeemed their promises to the oppressed races than the Arabs. Owing to the tremendous sacrifices of the Allied Nations, and more particularly of Britain and her Empire, the Arabs have already won independence in Iraq, Arabia, Syria, and Trans-Jordania, although most of the Arab races fought throughout the War for the Turkish oppressors.... [In particular] the Palestinian Arabs fought for Turkish rule.[13]

Jan Smuts, a member of the British War Cabinet, talked about the cabinet's decision to call for a Jewish homeland in Palestine:

> It was naturally assumed that large-scale immigration of Jews into their historic homeland could not and would not be looked upon as a hostile gesture to the highly favoured Arab people who, largely as a result of British action, came better out of the Great War than any other people.[14]

THE BRITISH TURN AGAINST THE JEWS

As I said, at first there was a great deal of support for the establishment of a Jewish homeland in the Middle East. But then, as had happened so often before, the tide of public opinion turned against the Jews. Nazi Germany wasn't the only country in the world where Jews were blamed for the economic troubles that were unleashed by the Great Depression.[15] The world needed a scapegoat, and it found one in the descendants of Abraham.

We make a mistake if we believe that other countries of Europe, or even the United States, went to war against Hitler's Germany in order to save the Jews. The war came about because of Hitler's aggressions against his neighbors. If he had left his neighbors alone, I doubt that anyone would have raised a finger to stop his murder of innocent Jews.

But I'm getting ahead of the story. When the British first put forward the idea of establishing a Jewish homeland in the Middle East, most felt there would be little opposition from the Arabs who lived in the region. After all, the Allies' victory in World War I had liberated the Arabs from the Ottoman Empire. For the first time in many years they were free, and they largely owed their freedom to the British.

Another reason most people thought a Jewish nation would be welcome in Palestine was that there were already a number of predominantly Arab countries there: Syria, Iraq, Lebanon, Egypt, and Saudi Arabia, to name just a few. And there was also a feeling that a Jewish state would be welcome because there was plenty of room in the Middle East.[16] As history relates, all those optimistic feelings were wrong. There has been constant fighting in the Middle East since Israel's first day as a nation and, actually, even before that day.

During World War I the vast majority of Arabs fought on the side of the Central Powers—Germany, Austria-Hungary, and Turkey. Despite this, there was no widespread animosity toward the Arabic people. This was not true of the Jews, who generally fought on the side of the country they called home. For instance, an estimated one hundred thousand Jews fought for Germany.[17] Even so, when the war ended and Germany was defeated, many Germans pointed to the Jews' "betrayal" as one of the primary reasons for Germany's loss.[18] As I said earlier, when the world needs a scapegoat, the Jews are often chosen to fill the bill.

Meanwhile an estimated half a million Jews fought in the Russian army,[19] where they were accused of collaborating with the enemy (in other words, the Germans).[20] Approximately forty thousand fought for Britain,[21] where their loyalty was publicly called into question. As a side note, another quarter of a million Jews fought in the US military during the war.[22]

After the war, despite the Jewish service in the British armed services, public opinion began to turn against the Jews. As Benjamin Netanyahu put it, "The will of British policymakers to actually implement the Balfour Declaration had begun to evaporate."[23] Netanyahu adds that "Britain tore off Transjordan from the Jewish National Home in 1922: With one stroke of the pen, it lopped off nearly 80 percent of the land promised the Jewish people, closing this area to Jews for the remainder of the century."[24]

Such actions on the part of Britain prompted Franklin Roosevelt to ask why the British were now "reneging" on their promise to the Jews. "I was at Versailles, and I know that the British made no secret of the fact they promised Palestine to the Jews," he said.[25]

Some British leaders were open in their animosity toward the Jews. General Edmund Allenby, who had led the fight to liberate Palestine from the Ottoman Empire, refused to allow the Balfour Declaration to be published in Palestine.[26] On August 4, 1918, the British authorities in Palestine received a cable from the Foreign Office in London reminding them that the Balfour Declaration was official British policy.[27] It had no effect. In fact, Allenby's successor, General Arthur Money, "ordered that government forms should be printed in English and Arabic only and refused to stand for the playing of 'Hatikva,' the Jewish national anthem."[28] Furthermore, the military governor of Jaffa, Lieutenant-Colonel J. E. Hubbard, reportedly said that if the Arabs wished to riot against the Jews, he wouldn't stop them.[29]

What prompted so many members of the British government to turn against the Jews? First and foremost, that centuries-old evil of anti-Semitism seems to have been very much at play. Zionist leader Vladimir Jabotinsky, who had consistently urged cooperation with the British government, believed that the British government "had been swept up in 'an unprecedented epidemic of anti-Semitism.'"[30] He added, "Not in Russia, nor in Poland had there been such an intense and widespread atmosphere of hatred as prevailed in the British army in Palestine in 1919 and 1920."[31]

Reportedly British officials even met with Arab militants, urging them to show the world that they would not accept Jewish domination of Palestine. Specifically Arabs were urged to riot on Easter Sunday in 1920 and told that if they could create enough violence, the British government would be forced to abandon its plan to create a Jewish homeland in the Middle East.[32] Posters went up in Jerusalem announcing, "The Government is with us, Allenby is with us, kill the Jews; there is no punishment for killing Jews."[33]

The rioting began right on schedule and lasted for three days, during which six Jews were killed and over two hundred were injured.[34] When the mayhem came to an end, "the British had arrested two Arabs for raping Jewish women and twenty Jewish men (including Jabotinsky) for having organized a Jewish self-defense unit."[35]

There is another, more pragmatic reason why the British turned against the Jews: they were convinced it was in their best interest to do so. As Benjamin Netanyahu writes:

> It took a mere twenty years for Britain to be transformed from the sincere protector of the Jews and the guarantor of their national restoration to one of the principal opponents of the restoration, abandoning the Jewish nation at the brink of annihilation. The engine for this transformation was the idea that it was in the interest of Britain to concede to the demands of the Arabs in their hatred of the Jewish nation. Like the British, who were told that they would earn the gratitude of the Arabs if only they would prevent the immigration of the Jews to Palestine, America is now told that it will earn that same gratitude if only it will force Israel to give up the West Bank and curb immigration.[36]

THE BLACK HAND

The years between World War I and World War II and the beginning of the Holocaust were not peaceful ones in the Middle East. In 1930 Sheikh Izz ad-Din al-Qassam traveled from Syria to Palestine and established an anti-Zionist organization called the Black Hand. He enlisted hundreds of Arabs to fight the Jews and the British with bombs, guns, and ammunition to start what was in effect a guerrilla war.[37]

For the most part the British left the matter for the local police to handle. Then, in November of 1935, two of Qassam's men engaged in a gunfight with a Palestine police patrol, and a policeman was killed.[38] It really was a case of mistaken identity because the police were not looking for terrorists but rather some thieves who had been stealing produce from local farms and orchards.[39]

Shortly after the shoot-out Qassam was tracked down and killed by British police.[40] His death ignited a flame of outrage that burned rapidly through the Arabic community in Palestine. Thousands turned out to pay their respects as Qassam's body was transported to his grave in the city of Haifa.[41]

In 1936 two Jews were murdered on the road that connected Tulkarm and Nablus, and on the next day, presumably in retaliation, two Arabs were killed near Petah Tikvah, a Jewish town.[42] Two days later, in the city of Jaffa, "dozens of Jews were attacked in the streets. Nine were beaten, stoned, or stabbed to death,"[43] and the violence continued for several days. Police opened fire to keep an Arab mob from "invading" Tel Aviv, "and armoured cars were brought in."[44]

Three days later, on April 20, the Arab National general strike began,[45] supported by a new group calling itself the Arab Higher Committee.[46] The strikers had "three basic demands: cessation of Jewish immigration [to Palestine], an end to all further land sales to the Jews, and the establishment of an Arab national government."[47]

That summer many Jewish civilians were murdered, thousands of Jewish-owned farms were destroyed, and some small Jewish communities disappeared as their residents fled to safer areas.[48] The violence continued well into the following year.

Despite initial reluctance on the part of the British, it soon became apparent that a full-scale military response was necessary to end the violence and restore order in Palestine. By the time the violence had come to an end, more than five thousand Arabs and four hundred Jews had been killed, and an estimated fifteen thousand Arabs had been wounded.[49]

These latter numbers may have been much higher if not for the fact that Jews in Palestine were following a policy of what they called *havlaga*, or restraint, with regard to Arab attacks. This meant that rather than taking matters into their own hands, they turned the situation over to

British authorities. This was done for a number of reasons, including the fact that the Jews wanted to have good relations with their Arabic neighbors and didn't want to stir up more conflict.[50]

Also, the Jews were concerned about world opinion, and they wanted to make sure the British did not see the situation as a Jew-versus-Arab conflict but rather as a one-sided attack on the Jews. This was especially important because at this time there was no official Jewish homeland in the Middle East.

In their book *The Encyclopedia of the Arab-Israeli Conflict*, Spencer C. Tucker and Priscilla Roberts wrote the following:

> When the Arab Revolt began in 1936, the policy of havlaga came under great scrutiny. At first trying to maintain the policy as the violence became widespread, Jewish leaders including David Ben-Gurion, Vladimir Jabotinsky, and Chaim Weizmann urged calm and the continuation of self-restraint. Believing that the uprising would be short-lived, they figured to outlast the attacks. But the Arab revolt endured, taking more and more Jewish lives and destroying much of their property. By mid-1937, many Jews in Palestine began to call for a more proactive response to Arab attacks.[51]

This essentially was the end of havlaga. Because it did not seem to lead to peace but rather to more conflict, it was discarded in favor of a new policy that might be described as "Hit me, and I'll hit you back—harder."

CHAPTER 4

WHO REALLY "OWNS" THE LAND OF ISRAEL?

It is manifestly right that the Jews, who are scattered all over the world, should have a national center and a National Home where some of them may be reunited. And where else could that be but in this land of Palestine, with which for more than 3,000 years they have been intimately and profoundly associated?

—WINSTON CHURCHILL

ONE OF THE major issues causing such hatred and strife in the Middle East today is the question of who really belongs there. The Jews insist that the land was given by God to their ancestor Abraham. The Arabs say the Jews no longer have any claim to the land because they were driven out of Palestine nearly two thousand years ago.

Arabs claim that over the centuries ownership of the land has transferred to them because they have been there building homes, planting fields and orchards, and raising sheep and other animals. They believe it is not right that the Jewish people have now come back to Palestine and demanded that their land be returned. The Jews say this is a misrepresentation. There have always been Jewish families in the land now called

Israel, and millions of Jews around the world have always had a deep desire to return there.

There are other differences between the attitudes of Jews and Arabs. Arabs, in general, want the Jews completely out of the Middle East. They want it all for themselves. The Jews, on the other hand, seem more than ready to share with their Arab neighbors. In fact, there are an estimated 1.8 million Arabs living in Israel today, making up more than 20 percent of the country's population.[1]

These people hold Israeli citizenship and receive all the rights and benefits that are accorded to other Israeli citizens. I have never heard any Jewish person demand that these Arabs leave Israel. Nor have I heard any Jew say that he or she won't rest until Lebanon, Syria, Jordan, or any other Arab country is wiped off the map. Israelis don't want *all* the land. They do want to be free from terrorist attacks and able to live in peace with their neighbors.

You may be thinking, "OK, if there are 1.8 million Arabs in Israel, how does that compare with the number of Jews in Arab countries—say Lebanon, Jordan, and Syria?" The answer is that fewer than one hundred Jews were believed to live in Lebanon early in this millennium.[2] There are fewer than one hundred in Syria as of 2017, down from an estimated forty thousand in 1948.[3]

Here is what the Jewish Virtual Library has to say about Jewish life in Syria:

> In 1944, after Syria gained independence from France, the new government prohibited Jewish immigration to Palestine, and severely restricted the teaching of Hebrew in Jewish schools. Attacks against Jews escalated, and boycotts were called against their businesses.
>
> When partition [of Palestine into Arab and Jewish states] was declared in 1947, Arab mobs in Aleppo devastated the 2,500-year-old Jewish community. Scores of Jews were killed and more than 200 homes, shops and synagogues were destroyed. Thousands of Jews illegally fled Syria to go to Israel.[4]

Afterward the Syrian government's persecution of Jews grew worse, with restrictions on Jewish movement, employment, and driving. Jews were not permitted to purchase property, and their "bank accounts were frozen."[5] Jews lived in great fear, and some were surveilled. Most could not travel overseas, and those who did had to leave behind a monetary bond and family members "who served as hostages."[6]

Clearly Arabs in Israel are treated much better than Jews are treated in most Arab countries. But aside from that, the question under discussion is this: Who really "owns" the land called Israel? Consider this:

> The Jewish presence in "the Holy land"—at time tenuous—persisted throughout its bloody history. In fact, the Jewish claim...to the land now called Palestine does not depend on a two-thousand-year-old promise. Buried beneath the propaganda—which has it that Jews "returned" to the Holy Land after two thousand years...is the bald fact that the Jews are indigenous people on that land who never left, but who have continuously stayed on their "Holy Land."[7]

A HISTORY OF JEWS IN THE MIDDLE EAST

There is copious historical evidence that large numbers of Jews continued to live in Palestine for centuries after the destruction of Jerusalem in AD 70.

For example, Joan Peters writes that when Muslims entered Jerusalem in the seventh century, they found a very strong Jewish presence. "We have evidence that Jews lived in all parts of the country and on both sides of the Jordan, and that they dwelt in both the towns and the villages, practicing both agriculture and various handicrafts."[8]

Peters says that although the crusaders of the eleventh century were "merciless" in their attempts to eradicate the Jews from the Holy Land, they did not succeed, and in Galilee, a number of Jewish villages survived intact.[9] In the fourteenth century a visiting Christian monk, Jacques of Verona, wrote of "the long established Jewish community at the foot of Mount Zion in Jerusalem."[10]

He said, "A pilgrim who wished to visit ancient forts and towns in the Holy Land would have been unable to locate these, without a good guide who knew the Land well, or without one of the Jews who lived there. The Jews were able to recount the history of these places since this knowledge had been handed down from their forefathers and wise men."[11]

Peters' extensive research uncovered numerous other examples of thriving Jewish settlements in Palestine:

- **In 1438** a rabbi from Italy was chosen as spiritual leader of the Jewish community in Jerusalem.[12]

- **In 1488** Obadiah de Bertinoro founded the Jerusalem Rabbinical school. The school dealt primarily with matters that were important to Jews living in the Arab world.[13]

- **In 1563** the first Jewish printing press outside of Europe was instituted in Safed, which is now located in northern Israel.[14]

- **In 1839** a dispatch from the British Consulate in Jerusalem reported that there were many Jews living in Palestine.[15]

- **In 1862** British Consul James Finn reported that "with regard to pure Hebrew, the learned world in Europe is greatly mistaken in designating this a dead language. In Jerusalem it is a living tongue of everyday utility."[16]

This is only a sampling of the historical reports that contradict the claims of a time when there were not many Jews in Palestine. That is not to deny the obvious fact that millions of Jews have returned to Israel over the past 150 years and especially since the end of World War II and the establishment of the State of Israel in 1948. I believe this is a direct fulfillment of Bible prophecy. My point is that Jewish people around the world have always thought of Israel as their home, and many have continued to live there, even during times of great persecution and distress.

The Jewish people are not late arrivals to the Holy Land, and they do have a right to think of this land as their homeland.

WHO ARE THE TRUE IMMIGRANTS?

Another reason some people give for opposing Israel is that they believe the Jews who have immigrated to Israel have taken away land from hard-working Arabs who have lived on and farmed the land for generations.

Upon closer inspection this assumption seems unwarranted. For one thing, when Jews began returning to Palestine, they came to a land that was largely desolate, sparsely settled, and unproductive. Jewish immigrants worked very hard, and as God blessed them, they began to see biblical prophecies coming true, such as this one: "I will open rivers on the bare hills and springs in the midst of the valleys. I will make the wilderness a pool of water and the dry land into fountains of water" (Isa. 41:18, TLV).

Furthermore, it is incorrect to assume that when Jewish families settled in Palestine, they took over land that did not belong to them. In fact, the newcomers paid fair and sometimes exorbitant prices for their property. Many "Jews actually went out of their way to avoid purchasing land in areas where Arabs might be displaced."[17] They built their homes and farms on land that was "uncultivated, swampy, cheap and, most important, without tenants."[18]

David Ben-Gurion was instrumental in the founding of Israel and served as the first prime minister. In 1920 he expressed concern about the impact of Jewish immigrants on Arab farmers (*fellahin*), saying that "under no circumstances must we touch land belonging to *fellahs* or worked by them.... Only if a *fellah* leaves his place of settlement should we offer to buy his land, at an appropriate price."[19]

According to author Mitchell G. Bard, director of the Jewish Virtual Library, "It was only after the Jews had bought all of this available land that they began to purchase cultivated land. Many Arabs were willing to sell because of the migration to coastal towns and because they needed money to invest in the citrus industry."[20]

Following a "survey of landlessness" in 1931, the British offered plots of land to "Arabs who had been 'dispossessed.'"[21] Claimants submitted in excess of three thousand applications, 80 percent of which were deemed to be from Arabs who were not landless and therefore not qualified. Of six hundred landless Arabs, one hundred accepted the offer.[22]

As the Jewish newcomers gave their blood, sweat, tears, and every ounce of their energy to restoring the land, and as God blessed them, fields that had been desolate and unproductive began to produce bountiful crops. What had been a wasteland was being restored as the biblical land of milk and honey. And although I don't have any hard and fast figures for this, it would seem that as this happened, it increased the draw for Muslims to move there from their native lands.

For example, in 1922 the Jewish population of Palestine was set at

84,000.[23] By 1945 there were 554,000 Jews in Palestine, and according to the Anglo-American Committee of Inquiry, 75 percent of them were immigrants.[24]

Meanwhile the committee reported that the number of Arabs had grown at an even greater rate than had the number of Jews.[25] This was attributed entirely to an increase in the birth rate among the Arab population. Joan Peters says that "the so-called 'unprecedented' rate of 'natural increase' among the non-Jews was never satisfactorily broken down or explained."[26]

Furthermore, over the previous two hundred years the Arab population of Palestine had remained roughly the same.[27] This is easy to understand when you consider the harsh climate and terrain of much of this part of the world. There were few doctors or hospitals. Life expectancy was short, and many children died in the first few years of life. In other words, the situation was the same as that which tragically confronts people in many of the world's developing countries today.

Why, then, did "natural population growth" suddenly zoom upward in the second quarter of the twentieth century?[28] Yes, there were improvements in living standards in Palestine during this period, most of them brought on by the Jewish arrivals who built hospitals, clinics, and schools; installed irrigation systems to provide water for drinking, bathing, and farming; and made other improvements to the infrastructure.[29]

This is not meant to be a criticism of the Arabs who lived in this area. Many of them were shepherds and nomads—wanderers who raised sheep, camels, and other animals and lived off the land. The Jewish pioneers were farmers who settled in one area, built homes, planted crops, and established cities. I am not trying to say that the Jewish way of life was superior to that of their Arab neighbors but rather that Jews and Arabs are two different peoples with two different lifestyles and cultures.

But it does seem that many Arabs from neighboring countries were coming to Palestine at this time, and it seems likely that many were drawn by the improvements that resulted from the Jewish presence in the land. In 1939 Winston Churchill said, "The Arabs have crowded into the country and multiplied till their population has increased more than even all world Jewry could lift up the Jewish population."[30]

A MULTITUDE OF LANGUAGES

In 1931 a census of Palestine found that a total of fifty-one languages were spoken by "non-Jews" who lived there. Twenty-three of these were spoken by Muslims, and twenty-eight by Arab Christians. In addition to this, non-Jews in Palestine reported coming from twenty-four different countries around the world. In Jerusalem alone the Arabic population represented twenty countries.[31]

There were Jews in Palestine who came from countries all over the world, including the United States and Canada. There were also Arabs who came from the United States, Canada, France, and many other lands. Of course, it cannot be accurate to say that the Arabs who were living in Palestine at that time were natives of the region but that they also came from twenty-four countries around the world.[32] If the latter is true, and the evidence seems to show that it is, then the former cannot also be true. This weakens the Arabs' claim that "this land belongs to us because we have been here for generations." Although there have been Arabs in Palestine for centuries, Jews have been there too.

MUCH OF WHAT YOU KNOW MAY NOT BE TRUE

Many Americans have come to believe the following myths about the current situation in the Middle East:

- **The Palestinian people have always identified with the land.** The truth is that in the two centuries before the State of Israel was founded, many Arabs were wandering all over the Middle East, struggling to survive in a land that had been devastated by drought and war.

- **The Jews returned to Israel in 1948 after two thousand years away and displaced the Arabs when they did.** The truth is that there have always been Jews in the area where Israel now exists. In fact, until the country now known as Jordan was removed from the area that was designated as "the Jewish National Home,"[33] Jews lived both east and west of the Jordan River.

35

- **The Arabs were settled in Palestine prior to the Jews' arrival. Israel sits on Palestinian land.** Actually, prior to the middle of the twentieth century the Arabic-speaking people in Palestine generally thought of themselves as Ottomans, Turks, Southern Syrians, or Arab people but never as Palestinians. And from the establishment of Jordan in 1921 until 1967, Arabs living in the area known as the West Bank were considered Jordanians, not an independent Palestinian people.

- **Before the establishment of Israel, Jews and Arabs lived peacefully side by side throughout the Middle East.** Sadly this has never been the case. A close inspection of the history of the Middle East shows that there has often been violence between Arabs and Jews and persecution of Jewish populations in many Muslim nations long before the modern nation of Israel existed. To say, as some Muslim leaders have, that if Israel were removed, Arabs and Jews would go back to living in peace is like yearning for "the good old days" that never really existed.

- **The Palestinian people, like other Arabs, have nothing against Jews. It is Zionism that they hate.** As I discussed earlier, there was a time when Zionism was very nearly universally applauded. As Benjamin Netanyahu writes, "Many nations and peoples had admired the tenacity, courage, and moral strength of the Zionist movement. They had marveled at Israel's achievement in rebuilding a modern state on the ruins of an ancient homeland. They had applauded the ingathering of the exiles from a hundred lands and the seemingly miraculous revival of an ancient tongue.... Israel and Zionism had served as a shining example of the independence and progress that so many other nations, coming out from under the heel of empire, hoped to achieve."[34]

In 1975, during a conference on the rights of women in Mexico City, the Soviet and Arab blocs of the United Nations somehow persuaded and intimidated the participating countries into approving a resolution that equated Zionism with racism.[35] This same resolution was confirmed by the United Nations General Assembly a few weeks later, on the thirty-seventh anniversary of Kristallnacht, when Nazi thugs attacked Jews throughout Germany, breaking store windows, torching synagogues and residences, and killing approximately one hundred Jews in the process.[36]

On what grounds was Zionism regarded as racist? It was said to be anti-Arab, anti-Muslim, and a movement against people of dark skin, even though thousands of the immigrants who have been welcomed into Israel are dark-skinned Jews from Ethiopia.

A Few More Words About Zionism as Racism

Just before the "Zionism is racism" resolution was passed by the General Assembly of the United Nations, the US ambassador to the UN, Daniel Patrick Moynihan, warned his colleagues that they were about to make anti-Semitism a part of international law:

> There will be time enough to contemplate the harm this act will have done the United Nations. Historians will do that for us, and it is sufficient for the moment only to note one foreboding fact: A great evil has been loosed upon the world.... The proposition to be sanctioned by a resolution of the General Assembly is that "Zionism is a form of racism and racial discrimination." Now this is a lie. But it is a lie which the United Nations has now declared to be a truth—and so the actual truth must be restated.... The United States of America declares that it does not acknowledge, it will not abide by, it will never acquiesce in this infamous act.[37]

As it happens, the resolution equating Zionism with racism was reversed by the United Nations in 1991, by a very wide margin of 111 to 25, with 17 abstentions.[38] The law lived for sixteen years and then was replaced.

But even today I hear people say, "Zionism is racism," and then point to the UN resolution to prove that this is so. In fact, I saw a news article recently about a forum called "Zionists Are Racists," which was held at Columbia University in New York City.[39] Apparently those students have yet to hear that a closer look at the situation revealed that Zionists are not racists after all. Instead, they are Jews who long to return to their ancestral homeland and build a good life there for themselves and their children. They don't want to take anybody's land or shove anyone out of the way. They don't look down on people who have hair or skin of a different color, or who come from a different ethnic background. They merely want the right to go home and live out their lives in peace.

It doesn't really surprise me anymore that some people still insist that Zionism is inherently racist and that a US resolution backs their claims. This is similar to what happens when someone is arrested for a heinous crime. The story of the arrest makes the front page of all the newspapers. It's on the radio and TV. But when the police discover that they arrested the wrong person, he or she is quietly let go—and I mean *quietly*. A tiny story might appear on page sixteen of the local paper, if at all. The arrest of the suspect is big news. The release of the suspect, not so much.

Bad news travels fast, and for some reason people seem inclined to believe it. Trying to undo the damage it causes is like trying to get toothpaste back into the tube after you have squeezed it out. It simply cannot be done.

As Benjamin Netanyahu said, "We must remember that the Arabs had a full sixteen years to drive home their racism message, and that even after its formal renunciation, this defamation lives on in the minds of many nations and their leaders. I stress again that, for the first time in history, a world body had given its stamp of approval to the libeling of an entire people."[40]

CHAPTER 5

THE HOLOCAUST AND BEYOND

Wherever men or women are persecuted because of their
race, religion, or political views, that place must—at
that moment—become the center of the universe.
—ELIE WIESEL

N 1933, WHEN Adolf Hitler came to power, there were an estimated 15.3 million Jews in the world.[1] In 1945, when World War II came to an end, some 40 percent of them had been killed. Hitler's Final Solution, implemented between 1941 and 1945, resulted in the murders of six million Jews,[2] which computes to roughly one death every twenty seconds.

The sad truth is that there seemed to be little sympathy for the Jewish people after the horrors they endured during the Holocaust. And what sympathy there was faded quickly, within a generation. Families had been torn apart. Innocent men, women, and even children endured years of torture and abuse in concentration camps.

All of this went on while most of the rest of the world ignored it or did little to stop it. Once the world became aware of what the Jews had been through, it would seem to me that a universal movement to help ensure their security and safety should have followed.

Instead, as soon as large numbers of Jews began immigrating to Israel, many people and nations around the world turned against the idea of a Jewish homeland. The British, who were in control of Palestine after

World War II, severely limited Jewish immigration to Palestine.[3] Instead of being allowed to make Aliyah to Israel, Jewish people were herded into internment camps on Cyprus.[4] No, they weren't concentration camps, but they were camps nonetheless, and a camp is not a home.

Netanyahu writes of the injustice:

> The extent of the British betrayal of the Jews can be understood only in the context of what was happening in Europe in the 1930s and thereafter. Responding to pressure from the Arabs, the British restriction of Jewish immigrants (there was no analogous restriction on Arab immigration) cut off the routes of escape for Jews trying to flee a burning Europe. Thus, while the Gestapo was conniving to send boatloads of German Jews out onto the high seas to prove that no country wanted them any more than Germany did, the British dutifully turned back every leaking barge that reached Palestine, even firing on several.[5]

Colonel Richard Meinertzhagen, then British chief of intelligence in the Middle East, was one of the few loud dissenting voices who objected to his country's shabby treatment of the Jews:

> The Nazis mean to eradicate Judaism from Germany and they will succeed. Nobody loves the Jews, nobody wants them and yet we are pledged to give them a home in Palestine. Instead we slam the door in their faces just at the moment when it should be wide open.... The action of His Majesty's Government in Palestine is very near to that of Hitler in Germany.[6]

I realize that some who are reading this might say, "This is old news, ancient history. What does this have to do with the situation in the Middle East today?"

The answer is, "Plenty."

As Spanish philosopher George Santayana said, "Those who cannot remember the past are condemned to repeat it."[7] There are important lessons for today to be learned from the world's past treatment of the Jews. Again and again throughout history the Jewish people have been blamed for the world's troubles. They have been persecuted and slaughtered without cause and then accused of bringing it on themselves. Every time, they have emerged stronger than ever as a people, and their enemies have been judged.

You may remember that we talked earlier about God's promise to Abraham: "My desire is to bless those who bless you, but whoever curses you I will curse" (Gen. 12:3, TLV). As you read those words, remember that God never breaks a promise.

In my book *A Rabbi Looks at the Last Days*, I talk about my friend Bill Koenig, who wrote a book called *Eye to Eye*, in which he showed how the United States has been blessed or cursed according to its treatment of Israel. Koenig presents a compelling case that whenever the United States has tried to force Israel to give up land for peace, or has turned against Israel in other ways, we have been hit by floods, hurricanes, terrorist attacks, and economic downturns.[8]

One example of how God curses those who curse Israel: Koenig writes about what happened in the United States between May and August of 2011, after the Obama administration called for a new Palestinian state to be created in the Middle East based upon "1967 borders with agreed upon land swaps."[9] Prime Minister Netanyahu quickly made it clear that these conditions were not acceptable to Israel because they would result in the establishment of indefensible borders that would threaten Israel's very existence.

Shortly after the American administration stated this position, an EF5 "monster" tornado struck Joplin, Missouri, killing about 160 people and injuring a thousand others.[10] It was the deadliest tornado to strike the United States in decades.[11] Just a few weeks later Hurricane Irene made landfall in North Carolina and then charged up the coast, causing catastrophic flooding, wind damage, and power outages across the Northeast. Forty-one Americans died, and property losses due to flooding alone were estimated at more than $7 billion.[12]

Other examples can be found in *Eye to Eye*. Now, I want to make clear that I don't believe for a second that God personally sent these storms to kill people and wreak havoc. I believe instead that He merely lifted His hand of protection because we had turned against Israel, and the result was disaster and death.

As I said in *A Rabbi Looks at the Last Days*, "Only in the world to come will we know how often [God] has stretched out His hand to protect us, individually and as a nation."[13] I believe that His continued protection is contingent on our support of the Jewish people and the nation of Israel. I also believe that we should never make the mistake of saying that the United States would never turn against the Jews. It has happened before, and it could happen again.

In May of 1939 the German ocean liner *St. Louis* sailed from Hamburg with 937 passengers, almost all of whom were Jewish. When they reached the port of Miami in June, they were turned away and denied entry. The ship was forced to return to Europe, where more than one-fourth of its passengers lost their lives in the Holocaust.[14]

Hundreds of thousands of Jewish immigrants applied for asylum in the United States, but only a small fraction of these requests were granted. The State Department opposed accepting Jews into the country on the basis that there might be Nazi spies hiding among them.[15] According to *Smithsonian* magazine, "Until the very end of 1944—by which time photographs and newspaper reports had demonstrated that the Nazis were carrying out mass murder—Attorney General Francis Biddle warned Roosevelt not to grant immigrant status to [Jewish] refugees."[16]

All during this time the Arab propaganda machine was operating at full speed, claiming that the Jews had not lived in the Middle East for nearly two thousand years and did not belong there. It was also said that the arrival of the Jews would uproot Arab families from their land and create thousands of refugees.

And yes, the refugees are still there to this day. But where did they really come from?

THE REFUGEES

We have already talked about Joan Peters' important book *From Time Immemorial*. Her scholarly, well-documented work explodes the myth that the Jews do not belong in the Middle East and that Israel was carved out of Arab land.

Peters discovered, among other things, that many of the Palestinian refugees were relative newcomers to Palestine. In fact, there was a massive immigration of Arabs into Palestine in the 1940s, as Peters explains:

The whole fabric of historical presuppositions unraveled upon close inspection. What began as a closer look at the refugees led to reflecting on the lengths the Arabs were willing to go to, including their cruel indifference to the well-being of their own brethren, in their hostility toward a Jewish state.[17]

Peters' research revealed that many of the refugees fled their lands in Israel not because they were expelled or mistreated by the Jews, but because leaders of the surrounding Arab nations urged them to flee prior to the Arabs' attack on Israel. Peters clarifies:

> At the time of the 1948 war, Arabs in Israel too were invited by their fellow Arabs—invited to "leave" while the "invading" Arab armies would purge the land of the Jews. The invading Arab governments were certain of a quick victory; leaders warned the Arabs in Israel to run for their lives.[18]

Some Jewish communities urged their Arab residents not to leave. For example, the Jewish Haifa Workers' Council issued this appeal to the Arab members of the community:

> For years we have lived together in our city, Haifa....Do not fear: Do not destroy your homes with your own hands,...do not bring upon yourself tragedy by unnecessary evacuation and self-imposed burdens....But in this city, yours and ours, Haifa, the gates are open for work, for life and for peace for you and your families.[19]

It is hard to know how many Arabic residents of Palestine listened to such appeals, but many did not. According to a research report by the Institute for Palestine Studies (an Arab organization), the majority of the refugees who left Israel in 1948 were not expelled by the Jews, and more than two-thirds left their homes without any interaction with Israeli troops.[20]

Joan Peters adds this:

> After the Arabs' defeat in the 1948 war, their positions became confused: some Arab leaders demanded the "return" of the "expelled" refugees to their former homes despite the evidence that Arab

leaders had called upon Arabs to flee. At the same time, Emile Ghoury, Secretary of the Arab Higher Command, called for the *prevention* of the refugees from "return." He stated in the Beirut Telegraph on August 6, 1948: "It is inconceivable that the refugees should be sent back to their homes while they are occupied by the Jews. It would serve as a first step toward Arab recognition of the state of Israel."[21]

In other words, it wasn't the Israelis who created the plight of the Palestinian refugees, but rather their Arab brothers. As King Hussein of Jordan said in 1960, "Since 1948, Arab leaders have approached the Palestine problem in an irresponsible manner.... They have used the Palestine people for selfish political purposes. This is ridiculous and, I could say, criminal."[22]

In his autobiography, published in 1972, Khalid al-Azm, Syria's former prime minister, made an even harsher assessment:

> Since 1948, it is we who demanded the return of the refugees...while it is we who made them leave....We have rendered them dispossessed.... We have accustomed them to begging.... We have participated in lowering their moral and social level.... Then we exploited them in executing crimes of murder, arson, and throwing bombs upon men, women and children—all this in the service of political purposes.[23]

The truth is that while the world's attention has been focused on the plight of the Palestinians for all these years, millions of Jews have fled from harsh treatment and persecution in Arab countries. Those Jews left behind millions of dollars in assets and had to start over in Israel. If you look at the total dollar amount of what was left behind, the Jews gave up far more than the Palestinians did.[24] This is not meant to minimize what the Palestinian people have endured; they have suffered a great deal. But the question is, Who is to blame?

TRADING PLACES

In essence, Jews and Arabs living in Israel have changed places. This is similar to what happened in India and Pakistan in the 1950s. In those years millions of Sikhs and Hindus moved from Pakistan to India, and millions of Muslims went from India to Pakistan.[25]

A similar shift of population occurred in 1922, with approximately two million people going from Greece to Turkey and vice versa.[26] A proposal to do the same thing in the Middle East was put forth in the 1930s by Mojli Amin, a member of the Arab Defense Committee for Palestine. He proposed that "all the Arabs of Palestine shall leave and be divided up among the neighboring Arab countries. In exchange for this, all the Jews living in Arab countries will go to Palestine."[27]

He also suggested that special committees should be set up to deal with liquidation of property that was left behind and added, "I fear, in truth, that the Arabs will not agree....But in spite of this, I take upon myself the task of convincing them."[28]

He was right; his proposal would not be accepted.[29] But most of what he suggested happened anyway. The difference was that the transition was not smooth; those who went from one country to another were not compensated for lost property, and hundreds of thousands of refugees were created in the process.

WOULD THERE BE PEACE WITHOUT THE JEWS?

There is a myth that the Arabic people of the Middle East would live in peace together if Israel would just disappear. Tiny Israel, they say, is the boil that stirs up all the hatred and violence there. But consider these events that have nothing at all to do with Israel or the Jews:

- **1961**: The first Kurdish-Iraqi War erupts in northern Iraq.

- **1963**: A military coup in Iraq brings Abdul Salam Arif to power.

- **1967**: A Kurdish revolt in Western Iran is crushed by the Iranian military.

- **1968**: A coup in Iraq brings General Ahmed Hassan al-Bakr to power. Saddam Hussein is installed as vice president.

- **1974**: The second Kurdish-Iraqi War erupts.

- **1975**: The Lebanese civil war begins. It lasts for fifteen years and results in an estimated 120,000 deaths.

- **1976**: Syria invades Lebanon.

- **1980**: War begins between Iran and Iraq. An estimated one million are killed during the eight-year conflict, including thousands who fall victim to Iraq's chemical weapons.

- **1983**: The second Sudanese civil war begins. The conflict continues for twenty-two years and claims an estimated two million lives.

- **1990**: Iraq invades Kuwait. The First Gulf War begins, resulting in more than one hundred thousand Iraqi military deaths.

- **1991**: Civil war in Algeria begins. It claims an estimated two hundred thousand lives.

- **1994**: Civil war begins in Yemen.

- **2011**: Civil war breaks out in Syria. Fighting still rages, and more than four hundred thousand Syrians have died.

This is not a full list of the wars, invasions, massacres, and other humanitarian tragedies that have taken place in the Middle East over the past sixty years. It more than makes my point, and because Israel has not been involved in any of these conflicts, the presence of Israel clearly is not the primary cause of war and strife in that part of the world—not even close.

It is ludicrous to think that Israel's annihilation would usher in an era of peace. The truth is that the Arab countries of the world have spent more time fighting each other than they have Israel. This continues today, with Shiite and Sunni Muslims slaughtering each other in record numbers.

CHAPTER 6

YASSER ARAFAT AND THE PLO

We plan to eliminate the State of Israel and establish a purely Palestinian state. We will make life unbearable for Jews by psychological warfare and population explosion. We Palestinians will take over everything, including all of Jerusalem.

—YASSER ARAFAT

T WAS AT a 1964 Arab League summit in Cairo that a new group dedicated to the "liberation of Palestine" through armed struggle was born. The Palestine Liberation Organization (PLO) later stated in the Palestinian National Charter that "Palestine with its boundaries that existed at the time of the British Mandate is an indivisible territorial unit."[1]

It is impossible to understand current events in the Middle East without having this background. The real issue here is not borders or mandates, or land that was won or lost through war. The issue is the very existence of Israel. The Palestinian National Charter of 1964 says, "The claims of historic and spiritual ties, ties between Jews and Palestine are not in agreement with the facts of history."[2] The charter talks about the "sacred national goal" of Palestinian liberation by way of an ongoing "holy war" to eliminate Zionism and "liberate Palestine."[3]

Yes, the charter is more than fifty years old, but the wording has never been changed. It essentially calls for the elimination of Israel, claiming in Article 17 that Israel's establishment was "illegal."[4] This was the claim when the charter was first written and approved, and this remains the claim today. In the Palestinians' view, this is not about two states living side by side. Rather, it is about one state only, and that state is Palestine.

When the charter was written, the territories that are under dispute today—the Gaza Strip and the West Bank—were under the control of Egypt and Jordan, respectively. Yet neither of those countries was willing to give up those lands to be used for a Palestinian homeland. It was only after they were won by Israel—in a war the Israelis did not start and did not want—that they became "necessary" for a Palestinian state.

The person most strongly linked to the PLO was an Egyptian named Mohammed Yasser Abdel Rahman Abdel Raouf Arafat al-Qudwa al-Husseini, better known as Yasser Arafat. He ran the organization for thirty-five years until his death in 2004. During that time he was responsible for thousands of deaths of both Jews and Arabs. From its beginning, the PLO was a terrorist organization, and Arafat found terrorism to be quite profitable, amassing a personal fortune estimated to be in the billions of dollars—most of it coming, apparently, from donations to support the Palestinian "cause."[5]

Here is how the *Atlantic Monthly* started an article about Arafat in 2002:

> Yasir Arafat claims that he was born in Jerusalem, but he was actually born in Cairo. He claims to belong to the prominent Jerusalem family of Husseini, but he is at best only distantly related to it. He claims that he turned down a chance to go to the University of Texas, but according to one biographer, the Palestinian-born writer Saïd K. Aburish, it is highly unlikely that he was ever accepted. He claims to have disabled ten Israeli armored personnel carriers in the 1948 Arab-Israeli war, but Israel didn't even have ten APCs in the sector he was in. He claims to have made millions as a businessman in Kuwait, but this, too, is almost certainly untrue.[6]

In other words, he wasn't exactly the epitome of a statesman.

The event that first brought worldwide notoriety to the PLO was the attack on Israeli athletes at the 1972 Olympic Games in Munich, Germany. Eleven Israeli athletes and coaches were killed.[7]

Although Arafat was hailed as a hero by the Palestinian people, he was a very unpopular fellow as far as most Arab leaders were concerned. He was expelled from Syria.[8] King Hussein of Jordan also expelled him after the PLO was linked to attempts to assassinate him. The expulsion came only after a series of bloody battles in which an estimated fifteen thousand people were killed.[9] Following his ouster from Jordan, Arafat moved his headquarters to Lebanon, from which he continued to launch attacks against Israel.

In 1982 the Israeli army invaded southern Lebanon[10] in an attempt to destroy the bases Arafat was using to launch constant missile attacks on Israel. The PLO had armed itself with thousands of missile and rocket launchers and was striking northern Israel with artillery fire almost daily. It didn't take long for Israel to overrun the PLO positions in southern Lebanon, move deeper into the country, and surround the organization's headquarters in Beirut. When Syria launched an air attack in defense of the PLO, the Israelis shot down more than eighty planes without suffering a single loss of their own.[11] (Even though the Syrian government hated Arafat, they obviously hated Israel more.)

The PLO might have been destroyed had the United States not stepped in, brokered a cease-fire, and offered Arafat and his fighters safe passage to Tunisia, where they remained for the next roughly eleven years.[12] During that time Arafat survived a number of internal power struggles and at least one Israeli bombing of his headquarters in Tunis.[13] He continued to call for a Palestinian state and to plan and carry out terrorist attacks on Israel. Eventually he did tone down his rhetoric, but a skeptic might wonder if he did it to gain recognition and financial support from the world community.

Following the signing of the Oslo Accords in 1993, Arafat shared the Nobel Prize with Israel's Prime Minister Yitzhak Rabin and President Shimon Peres.[14] Among the guarantees of the Oslo agreement, the Palestinians agreed that they would recognize Israel's right to exist and stop launching terrorist attacks on the Israeli people. In return for this, there would be a gradual transition to Palestinian self-rule.[15]

Despite their promises, Arafat and the PLO never amended their charter to recognize Israel's right to exist, nor did they stop the violence against Israel. Instead, Arafat continued to try to play both sides of the fence, convincing many Western leaders and their governments that he was a man of peace while continuing to plan and fund terrorist attacks against military targets and innocent Jewish citizens in Israel.

As seems to be true with the vast majority of Arab and Palestinian leaders, Arafat remained focused on the utter destruction of Israel. This focus was clearly seen at the Camp David peace talks held in 2000, when Israel's Prime Minister Ehud Barak offered to give up all of Gaza plus 94 percent of the West Bank. This was a much larger concession than anyone expected, but Arafat turned it down flat. His rejection of the proposed deal seemed to show that Arafat was not really after a just peace that would benefit both Palestinians and Israelis. Rather, his goal was to see Israel disappear.

Had he not been so full of hatred for Israel, he might have done some very good things for the Palestinian people. After all, he was a master fund-raiser who brought in billions of dollars for the Palestinian cause. But it seems that most of that money was used on bombs, bullets, and propaganda. Very little went to improving the lives of the Palestinian people. Most of them lived in abject poverty when Arafat came on the scene in 1964, and most of them were still living in poverty when he died forty years later.[16]

After Arafat died in 2004, he was replaced by Mahmoud Abbas, who continues as president of the Palestinian Authority despite the fact that his term of office expired in 2009 and there have been no further elections.[17]

The Intifadas

It was during the heyday of Yasser Arafat, during the winter of 1987, that tensions boiled over between Palestinians and Israelis and the first intifada, or uprising, occurred. In Arabic, *intifada* means "to shake off,"[18] or get rid of. It has the idea of a dog shaking all over in an attempt to get rid of his fleas; the intifada was a Palestinian attempt to shake the Jews out of Palestine.

It all began when a Jewish worker was stabbed and killed in Gaza. A day or so later an Israeli tank transport driver lost control and ran into another vehicle, killing four Palestinians. It was a tragic accident, but a rumor quickly spread that the accident had been an intentional act of revenge for the murder of the Jewish worker.

Angry Palestinians began throwing stones and setting fires, and soon rioting had engulfed Gaza, the West Bank, and Jerusalem. Mobs filled the streets, burning tires, destroying vehicles, and throwing stones and Molotov cocktails at Israeli soldiers trying to maintain order. Rioters also bombed the US Consulate in Jerusalem. The violence continued on not for days, weeks, or months, but for six long years.[19]

During that time hundreds of Palestinians were killed or wounded in attacks on Israeli troops, and many more were killed by other Palestinians after being accused of collaborating with "the enemy."[20] It is still impossible to get an accurate account of casualties, but it is estimated by the Israeli human rights group B'Tselem that as many as two thousand people died during the six years of sporadic fighting and violence.[21]

Although the violence of the intifada was aimed primarily at the Jews, many Christians were also targeted, especially those who lived in the West Bank. In Bethlehem, churches, businesses, and homes owned by Christians were firebombed and vandalized, and some Christians were beaten. Apparently Jews are not the only ones who are not welcome in the Holy Land.

Writing in the Catholic journal *Terra Santa*, "Father Georges Abou-Khazen wrote that Arab states have been pouring money into the effort to 'Islamicize' the country, and that he feared the complete eradication of the Christian presence in the Holy Land."[22] According to the priest, Christians were too terrified to speak out against the violence.[23] Did the campaign of terror directed at Christians work?

"In 1950, Bethlehem and the surrounding villages were 86 percent Christian."[24] By 2016 they were just 12 percent of the population.[25] In 2006 there were an estimated five thousand Christians in Gaza. Today, with the more radical Hamas in power, there are just over a thousand.[26]

Ronald Lauder, the president of the World Jewish Congress, wrote a *New York Times* op-ed piece about the plight of Christians in the Middle East:

> Why is the world silent while Christians are being slaughtered in the Middle East and Africa? . . . We have witnessed demonstrations over the tragic deaths of Palestinians who have been used as human shields by Hamas. . . . The United Nations has held inquiries and focuses its anger on Israel for defending itself against that same terrorist organization. But the barbarous slaughter

of thousands upon thousands of Christians is met with relative indifference.[27]

Lauder noted the disappearance of Christian communities with long-standing histories and professed the bond that Jews and Christians share. He decried the world's indifference to the violence waged against Christians and reminded readers that silence on the world stage has grave consequences.[28]

The Oslo Accords in 1993 produced six years of relatively peaceful times. Then a second intifada, much more deadly than the first, erupted in 2000. Over the next several years full-scale military conflicts resulted in the deaths of an estimated forty-eight hundred Palestinians and more than one thousand Jews.[29]

This intifada began shortly after the failure of the July 2000 Middle East Peace Summit at Camp David. As already noted, President Clinton had invited Israeli Prime Minister Ehud Barak and Yasser Arafat to the presidential retreat in Maryland in an attempt to move peace negotiations forward. The talks, though hopeful at first, failed to produce any agreement when Arafat refused the major concessions offered by Israel. It was later alleged that Arafat himself had played a major role in launching the unrest in an attempt to gain more concessions from Israel.[30]

It is reported that at one point during the talks Clinton became so agitated by Arafat's behavior that he snapped, "A summit's purpose is to have discussions that are based on sincere intentions and you, the Palestinians, did not come to this summit with sincere intentions," and then he got up and walked out of the room.[31] When the peace talks collapsed, Clinton publicly blamed the Palestinians for their failure.[32]

During the five years following the summit, off-and-on fighting between Israeli troops and Palestinian militants continued, along with suicide bombings and missile and mortar attacks against Jewish civilians in Israel. An uneasy truce was declared in February 2005, which was generally considered to mark the end of the second intifada.

The Killing Continues

In 2017 further unrest in Jerusalem broke out, stemming from the murder of two Israeli police officers at the Temple Mount by Arab-Israeli radicals.[33] The violence resulted not because of the murders but because the Israeli government reacted to them by installing metal detectors and increasing other security measures.[34] After this was done, Palestinian Authority leaders and Islamic clerics in Jerusalem declared a "Day of Rage" and encouraged protests calling for the security devices to be removed.[35]

According to Arutz Sheva (Israel National News), an Israeli TV station (Kan 11) reported that the Palestinian Authority, under Abbas' direction, offered monetary and other incentives to those who were willing to participate in violent protests against the Israeli security measures.[36] The benefits were said to include "cash payments of $1,000 a month for up to three months, as well as exemptions from payments to the Jerusalem District Electricity Company, which provides electricity to some predominantly Arab neighborhoods in Israel's capital."[37] Cash and college tuition payments were also offered to certain groups, among them merchants and students in the Old City of Jerusalem.[38]

And so it would seem that even though Yasser Arafat is gone, the spirit of the man lives on. The question of the future of the Palestinians was set in motion more than sixty years ago when they and the Arab nations of the Middle East rejected the United Nations plan to create Israel and launched war to destroy the Jewish state. Today they remain a people without a country, and most of them are still committed to the eventual annihilation of Israel.

CHAPTER 7

A MONSTER CALLED ISIS

The spark has been lit... and its flames will blaze...
until they consume the Armies of the Cross.

—ABU MUSAB AL-ZARQAWI

N THE AFTERMATH of attacks on the United States on September 11, 2001, many Americans became obsessed with the idea of finding Osama bin Laden, killing him, and thereby destroying al Qaeda, the terrorist group he founded. The feeling was, "Destroy bin Laden, and you destroy al Qaeda. Then we can go back to living together in peace."

It is easy to see why people felt that way. Bin Laden was the so-called mastermind behind the deadly terrorist attacks that killed nearly three thousand people. He was the one who taunted us with videotaped threats, gloated over the deaths and suffering he had caused, and threatened more bloodshed. He was the head of the evil snake. The solution seemed simple: cut off the head, and the snake will die.

Despite our government's efforts to find him, bin Laden eluded capture for nearly ten years. Then, in the spring of 2011, he was tracked to a compound of fairly modest size in Abbottabad, Pakistan. Early on the morning of May 2, 2011, the compound was invaded by US Navy Seals, and bin Laden was shot and killed. As far as most Americans were concerned, this evil man got exactly what he deserved. Well, maybe not *exactly*. For many, his death was too quick, too easy. He didn't even begin to pay for all the pain he had caused, but at least we could all breathe easier now that he was gone.

Sadly Osama bin Laden's death did not bring an end to America's or the world's constant battle with terrorism. We didn't know that something even more evil than al Qaeda was preparing to strike. That something was an organization known as ISIS, or the Islamic State. We rarely hear of al Qaeda these days, but until recently ISIS was constantly in the news because of the savagery it unleashed on innocent men, women, and children all over the world.

ISIS is a sadistic and cruel organization that seems to take absolute delight in spilling blood. Beheadings, crucifixions, executions of children, eradication of entire communities, rape—ISIS has done it all. Its leaders have no compassion, no respect for human life, and no human decency. ISIS is the epitome of Sunni Muslim hatred toward everyone who is not a Sunni Muslim—and especially the Jews. An article in an ISIS newspaper, *al-Naba*, is quoted as saying that "jihadis should focus first on toppling the Arab regimes, which it believes defend Israel" and only then confront Israel's military.[1]

On religious grounds, however, the article encourages Muslims to return Palestine to Islam, assist the Palestinians in their fight with Israel, and wage continued jihad against Israel, Israelis, and their interests.[2]

FROM STREET THUG TO TERRORIST LEADER

ISIS' roots formed under the leadership of Abu Musab al-Zarqawi,[3] but it was not known as the Islamic State during his heyday. At the time, the organization was best known as Al-Qaeda in Iraq (AQI).

Zarqawi, a Jordanian, was radicalized while being imprisoned "for drug possession and sexual assault."[4] After his release in the late 1980s he relocated to Afghanistan to fight against Soviet occupation of Afghanistan,[5] but he arrived too late for the fight.[6] During the 1990s he again spent time behind bars, this time for advocating the overthrow of the Jordanian government and trafficking in propaganda to be "published on Salafi websites."[7] "A few of Zarqawi's tracts had caught the attention of Osama bin Laden in Afghanistan," and the two reportedly met after Zarqawi's release from prison in 1999.[8]

Reportedly the two men did not get along particularly well. Bin Laden was suspicious of Zarqawi, and they "disagreed about several targeting and tactical issues.... Zarqawi preferred to target his 'near enemies,' such as Israel and the Jordanian government."[9] Although bin Laden shared Zarqawi's hatred of Israel, he preferred to focus on the "far enemy," the United States.[10]

Zarqawi despised the Shiites in a way bin Laden did not.[11] For Zarqawi, Shiites were just as bad as Christians and Jews. They were infidels, worthy of death.[12] The major issue was that Shiites believe the "doctrine that Muhammad's son-in-law and some of his male descendants were infallible and the only legitimate political and religious leaders of the early Muslim community."[13] Sunnis do not believe this. It might seem a trivial matter to most of us, but not to "fundamentalists" like Abu Musab al-Zarqawi.

Osama bin Laden believed all Muslims should work together. Perhaps after all Christians and Jews were eliminated, it would have been acceptable for Muslims to kill each other.

THE MURDER OF NICHOLAS BERG

In May of 2004 the world got its first good look at the depravity of Zarqawi and his followers. A twenty-six-year-old American named Nicholas Berg was taken captive and viciously murdered on camera.[14] The incident was witnessed on computer monitors around the world. Berg, dressed in an orange jumpsuit, sat on a blanket, his arms and legs bound with ropes. A man dressed in black from head to foot, including a ski mask, stood behind Berg. US intelligence officials immediately recognized him as Zarqawi. Four other men, also dressed completely in black, stood behind him.

Zarqawi produced a large knife and jumped on Berg. As the other men helped to restrain their helpless victim, Zarqawi grabbed Berg's hair with his left hand and began cutting his throat with his right. Berg screamed, but was quickly silenced as Zarqawi continued to slash and cut.[15]

Finally, "one of Zarqawi's companions…lifted the head" for the world to see and set it down on its owner's back.[16] Berg's death was the first of many such "staged" executions. There were also kidnappings for ransom and even the videotaped burning alive of a Jordanian Air Force pilot named Muath al-Kasasbeh.

Meanwhile, many young Islamists who answered Zarqawi's call for soldiers were sent to school to learn how to carry out suicide bomb attacks. For Zarqawi and his ilk, these young lives were expendable, even though the Quran expressly forbids suicide. He praised suicide attacks as being one of the "most deadly weapons" in the jihadists' arsenal, adding that "these kinds of operations are of little effort for us; they are uncomplicated and are the least costly for us."[17]

In his book *The ISIS Apocalypse*, William McCants describes the ISIS method:

> Islamic State has deliberately provoked the anger of Muslims and non-Muslims alike with its online videos of outrageous and carefully choreographed violence.... The State revels in gore and wants everyone to know it. And yet it has been remarkably successful at recruiting fighters, capturing land, subduing its subjects, and creating a state. Why? Because violence and gore work.[18]

ISIS AND THE END TIMES

Many of Zarqawi's attacks targeted Muslims, such as the bombing of a hotel in Amman, Jordan, that killed dozens of civilians in November 2005.[19] "On February 22, 2006, [his organization] AQI bombed the Askariyah Shrine, also known as the Golden Mosque in Samarra," Iraq.[20] In response, "at least 27" Sunni mosques in Baghdad were bombed, "and violence between Shiites and Sunnis escalated" throughout Iraq and the Middle East.[21]

Bin Laden disliked Zarqawi's approach (especially regarding "targeting and tactical issues")[22] and believed in winning the hearts and minds of the people—even if he did it by killing Americans and other non-Muslims.[23] Zarqawi didn't care what people thought. He was perfectly happy to rule by force.

There were other points of contention between them. Bin Laden was not guided by ancient Muslim prophecies. He did not have an apocalyptic point of view or think the end times were upon us.[24] Zarqawi, however, believed in and was preparing for the cataclysmic battle that is to usher in the reign of the Muslim savior, the Mahdi. In other words, he was preparing for what Christians call Armageddon and was expecting to fight against the Christians in that battle. Since he believed that millions of people would be killed in the final fight, it didn't matter to him how many he killed now. In fact, killing "infidels" was one of the ways he could usher in the final battle and then the Mahdi's reign. He bragged that his soldiers would set off flames that would "consume the Armies of the Cross in Dabiq,"[25] the village prophesied to be the site of the final event.

He was so fanatical about this that it wouldn't have bothered him at all to touch off a nuclear war. You can be sure that today's leaders of ISIS feel the same way.

In his book *ISIS, Iran and Israel* reporter Chris Mitchell writes, "What makes the beliefs of Iran and ISIS so toxic is the idea that they can hasten the return of the Islamic messiah through violence or weapons of mass destruction."[26] He further quotes Ayatollah Hassan Mamduhi quoting Ayatollah Aziz-Allah Khoshwaqt, saying, "The return of the Mahdi is conditional on what our nuclear scientists are doing."[27]

Mitchell also quotes Ryan Mauro of the Clarion Project regarding these views:

> One of the interesting developments I've seen, particularly with ISIS and other jihadists, is how much they're wrapping themselves in end-time theology. When a jihadist says something like, "We're going to break the cross," or "America, we condemn you for being the protector of the cross," they're referencing an end-time prophecy....They're saying that they're creating the conditions for their version of Jesus (far different from the Bible's version) to show up and help them conquer the world.[28]

It's quite interesting to me that Muslims actually believe the Messiah will descend to earth to fight for them in the last days. McCants quotes *Sunan Abu Dawud*, a Hadith volume:

> There is no prophet between me and him, meaning Jesus. Verily, he will descend. When you see him you will recognize him as a man of medium height, reddish to fair, wearing two light yellow garments. His head will appear to be dripping though it is not wet....In his time, God will destroy every religious community except Islam. He will destroy the Deceiving Messiah. He will dwell on earth for forty years. When he dies, the Muslims will pray for him.[29]

UNITED IN HATE

Despite bin Laden's disagreements with Zarqawi, he is reported to have given Zarqawi funds to establish "a training camp in Herat [Afghanistan], where Zarqawi trained between two thousand and three thousand Salafi terrorists by October 2001."[30] Many of these fighters moved into Iraq, where they launched terrorist attacks against American soldiers and Shiite civilians. They didn't care much for Saddam Hussein.[31] He was far from a saint or a religious person. But at least he was a Sunni—and they couldn't stomach the idea of having Shiites in power.

On several occasions Osama bin Laden and some of his lieutenants told Zarqawi to stop killing Shiites. But he wouldn't listen. "Zarqawi's hatred of the Shi'a [Shiites] was all-consuming. To his mind, the Shi'a were not just fifth columnists, selling out the Sunnis to the Americans. They were servants of the Antichrist, who will appear at the end of time to fight against the Muslims."[32]

McCants then explains:

> Although al-Qaeda's leaders downplayed the apocalypse, some of their followers celebrated it.... Senior al-Qaeda officers also cited Islamic prophecies. "The Islamic armies must gather, rely on God, and support His religion and their brothers in Jerusalem," wrote Fadil Harun, Bin Laden's man in Somalia. The "awaited Mahdi" would then appear and lead "an ideological struggle, which will continue until the [Final] Hour as long as an inch of Muslim land in the Holy Land is under the control of the enemies."[33]

The goal of ISIS, al Qaeda, and all Islamic extremist groups is to usher in a Muslim caliphate, from which a caliph will rule the Muslim world. What exactly is a caliphate? And what is a caliph, for that matter? Robert Spencer writes, "The caliphate in Islamic theology is *the* Islamic nation, embodying the supranational unity of the Muslim community worldwide under a single leader, the caliph, or 'successor,'—that is, the successor of Muhammad as the spiritual, political, and military leader of the Muslims."[34]

He goes on to say that ISIS has resonated with many Muslims by proclaiming itself to be the caliphate.[35] They understand the prophetic importance of this. ISIS is saying, in essence, that the end times are here and the kingdom of Allah is being restored. "The only earthly authority to which any Muslim owes allegiance, according to Sunni Muslim theology, is to the caliph. This has proven already to be an extraordinarily powerful claim."[36]

When Zarqawi was killed in an American air strike on June 7, 2006, many Americans and other members of the anti-terrorist coalition breathed a sigh of relief. With its leader gone, some doubted that his organization could survive. For several years it seemed that this was true. Although AQI continued to kill civilians, and occasionally coalition soldiers, through suicide bombings and other terrorist attacks, it seemed clear that coalition forces had won the battle for the hearts and minds of the Iraqi people.[37]

Shiite Muslims were the vast majority in Iraq, and they had joined the fight against "insurgent" Sunnis. Many AQI leaders were killed, and it seemed to be a matter of time before the group was completely purged from Iraq.

Tragically there was still a feeble heartbeat in that corpse—and it was about to return to life with a vengeance.

THE REBIRTH OF ISIS

By December of 2011, AQI was barely breathing and on life support. Hundreds of top leaders had been killed.[38] Communications had been cut off. Nine years and thousands of deaths after al Qaeda's murderous attack on the World Trade Center there was reason for optimism. It seemed that the tide had finally turned in the war on terror. Sporadic violence continued, but the worst was certainly past.

Then two things happened that breathed new life into al Qaeda in Iraq.

1) Coalition troops were withdrawn from Iraq in 2011.

2) The Arab Spring swept through the Middle East.

At the time, both were seen as reasons to celebrate. The withdrawal of coalition troops seemed to mean that Iraq could handle its own issues without the support of foreign troops. This was especially good news for the American people, who had grown weary after nine years of war with Iraq and Afghanistan and wanted to see our young men and women come home. As far as the Arab Spring was concerned, it appeared to be a great day for Arab countries throughout the Middle East, who were rising en masse to overthrow bloody tyrants no thinking person wanted in power anyway.

AQI attacks ramped up in 2012, brought on in part by the new Iraqi government's lack of inclusion of Sunni Muslims.[39] This increased Sunni support for terrorist organizations such as ISIS and brought increased bombings and other attacks on Shiite neighborhoods. Civilian deaths in 2013 doubled those in 2012. At the close of 2013 "a local uprising" cleared much of Anbar province of Iraqi security forces, following the latter's attempt "to clear a protest camp in Ramadi."[40] AQI was then able to march in and take control.

In April 2013 Abu Bakr al-Baghdadi "changed the group's name to the Islamic State in Iraq and Syria (ISIS)."[41] In February of the following year al Qaeda officially renounced all ties with ISIS.[42] Both organizations believed in murdering innocent men, women, and children in order to spread Islam throughout the Middle East and the world. They just disagreed on how to do it and on which of them was really "Number One." ISIS leaders expected all jihadists everywhere to look to ISIS as their leader; al Qaeda was not ready to comply.

Even after the split ISIS continued to grow,[43] and at an incredible rate. Foreign fighters poured into Syria to fight under the black flag of ISIS. Fighters came not only from Arab or Middle Eastern countries; thousands came from European countries such as England and France, and hundreds from the United States.[44] Whereas al Qaeda was a shadowy, clandestine organization that plotted occasional terrorist attacks, ISIS had become an actual army—and for a while a seemingly unstoppable one.

ISIS troops stormed across Iraq, defeating enemies and gobbling up large chunks of territory.[45] In January of 2014 Iraqi troops were driven out of Fallujah. Five months later the black flag was raised over Mosul. In Mosul, as in other cities they conquered, Sharia law was put into effect, and a bloodbath took place. Christians were told they could either convert to Islam, pay a special tax, or die.[46] Abductions, mass killings, deployment of child soldiers, civilian executions—these are just a few of the atrocities documented in reports by two UN human rights agencies.[47] The warning was clear: don't try to defy us.

On June 29, 2014, AQI changed its name again, "this time to the 'Islamic State' (IS), declaring a Caliphate and naming its leader Abu Bakr al-Baghdadi the Caliph. It called upon all Muslims to declare allegiance to the new Caliphate."[48]

Speaking from beneath the dome of the Grand al-Nuri Mosque in Mosul, Iraq,[49] Baghdadi proclaimed himself to be a descendant of Muhammad and declared himself "Caliph Ibrahim," leader of the Muslim community.[50] There he declared Muslims' "return [to their] dignity, mights, rights, and leadership" and promised their revenge against "treacherous rulers—the agents of the crusaders and the atheists, and the guards of the Jews!"[51]

The caliphate that Baghdadi proclaimed looks absolutely nothing like the kingdom of God anticipated by those who are looking forward to the return of Jesus at the end of this present age. Christians and Messianic Jews look to an age of peace in which the world will be full of the knowledge of the Lord, and the lion will lie down with the lamb. In contrast, the Islamic State left behind it a trail of devastation, heartbreak, and death everywhere it went. People were tortured and killed for the slightest infractions of Sharia law. There was not a single drop of mercy, love, or forgiveness.

Who would welcome that type of kingdom with open arms?

Yet the ISIS onslaught continued. By October of 2014 the terrorists were reported to be within striking distance of the Baghdad airport.[52] The entire country of Iraq seemed ready to fall, and might have if not for a series of air strikes launched by coalition forces.

In *ISIS, Iran and Israel*, Chris Mitchell writes about two of hundreds of atrocities ISIS fighters have committed. In Palmyra, Syria, they "beheaded 81-year-old Kahled al-Assad, one of the Middle East's most prominent antiquities scholars" and strapped his body to a Roman column for all to see.[53] Mitchell also tells of two teenage boys who were crucified in the city of al-Mayadin for not fasting on Ramadan.[54]

Mitchell explains that beheading is deeply "ingrained in the religious culture of ISIS" and is supported by two verses from the Quran:[55]

> "Your (Muhammad's) Lord revealed to the angels: 'I am with you, give the believers firmness; I shall put terror into the hearts of the disbelievers. Strike above their necks and strike their fingertips'" (Sura 8:12). "So, when you meet those who disbelieve,

smite (their) necks till you have killed or wounded many of them"
(Sura 47:4).[56]

ISIS is like a snake that has the ability to regenerate itself. Each time
the head is cut off, a new one grows in its place. Hundreds of its top
leaders have been killed, many of them by United States drones and missiles. Yet somehow others rise up to take their place.

Now after years of horrific advances ISIS appears to be on the run in
the Middle East. Under the Trump administration there has been a significant escalation in bombings and military action.[57] Iraqi and Kurdish
forces have retaken many of the towns and cities that were under the control of the black flag. Baghdadi himself went "missing" for some time. It
was believed that he had been seriously wounded in a coalition air strike
or perhaps killed. He is reportedly recovering from serious wounds in
Syria.[58] Coalition forces continue to hunt for him.

Although ISIS appears to be in withdrawal and is no longer at the
center of world attention, it is not necessarily finished. Many confused,
lost souls remain susceptible to the ISIS message of hate and destruction.
Millions of devout Muslims would gladly welcome the death of every
Christian and Jew in the world (and *every* non-Muslim, in fact) in order
to see Islam cover the earth.

The Islamic State's aim is the eradication of all whom they consider to
be nonbelievers. This means Jews, Christians, Shiite Muslims, Buddhists,
Hindus, and members of other religions. Thousands of Christians have
been slaughtered by ISIS already. Others are being persecuted in various
ways. In August of 2015 ISIS captured the Syrian town of al-Qaryatain,
which had been home to many Christians. ISIS officers said they would
spare the Christians' homes and lives, but only if they were willing to
"sign a dhimma (Sharia social contract) in order to remain in the town
and not face death."[59]

Such contracts can forbid gun ownership, the building of "churches,
monasteries, or hermitages," displays of the cross in Muslim communities, "acts of aggression against ISIS," the public performance of religious rites, and other activities.[60] They also require Christians to "respect
Muslims," pay special taxes, and obey the "ISIS dress code and commerce

guidelines."[61] As harsh as these rules seem, they are quite lenient compared with the "convert or die" choice many Christians face.

As Believers, we need to be in diligent prayer for our Christian brothers and sisters in the Middle East who have been victims of ISIS. Many have lost family members or been maimed for life. Following are some prayer points:

- Pray that God will thwart ISIS' plans to harm innocent men, women, and children, and that ISIS will not be allowed to reemerge in Syria, Iraq, and other areas of the Middle East.

- Pray that God will protect Christians and Jews around the world (and especially in the Middle East) who are in immediate danger under the threat of ISIS cruelty.

- Pray that the Lord will change the hearts and close the ears of those who might otherwise be susceptible to ISIS' propaganda.

- Pray that God will find a way to use for good what ISIS intends for bad. Also pray that God will cause its attacks to boomerang and that the bombs and bullets they intend for others would fall upon their own heads. (See Balaam's story beginning in Numbers 22. He tried three times to pronounce a curse on the Israelites but blessed them instead.)

- Finally, pray that the Holy Spirit will reveal Jesus to the members of ISIS and they will be converted to faith in Him. Abraham Lincoln once said that the best way to get rid of an enemy is to turn him into a friend. God can convert the worst of ISIS killers, just as He converted Saul of Tarsus on the road to Damascus. One minute Saul was persecuting and killing followers of Yeshua. He described himself as the "chief of sinners." But the minute Jesus appeared to him, everything changed. God's love can change the hearts of all who hate Him.

CHAPTER 8

THE WAR AGAINST CHRISTIANS

In the early 21st century we estimate that on average over the 10-year period from 2000–2010 there were approximately 100,000 Christians killed each year (1 million total).
—CENTER FOR THE STUDY OF GLOBAL CHRISTIANITY,
GORDON-CONWELL THEOLOGICAL SEMINARY

YOU HAVE PROBABLY heard this thought-provoking quote from Lutheran pastor Martin Niemöller, who was imprisoned for speaking out against Adolf Hitler's reign in Nazi Germany:

First they came for the socialists, and I did not speak out—
Because I was not a socialist.
Then they came for the trade unionists, and I did not speak out—
Because I was not a trade unionist.
Then they came for the Jews, and I did not speak out—
Because I was not a Jew.
Then they came for me—and there was no one left to speak for
me.[1]

Several versions of this quote exist because it is based on lectures Niemöller gave about his experiences during the Nazi regime. He saw how "good people" stood aside and did nothing while the Nazis jailed and even killed their neighbors (simply because they considered them to be different or "inferior" in some way). You may have heard a version of the quote that says, "They came for the Jehovah's Witnesses," or "They came for the Communists." Niemöller often purposefully chose groups that were not held in universal acclaim. He knew that some people's first reaction might be, "Well, it's OK if they want to persecute the Communists or the Jehovah's Witnesses. After all, I don't like Communism, and I'm tired of people ringing my doorbell and trying to give me a copy of *The Watchtower*."

That was Niemöller's point. If we turn our backs and look the other way while *anyone* is being persecuted, we are in great danger of being persecuted ourselves. Yet I have heard many people, especially Christians, say that the struggles taking place in the Middle East do not concern them. "This is between the Muslims and the Jews," they say. "Let them work it out."

As a Jew who grew up with a deep awareness of the Holocaust and the fact that the world stood by, watched, and did almost nothing, I am very sensitive to this issue. As followers of the Lord, we cannot sit back and allow indifference and apathy to numb us to the realities our brothers and sisters are facing far from our homes. We must speak out and be their advocates.

The truth is, what's going on in the Middle East today concerns *all* people of faith, and especially Christians. To put it as bluntly and clearly as I possibly can: *Christians in the Middle East are being persecuted, tortured, and killed in unprecedented numbers. If we Americans remain silent or refuse to do anything about it, we are standing on the side of their enemies.*

Across the Middle East, Christian populations are being decimated. The British newspaper *The Telegraph* recently published an article with the headline "Christianity 'Close to Extinction' in Middle East." Its subhead proclaims, "Christianity faces being wiped out of the 'biblical heartlands' in the Middle East because of mounting persecution of worshippers, according to a new report."[2] Reporting on a study, the article says, "The most common threat to Christians abroad is militant Islam."[3]

According to *The Telegraph*, the study revealed that "Christians suffer greater hostility across the world than any other religious group," with some two hundred million Believers "socially disadvantaged, harassed, or actively oppressed for their beliefs."[4] The report adds that most of the persecution Christians face occurs in predominantly Islamic nations, and it estimates that as much as two-thirds of Middle East Christians "have left the region or been killed" in the past one hundred years.[5]

In most of the Middle East, Christians have been persecuted for centuries—at least since Muslims became the dominant power there. But now, that persecution is reaching a fever pitch.

Are we taking a stand? Back in 2014 when President Obama announced the beginning of air strikes against ISIS troops in Iraq,[6] I was surprised to hear some Christian friends say forcefully that they thought it was a mistake. Even though ISIS troops were sweeping through Iraq, slaughtering countless innocent civilians (especially Christians and Shiite Muslims), their reaction was, "This doesn't concern us, and we shouldn't get involved."

Thankfully we did get involved. I can't even begin to imagine what the death toll would have been if we had stood aside and let ISIS continue its push toward Baghdad unchecked. As it is, ISIS has butchered thousands of people in the Middle East, many of them women and children.

I am certainly not in favor of war. I also understand why Americans are wary of "getting involved" in another conflict overseas. Too many young Americans have given their lives in places such as Iraq, Afghanistan, and Vietnam. But I also believe that we must do what we can to help innocent people who are being brutalized and martyred because of their faith.

This is happening on a regular basis in places such as Gaza, Iraq, Iran, Egypt, Sudan, Syria, and other countries around the world. In the United States, Believers sometimes think they are being persecuted when store clerks say "Happy holidays" instead of "Merry Christmas," or when courts rule that crosses in city and state seals are unconstitutional.

Yes, I agree that those are forms of discrimination and persecution. But while we get riled up about those things, we need to remember that Believers in some parts of the world are being beaten, stabbed, shot, and even crucified for their faith. It is rarely dangerous to be a Believer in the United States. In some parts of the world people take their lives in their hands every time they attend church or hold a Bible study in their homes. There is a war against Christianity, and they are its innocent victims.

Killed Because He Sold Christian Books

A young husband and father named Rami Ayyad managed a Christian bookstore in Gaza called The Teacher's Bookshop.[7] His store was the only one of its kind in Gaza. Some people thought that was one store too many. He started receiving phone calls from people who said they were going to kill him if he didn't shut it down.

Ayyad was a committed Christian who refused to be deterred by their threats. Then one night Ayyad noticed a car following him as he drove home from work. He figured someone was trying to scare him, and he shook it off. The next day he was kidnapped while locking up the bookstore for the evening. Later that night he called his wife on his cell phone and told her that he was being held but expected to be home soon.

He never made it. His body was found the next day in an alley not far from The Teacher's Bookshop. The young, hardworking husband and father of three had been stabbed and shot.

His widow, Pauline, had two small boys and was five months pregnant with a girl. Even in her time of grief, she faced threats from Muslim leaders. She remembers that one of the local clerics threatened to have her children taken away from her. "Your kids belong to me," he said.

Pauline desperately wanted to get out of Gaza and take her children to the West Bank, where she had friends and family. She knew that things would not be ideal there, but she also knew she would feel safer than she did in Gaza. Her fears were exacerbated by the fact that Gaza's Hamas government seemed to be constantly preparing for war with Israel. Tensions were high, and very few travel permits were being issued.

Thankfully when word of Pauline's plight spread, a number of American Christian organizations came to her aid, including the American Center for Law and Justice, an organization headed by my friend and fellow Messianic Jew Jay Sekulow. Through the efforts of all these organizations, Pauline and her children were able to move to Bethlehem, where they began a new life. She also started and leads a prayer group and Bible study, where she ministers to six other widows.

Pauline is an example of the power Believers have when they come together to help persecuted Christians in the Middle East and around the world. It grieves me to think about what might have happened to her and her children if not for caring people like you who came to her aid.

A BLACK FLAG FLIES IN SYRIA

The 220,000 residents of Raqqa, Syria,[8] didn't know what to think when the black flag of the Islamic State went up over their city. Then the executions began.

A young man accused of unspecified criminal activity was shot in the head, and his body was left in the public square for three days. Several others were crucified. Some had their heads cut off and placed on fence posts.

There were many new rules to obey. No one seemed to know for sure which behaviors were now criminal offenses.[9]

An eyewitness named Abu Ibrahim said, "People were frightened, which is what they wanted. They wanted everyone to be terrified of them."[10] The city's three Christian churches were padlocked. Crosses and other Christian symbols were either destroyed or covered.

Surely those who strive to be peacemakers in this part of the world have a long, hard job in front of them.

In his book *Destination Jerusalem*, CBN News Middle East Bureau Chief Chris Mitchell writes eloquently about the suffering Christians he has met in Iraq, Egypt, and other areas of the Middle East. In Erbil, the capital of Kurdistan, Mitchell and his crew met with a number of Christians who had fled Mosul (ancient Nineveh) and other cities under attack by the Islamic State. One woman told Mitchell, "ISIS bombed our churches and took our houses. We don't have anything here. No money. No ID. No travel documents."[11]

An older man reported, "They're [ISIS] using the sword to cut off hands and beheading others. I don't think that is the behavior of human beings, but wild animals do that." [12]

A middle-aged woman added, "They say, 'If anyone don't become like Muslim, we kill them, each one, from baby to woman to old man.'"[13] Another refugee said that when he and his family reached the ISIS checkpoint, the soldiers began yelling at him that they could kill him because he was a Christian. He didn't even seem to know how he had escaped them. "Jesus saved me," he said. Then he added, "We are sheep. We are sheep with the wolves."[14] He wept because he had lost everything and did not know how he would support his wife, son, and teenage daughter.

Mitchell also talked to Canon Andrew White, who formerly pastored St. George's Anglican Church in Baghdad. Several of his church members were killed by Islamic terrorists, and many more fled to escape the ISIS onslaught, hundreds of them to Mosul, where they thought they would be safe. Then one day ISIS stormed into the city.

White said, "They came in and they rounded all of them up. Not some, all of them. And they killed huge numbers. They chopped the children in half. They chopped their heads off. It was just so terrible what happened."[15]

He told Mitchell that one man had telephoned him in tears, saying that ISIS had ordered him to convert to Islam and that they would kill his children if he refused. He couldn't bear to see his children killed, so he did as they commanded.

"Does that mean Jesus doesn't love me anymore?" he cried.

"Elias, no; Jesus still loves you," White told him. "He will always love you."[16]

The vicar also told of four young girls who were ordered by ISIS soldiers to renounce their faith. "We can't," they replied. "We have always loved Jesus. We have always followed Him."

The soldiers gave them one last chance to convert to Islam, but they would not do it.

And all of them were beheaded.

"How do you respond to that?" White asked. "You just cry. That's what we have been going through. That's what we are going through."[17]

He also had some important words for Believers in the United States and other Western countries:

> We are one family, brothers and sisters together. We need your prayers for our protection. We need prayer for our provision. We need prayer for our perseverance, so we can keep going, and finally, we need prayer for peace.[18]

FIRES OF PERSECUTION BURN IN EGYPT

Mitchell also writes of his travels to Egypt, where dozens of churches have been bombed or set ablaze by radical Muslims, most of them allegedly members of the Muslim Brotherhood.

Egypt has the largest number of Christians of any Arab nation,[19] with about 10 percent of its population of ninety-five million said to be Believers in Jesus Christ.[20] Most of them are Copts (Coptic Orthodox), but there are also thousands of Roman Catholics, Evangelicals, and members of various denominations. Persecution is nothing new to Egypt's Christians, but it has been growing in intensity since the Arab Spring brought down the dictatorship of Hosni Mubarak.

Although the situation was bad for Christian Believers under Mubarak, it was even worse following Mubarak's replacement by Mohamed Morsi, a staunch member of the Muslim Brotherhood.[21] The situation remains difficult for Christians, as Egypt's current leader, Abdel Fattah el-Sisi, has not delivered on his promises for equality.[22] (More on this is coming in chapter 14.)

In Minya members of the Brotherhood went throughout the city painting large black Xs on businesses, homes, and cars that belonged to Christians.[23] Then they came back and set them all on fire. In this one day of violence some sixty Christian churches were burned in cities throughout Egypt.[24]

Mitchell writes that one of the most shocking things he saw was an orphanage that had been utterly destroyed by rampaging mobs. The facility, called Christ's Soldiers, had once served as home to two hundred young girls who had no moms or dads. Now it was broken, trashed, and virtually unlivable. The residents of the home had written a message of forgiveness on an outside wall. "You meant to hurt us, but we forgive you. Everything works out for good." Then they added these words from Matthew 5:44: "Love your enemies."[25]

Believers in Minya want to make it clear that some of their Muslim neighbors stood with them during the violence, trying to defend and protect them.[26] Many of these people have lived side by side in peace for generations. But peace seems to be harder and harder to find in our increasingly dangerous age.

Although Egypt is widely considered to be moderate in its attitude toward Christians, there have been an increasing number of deadly attacks that have met with almost no resistance on the part of the government. On at least one occasion Egyptian troops took part in a confrontation that left more than twenty Christians dead.

In one instance residents of Cairo's Christian neighborhood of Mokatam were viciously attacked without warning.[27] Into the wee hours of the morning armed gangs rampaged through the streets of this desperately poor neighborhood, using combustible propane tanks to burn homes, businesses, and vehicles, and shooting at anyone they happened to see. When the burning, looting, and shooting finally ended, ten people were dead and 130 were injured. Eyewitnesses reported that ambulances and fire trucks did not arrive until the next morning, hours after the attackers had fled.[28]

A few months later the Egyptian army crushed a protest in Cairo organized by a Christian youth group to call attention to a number of church burnings in Egypt. The Maspero Youth Group was also protesting what it saw as a failure on the part of the government to protect Christians from attacks. As the protesters marched through Muslim neighborhoods, they were pelted with stones. Then the army swept in. In the melee that followed, twenty-seven Christians were killed and three hundred people were injured. According to forensic reports, ten people were crushed by army vehicles. The other victims died from gunshot wounds and other injuries.[29]

State-run media falsely reported that the protesters had opened fire and called on citizens to come to the army's defense. One Muslim-owned TV station said (again incorrectly) that the protesters had burned a copy of the Quran, inflaming passions and resulting in attacks on the hospital where those who had been injured were being treated.

A couple of days later, when funerals were held, mourners were attacked by thugs who hurled stones and Molotov cocktails at them. The Christians were forced to flee and find shelter, and some of them called an emergency number to report that they were under attack and needed assistance.

No one came to help.[30]

How did the government finally respond to what amounted to a massacre of unarmed citizens? "In a televised speech, Prime Minister Essam Sharaf provided no explanation for the army's brutal tactics, blasting instead unseen forces he said had instigated the violence in an attempt to derail Egypt's transition to democracy."[31]

The "invisible hand" idea implied that either the United States or Israel had orchestrated the whole thing. At a press conference the Egyptian army blamed the Christian protesters.[32] That is interesting because Christians were very much in the forefront of the revolution that brought down the government of Egypt's longtime strongman, Hosni Mubarak. The members of the army denied that it was responsible for any of the deaths because they were not using "live ammunition" when they moved in to break up the protest.[33] General Adel Emara said the army would never run over people, "even when battling our enemy."[34] Nobody could explain the mangled corpses or all the bodies with bullet holes in them.

Finally a number of Christians were arrested and jailed for provoking the disturbance. They were held for several months before being released. No one else was ever charged.[35]

CHURCH BUILDERS BEWARE

If you live in Egypt and want to build a mosque, no problem. The government will do everything it can to make the process easy for you. But it is an entirely different story if you want to build a church.[36] Then you have to go through a laborious approval process that can take years, or even decades, to complete. Some church buildings have even collapsed while the Christians who met in them waited for government approval to erect a new building.[37]

In one tragic case Egyptian police moved in at three in the morning to stop the construction of an addition to St. Mary's Coptic Orthodox Church in Giza. While men were working on the roof and an estimated two hundred members of the congregation prayed in the sanctuary, police surrounded the building. Then, to show they meant business, they opened up with tear gas, rubber bullets, and live ammunition. By the time the shooting stopped, four Coptic Christians were dead and another fifty were wounded, some seriously. In addition to this, two hundred members of the church were arrested, even though church leaders insisted they had the proper permits for the construction. Government authorities denied this but could not prove their contentions.[38]

There are many other cases that show the low status accorded to

Believers in Egypt. Consider the case of a man named Maher el-Gohary, who filed to change his official religion from Muslim to Christian.[39] El-Gohary had become a Christian more than thirty years earlier but never went to the trouble of changing his registration. For one thing, I suppose he knew that it wouldn't be easy to do and wouldn't go over so well with Egyptian authorities. It was a lot more involved than walking into city hall and signing a piece of paper.

But now his daughter Dina was fourteen, and he wanted to change his official registration for her sake. The problem was that if he registered as a Muslim, she would be considered a Muslim as well. On her sixteenth birthday she would be issued an identity card listing her religion as Muslim, making it illegal for her to marry a Christian. Naturally el-Gohary didn't want that to happen.

The matter required a court hearing, but el-Gohary could not attend because he received many death threats when word got out about what he intended to do. When he hired a lawyer to act in his behalf, registry officials beat the man.

Dina had to go into hiding. When she ventured out one day to get water, some strangers threw acid on her. Fortunately she was not seriously injured, although her jacket was ruined. Finally the entire family was forced to flee Egypt.

That gives some idea as to what life is like for many Christians in Egypt today.

In another case a seventeen-year-old schoolboy was murdered by a teacher and some classmates after the teacher noticed that the boy had a tattoo of a cross on his wrist. The teacher, Usama Mahmud Hasan, asked the boy, Ayman Nabil Labib, to wipe off the cross, but the boy replied that he couldn't do so because it was a tattoo and not a drawing. He also told the teacher that underneath his shirt he wore a cross on a necklace.

The teacher then reportedly asked his students, "What are we going to do with him?" At this point a group of about fifteen students began beating and chasing him. When he tried to escape, a couple of school administrators forced the boy into a teacher's room, where the group of his classmates beat him to death. Two of the students have been charged with his murder, but neither the teacher nor the school personnel have been charged.[40]

Do you suppose this was the work of Islamic extremists and that most Egyptians would be shocked by such a tragedy? Think again. In 2010 the Pew Research Center asked the Egyptian people whether they thought people who converted from Islam to Christianity should be executed. Some 84 percent said they should be.[41] That same year a member of Egypt's Ministry of Islamic Endowments appeared on state-run television and said he believed that people who converted from Islam should be killed.[42]

The fact is that in Egypt and in many other countries around the world, committed Christians are dealing with the same prejudice and mistreatment that blacks faced in the American South just a few decades ago. In those days a black man could not get a fair trial, especially if the matter came down to his word against a white man's word. It might be clear that the black man was telling the truth, but no judge or jury was going to listen if a white man told a conflicting story. If a white man was charged with robbing or killing a black man, he invariably got away with it. On the other hand, think of how many black people were beaten or murdered because they didn't "know their place."

It was outrageous. Something had to be done to change the system. Thank God for men like Dr. Martin Luther King Jr., who stood up for equal rights for all Americans.

I bring this up not to talk about American history but rather to drive home the point that Christians in countries like Egypt are being treated as second-class citizens and worse. It seems the pervasive spirit of Shira has permeated Egyptian society. They need our prayers desperately.

We must not forget them.

CHAPTER 9

WHATEVER HAPPENED TO THE ARAB SPRING?

With the Arab Spring came a great deal of hope that there would be a change towards more moderation, and opportunity for greater participation on the part of women in public life, and in economic life in the Middle East. But instead, we've seen in nation after nation a number of disturbing events.

—MITT ROMNEY

JUST A FEW years ago it seemed that a new era of freedom was dawning in the Middle East. Arab countries were throwing off brutal dictators who held them captive for generations. The excitement that liberty brings was in the air of Egypt, Libya, Syria, and other countries throughout the region. But what happened? The beautiful dream became a horrible nightmare. Amnesty International explains:

The Middle East and North Africa [were] engulfed in an unprecedented outburst of popular protests and demand for reform. It began in Tunisia and spread within weeks to Egypt, Yemen, Bahrain, Libya, and Syria.

Long-standing authoritarian leaders were swept from power, including Hosni Mubarak in Egypt and Zine el-Abidine Ben Ali in Tunisia.

Many hoped that this "Arab Spring" would bring in new governments that would deliver political reform and social justice. But the reality is more war and violence, and a crackdown on people who dare to speak out for a fairer, more open society.[1]

TUNISIA, 2010

According to reports, the young man, just twenty-six years old, lived in the landlocked rural town of Sidi Bouzid in Tunisia. His mother was a widow, and Mohamed Bouazizi was the breadwinner for her and his six siblings.[2] Mohamed was unable to find regular work in his busy community of just under fifty thousand souls.[3] So he struggled to feed his family by selling fruit and vegetables from his wooden cart.

Selling his produce was always a tenuous enterprise for Mohamed, as he didn't have the permit the city required to run his business.[4] On a cold December day in 2010, he was approached by the police, who demanded that he hand over the contents of his cart. Mohamed refused. It is reported that one of the police officers, a woman, slapped him.[5] Not only was that humiliating to this poor, but proud, young man, but it also left him unable to buy the necessities his family needed that day.

An hour later Mohamed doused himself with gasoline and, in front of a government building, set himself on fire.[6] The choice of location for his shocking act was not random and illustrated just how frustrated, angry, and tired he had become with the situation in Tunisia. Within hours it became evident that many others felt the same way. Protests began almost immediately, and images of Mohamed's terrible sacrifice were widely shared on the internet.[7]

Soon people across Tunisia were calling for President Zine El Abidine Ben Ali to step down. Mohamed Bouazizi's death became the catalyst for the convergence of many groups demanding a change to the current political system. For the unemployed such as Mohamed as well as "human rights activists, trade unionists, students, professors, and lawyers,"[8] the time had come to stand together and say enough was enough. And so the Tunisian Revolution (also called the Jasmine Revolution) began.[9]

On January 15, 2011, mere weeks after Mohamed Bouazizi's death, Tunisia's President Zine El Abidine Ben Ali fled the country for exile in

Saudi Arabia.[10] He did not leave without a fight. His government used violence against the demonstrators and even offered some political or economic concessions. However, that seemed to only strengthen the insurgents' desire for a new and democratically chosen government.[11] In the end the protesters overwhelmed security forces, and Ben Ali had no choice but to flee.[12]

President Ben Ali's ignominious flight from the country must have seemed like a blessing from God, not just to the freedom-hungry citizens of Tunisia but to the many other pro-democracy Arabs in the region who were beginning to demonstrate en masse against other entrenched authoritarian regimes.[13]

EGYPT, 2011

Within days after Tunisia ousted its president, protests broke out in Egypt. Here again, attempts by the government failed to control protesters, despite violent crackdowns against them on the one hand and concessions offered on the other. It became obvious that the fragrance of freedom and democracy wafting in the wind was stronger to the protesters than the sting of tear gas and pepper spray from Egypt's military.

But would this desire for change last? Around the world that was the question in everyone's mind, especially after the government disabled the country's internet access, thus greatly hindering the protesters' ability to communicate with one another.[14]

Then came the turning point. The Egyptian army announced that it would not use force against the protesters. Without the support of his army, President Hosni Mubarak had no choice but to step down.[15] Thirty years of ruling with impunity came to a shameful end, with Mubarak being given a life sentence for the killings that occurred during the start of the Revolution.[16] (Six years after his detention, Mubarak was acquitted and released.)[17]

Though the military at first met with high public approval in Egypt, it was not long before clashes resumed between protesters and the military and security forces. This time it was because the country's latest administration seemed to be reluctant to transfer complete power to an elected government. Clashes continued until November 2011, when parliamentary elections proceeded and a new People's Assembly was put in place.[18]

The protests and resulting changes in Tunisia and Egypt acted like lightning rods and encouraged similar movements in the surrounding Arab nations. It appeared almost as if the ordinary working-class people (especially young people) had been waiting for such early signs of success. In rapid succession protests erupted in Yemen, Bahrain, Libya, and Syria.

REVOLUTION IN YEMEN

Some of the first protests outside of Tunisia and Egypt were in Yemen in the latter days of January 2011. In a surprising twist some of the country's influential leaders in the military and tribes actually decided to side with the pro-democracy activists. After demands for the abdication of President Ali Abdullah Saleh did not succeed, fighting broke out in Sanaa.[19] In June the president was hit in a bomb attack and left the country for medical care,[20] temporarily raising hopes with the protesters that he might not return and their demands would be met. These demands included the government's addressing issues of unemployment, the dire economic conditions, and rampant corruption.

However, Saleh returned after four months. Finally, in November 2011, he agreed to a phased power transfer through Abdrabbuh Mansur Hadi, the vice president.[21] Hadi took over the presidency after a presidential election in February 2012 in which he was the only candidate.[22] His presidency was not to last; he was forced to flee due to pressure by Houthi rebels in March 2015.[23]

For Yemen, what started as hope in its Arab Spring ended in the Yemeni Civil War. The Houthis, who began as a theological movement espousing peace and tolerance, now found themselves embroiled in an international conflict.

BAHRAIN

Bahrain was another country rife with demands for political freedom and economic reforms. Though the Shiites were in the majority in the country, they had long been marginalized by the Sunni government and so had joined forces with those protesting human rights issues.[24] However, unlike the protests in Tunisia and Egypt, these protesters did not originally intend to overthrow their government. What they really wanted was to be able to garner more political power and freedom for the Shiites, along with greater respect for human rights for all.[25]

Since 1982 the well-known Pearl Monument had stood in the center of the Pearl Roundabout in the heart of Bahrain's capital, Manama. Before its destruction the roundabout was the major intersection for traffic routes into the city and was surrounded by the Bahrain Central Market, the marina, and a large apartment complex. It was the natural choice for the protesters to meet and stage their demonstrations.

There the police made a raid in the early morning hours of February 17, 2011, to forcibly remove the protesters and their encampment. Four protesters were killed.[26] After that a number of protesters decided it was time to call for an end to the monarchy. That was when things took a turn for the worse. The following day as protesters came back to the roundabout, they were fired upon by army forces. One protester was killed.[27]

In the ensuing days thousands of protesters arrived at the roundabout, only to be met by fifteen hundred Saudi and United Arab Emirates troops hired by the Bahrain government.[28] The roundabout was not the only site of civil unrest in the country, and King Hamad bin Isa Al Khalifa declared a state of emergency and ordered the military to retake control of the situation.[29] After this, on March 18, government forces tore down the Pearl Monument altogether.[30]

For all intents and purposes, the crackdown on the Bahrain protesters, which included people from all walks of life, was nothing less than brutal. The raiding of Shiite neighborhoods, checkpoint beatings, and even denial of medical care were all methods of intimidation used by the police.

LIBYA

Protests against Colonel Muammar Gaddafi's forty-two-year control of the Libyan government began on February 15, 2011. Gaddafi threatened that if and when he answered with force, "everything will burn," and he vowed to "die as a martyr."[31] Gaddafi's son also spoke on television and warned of an impending civil war if the protests continued.[32] Protests did continue, and the death toll quickly rose into the thousands, prompting "international condemnation."[33]

Surprisingly the United Nations Security Council adopted Resolution 1973 on March 17, 2011, authorizing a no-fly zone over Libya and "all necessary measures" to protect its civilians.[34] Within two days the United States, the United Kingdom, and France conducted a bombing campaign against pro-Gaddafi forces.[35] Before long a coalition of some twenty-eight states from Europe and the Middle East had joined the intervention. The previously noted actions allowed the opposition forces to conduct an offensive, thereby capturing many towns across Libya's coast. This was a back-and-forth battle, with Gaddafi's military once again retaking many of the towns that the opposition forces had won.[36]

But Libya's Mediterranean coastline was not the only area of Libya caught up in the battle. Very heavy fighting was occurring to the west. For three months the rebel-held city of Misrata had been under siege by Gaddafi loyalists. Thanks to coalition air strikes, however, the siege of Misrata was finally broken.[37]

Opposition forces captured Tripoli in late August. Gaddafi and a number of his top officials regrouped in Sirte, which Gaddafi declared to be the new capital. Finally, in October, Sirte was taken by fighters and Gaddafi was killed.

Was it finally an end to the civil war? Unfortunately not, as there were multiple extremist groups vying for power.

SYRIA

On March 6, 2011, Syrian security forces arrested about fifteen children in Daraa, in southern Syria. These children were accused of writing anti-government slogans and were arrested. Rumors that these children were abused while they were under arrest filled the city's residents with rage, and soon there were protests throughout the city.[38]

On March 15 protesters gathered in the cities of Damascus, Aleppo,[39] Daraa, Hama, and Deir ez-Zor. In less than twenty-four hours there were widespread reports of arrests numbering in the thousands. There were also claims of casualties but no official figures. About one hundred thousand protesters gathered at the central square of Homs and called for President Bashar al-Assad to resign. Protests spread throughout the country and continued into July 2011.

The response of the Assad regime was one of complete and brutal defiance, with military operations strategically placed in several districts, especially in the North. Security forces were reported to have fired into crowds of protesters on more than one occasion.[40] Then, on July 31, Assad sent his army's tanks storming into a number of cities, including Hama, Deir ez-Zor, and Herak, which is near Daraa,[41] where the Syrian revolution was said to have started.

In spite of the crackdown by the Assad regime, the Syrian opposition army—called the Free Syrian Army—was able to take control of some of the regions. This was the case with the Baba Amr district in Homs[42] and by December some cities in Idlib and certain neighborhoods in Homs and Hama. The Free Syrian Army (FSA) continued to have some success through the end of 2011, taking over some areas near Damascus.[43]

Then, on January 30, 2012, President Assad's brother, Maher al-Assad, led the Syrian Army's fourth armored division and joined with the Republican Guard in Damascus,[44] determined to stop any further progress of the FSA, now only eight kilometers from the palace.[45] Additional fighting erupted close to the airport.[46] From then on the FSA was hard-pressed to hang on to the ground it had previously gained. By February 4 the Syrian Army attacked Homs with such a tremendous bombardment that "at least 300 people" were killed.[47] It was a great blow to the Free Syria Army and the citizens of Syria.

By the end of February, Assad and his armies had regained control over Madaya and Zabadani and had reentered Baba Amr amid heavy artillery and street fighting.[48] From that point on the opposition forces lost street after street and neighborhood after neighborhood. Soon only certain neighborhoods in Homs remained in their control.

Assad's vicious response to the protesters and the opposition army drew condemnation from human rights groups and international leaders around the world. Yet Assad never loosened his grip. Instead, his hold on power remained as strong as ever. He maintained the support of vital military units because those units were composed of members of Syria's Alawite minority, of which he was a member.[49]

What was the United Nations' stance on this humanitarian tragedy? As inadequate as ever. UN Security Council resolutions that were meant to put pressure on Assad in both October 2011 and February 2012 were vetoed by both China and Russia.[50] Those two countries also vowed to oppose any measure put forward by the UN that would lead to foreign intervention in Syria or the forcible removal of Assad.[51] Once again, a humanitarian tragedy was being played out right before the United Nations' eyes and, for all intents and purposes, was completely ignored. Even the Arab League's sending a delegation of peace monitors in December 2011 did next to nothing to reduce the violence.[52]

AFTER THE ARAB SPRING

So what did the Arab Spring accomplish? If Westerners were hopeful that its protesters were moderates hungering for Western-style democratic governments, they were soon disappointed. The so-called "spring" (a term possibly coined by Marc Lynch, an American professor of political science and international affairs at George Washington University[53]) soon gave way to a very cold and unforgiving winter.

Libya, Syria, and Yemen were thrust into "bloody civil war" and "economic stagnation."[54] The once promising "spring" morphed into instability in Egypt, Bahrain, and Iraq. All of this has the prospect of leading to continued instability in governments throughout the region.[55]

In trying to determine how much support the West should or shouldn't have provided the rebels, it might be wise to consider that perhaps we were viewing what was happening through our own wishful, rose-colored glasses. People in the West tended to believe that the revolts and demonstrations were led by people with a fervent desire for change to more democratic governments such as our own. Probably nothing could have been further from the truth.

As Joseph V. Micallef notes in his article "The Arab Spring: Six Years Later," these revolts were never really democratic movements. Although there were undoubtedly "some liberal-democratic groups" mixed in with the protesters, it was mostly "a reactionary movement...against secular Arab regimes."[56] In other words, most of the protests were "led primarily by conservative, religious and Islamist elements" of the population.[57] While we were blindly hoping for a turning away from Islamic-based governments, the opposite was actually happening.

Most regimes that came to power in the region between the 1950s and the 1970s had become repressive, ruling mainly through corruption and brutality. Post–World War II Arab regimes did little to improve the lives of their average citizens. In fact, as time went on, most of these governments became even more corrupt. In some ways, as Micallef opines, the West shares the blame for that.[58]

The Middle East map was largely the result of "post–World War I European dissection of the Ottoman Empire."[59] Treaties hacked up the Middle East without considering "ethnicity, religion, culture or historical association."[60] In fact, many of the borders were drawn to accommodate the victors' thirst for oil.[61] There was also a pervasive belief at the time that colonial rule actually benefited from "pitting various ethnic and religious groups against each other."[62] Perhaps the thought at the time was that it was better to have the groups fighting among themselves than to see them turn their discontent against their colonial rulers.

Although the Arab Spring might have held the promise of a flowering democratic "summer" for the Middle East as viewed by the West, it was never really a possibility. Instead, the Arab Spring became the bloody slaughter of hundreds of thousands of civilians and drove more than seven million people from their homes.[63] The destabilized territories have become training grounds for jihadists, with the resultant spread of illicit arms. The multitudes of Syrian refugees flooding Europe have caused major "security concerns" on that continent.[64] In oil-rich Saudi Arabia and other nations benefiting from oil profits, there has been a slowdown in economic growth because of the decline in the price of oil, resulting in high unemployment even in those countries.[65]

Did anything worthwhile result from the Arab Spring? Very little, if anything at all. In fact, further destabilization of the region is noteworthy. Predictions of a new and more democratic Middle East have devolved into even more brutal regimes with more mass killings and more refugees flooding into nearby nations.

The modern world with its easy access to the internet and social media outlets makes it easier than ever for tyrants and terrorists to rally like-minded individuals, for news "pundits" to spread lies and fear as much as legitimate information, and for those with evil intent to wreak devastating havoc as never before.

Will there ever be a lasting peace in the Middle East? Perhaps someday, but not as a result of the Arab Spring.

CHAPTER 10

THE UNITED NATIONS VS. ISRAEL

*Supporters of Israel feel that it is harshly judged, by
standards that are not applied to its enemies—and too
often this is true, particularly in some UN bodies.*

—Kofi Annan, Former United Nations Secretary-General

I T WAS UNDOUBTEDLY hoped by its founders that the United Nations would be a phoenix rising from the ashes of the destruction and carnage of World War II, a glimmer of hope desperately needed by the world's masses of war-weary citizens. This was not the first attempt at creating an international body to promote peace and cooperation between nations. It was hoped that this time, however, the mistakes from those past attempts might have been instructive and this United Nations might be the means to prevent future wars and genocide.

I think Winston Churchill's famous quote from 1946 expresses it best:

> We must make sure that [the United Nations'] work is fruitful, that it is a reality and not a sham, that it is a force for action, and not merely a frothing of words, that it is a true temple of peace in which the shields of many nations can someday be hung up, and not merely a cockpit in a Tower of Babel.[1]

Unfortunately we now know that Churchill's hope was not to become reality. In fact, it became clear fairly soon after its founding that the UN was—in spite of its lofty ideals and even loftier building—ill-equipped to carry out its mission of safeguarding global order and peace.

THE UN—ANYTHING BUT UNITED

Over the years it has been shown time and again that when it comes to facing aggressive nations or those nations' leaders, the United Nations is anything but united. The first part of Article 1 of its charter clearly states the organization's purposes:

> To maintain international peace and security, and to that end: to take effective collective measures for the prevention and removal of threats to the peace, and for the suppression of acts of aggression or other breaches of the peace, and to bring about by peaceful means, and in conformity with the principles of justice and international law, adjustment or settlement of international disputes or situations which might lead to a breach of the peace.[2]

Why has the United Nations failed so miserably to live up to its stated goals? Why has it stood by while groups deemed "unsuitable" by their countries' leaders are slaughtered?

One reason, stated by Kofi Annan, the United Nations' Assistant Secretary-General and Under-Secretary-General for Peacekeeping Operations during both the Bosnian and Rwandan genocides,[3] is that the UN possesses an "institutional ideology of impartiality even when confronted with attempted genocide."[4] In Rwanda eight hundred thousand people, most of them Tutsis, were believed slaughtered in a systematic crusade to exterminate them.[5] UN peacekeeping forces had been instructed to uphold "strict impartiality"[6] and thus they hunkered down in Srebrenica while the slaughter went on. Similarly seven thousand Muslims were "slaughtered in a UN 'safe haven.'"[7] How could UN peacekeeping forces have stood by and done nothing while these atrocities occurred?

As stated in Dore Gold's excellent exposé of the United Nations, *Tower of Babble,* "Diplomatic neutralism in the face of genocidal murderers is not amoral; it is *immoral.*"[8] There can be no neutrality when it comes to the mass slaughter of a people. In fact, remaining neutral in those types of situations is not remaining neutral at all; it is actually taking sides with the slaughterers.

Through its inaction in such times, the UN gives credence to dictators and autocratic rulers who have either violated UN resolutions (as in the case of Saddam Hussein, who ignored his pledges to allow weapons inspectors into his country in exchange for the Oil-for-Food Program intended to help feed the people of Iraq)[9] or engaged in the outright systematic murder of their own or their neighbors' people.

It must be acknowledged that the United Nations is a political rather than legal entity. Yet it has been endowed with enough moral weight that it must not stand idly by when aggressor nations turn their eyes against their neighbors. The trouble is that it has lost its moral direction. Why? Partly because its original members were survivors of World War II who had been impressed by the wise democratic leadership of Winston Churchill and Franklin Roosevelt. Yet by the 1990s only 75 out of 184 member states were "free democracies."[10] The result of this basic change is nowhere more apparent than in the organization's dealings with Israel.

THE UN AND THE CREATION OF ISRAEL

Certainly no people has deserved a homeland more than the Jews. The land God promised to Abraham and his descendants has been fought over more than any piece of real estate on the planet. Yet the Jews actually lived and ruled there for only a brief period before being scattered to all corners of the globe.

Only after the horrors of the Holocaust did a world body such as the United Nations take up the cause of creating a Jewish state. At that time Palestine was under British rule as decreed by the Palestine Mandate and confirmed by the League of Nations in 1922.[11] The Mandate system had been created after World War I to administer non-self-governing territories for the benefit and improvement of those populations. It was to be a temporary trust until such time as those territories could become self-governing.

After World War II ended and the whole world became aware of the extent of Hitler's persecution of the Jews, the United Nations Special Committee on Palestine (UNSCOP) took up "the question of Palestine."[12] The group went to Palestine in 1947 and met with Jewish and Zionist delegations.[13] Though invited, the Arab Higher Committee refused to attend any of the meetings.[14]

In the end UNSCOP recommended the establishment of independent Arab and Jewish states, with the city of Jerusalem to be controlled by an "International Trusteeship System."[15] Thus, Resolution 181 was adopted in November of 1947.[16] No immediate action was taken to bring about its implementation, however, and it wasn't until May 14, 1948, with the British withdrawal from the region, that the Jewish People's Council proclaimed the establishment of the Jewish state of Israel.[17] President Harry Truman announced the United States' recognition of Israel on that day.

Not everyone was rejoicing.

The Arab states of Egypt, Syria, Lebanon, Transjordan, and Iraq immediately declared what would become the first Arab-Israeli War. Outnumbered and outgunned, Israel still managed to win the war, much to almost everyone's surprise. What many people had failed to understand was that the Jews were not just fighting for their personal lives; they were fighting for the very existence of their cultural heritage and homeland, the homeland God had promised to them and their father Abraham thousands of years earlier.

Clearly there were many who hoped that Israel would be crushed by its enemies and that the question of a Jewish homeland would just go away. Sadly the United Nations has done little since 1948 to ensure that the tiny nation of Israel will continue to exist while surrounded by its enemies.

ARABS AND RUSSIANS AGAINST THE JEWS

Time and again since that first Arab-Israeli War the United Nations has passed resolutions attacking Israel. Since the mid-1970s, Arab nations, the Soviet Union, and a number of developing countries from around the world have joined together to form a pro-PLO lobby.

It should be noted, however, that changes in the United Nations began even earlier than the 1970s. In its infancy the organization "was dominated by the Cold War competition between"[18] the Soviet bloc in the East and the United States and its allies in the West. But the UN's membership increased from 82 member states in 1952 to 126 in 1968, so the two Cold War "blocs became outnumbered by a third" consisting largely of former colonies of the West that had won their independence since the war.[19]

This new bloc, called the Non-Aligned Movement, was "non-aligned far more emphatically with the West than with the Communist world."[20] As Cuba, Vietnam, Egypt, and many Muslim countries took leading roles, an anti-West flavor took over.[21] This was especially true in regard to the Middle East and its major area of concern: Israel. Soon this bloc of nations was pushing a new agenda, that of "advancing Arab claims and actions against Israel, including even legitimating Palestinian terrorism."[22]

It is also interesting to note that almost all of these countries are either autocracies or dictatorships. In the General Assembly they often vote as one to pass resolutions attacking Israel (the only democracy in the region) while giving their support to the Palestinians. The submission of resolutions against Israel by these countries has been relentless, and the passage of so many of them in the General Assembly has been shameful. Here is just a small sample of the many actions and resolutions introduced and/or passed by the General Assembly against the State of Israel:

- In 1974 the General Assembly invited the PLO to send a representative to speak to the Assembly. Before this only designated representatives of a legitimate government had ever been allowed to speak.[23] But here came Yasser Arafat, gun holstered to his hip, as if he were a rock star.[24] (He removed his sidearm before speaking to the General Assembly.) Then, with fiery words, he vowed his "resolve to build a new world…a world free of colonialism, imperialism, neo-colonialism, and racism in each of its instances, including Zionism." He received a standing ovation.[25]

- One week later the General Assembly passed Resolution 3236, which affirmed "the right of the Palestinian people to regain its rights by all means,"[26] thus giving a veiled legitimization to the murders and bombings of Israeli civilians by the Palestinian terrorists.

- Even though the UN attempted to pass a general treaty against terrorism after the September 11 attacks in 2001, the

Organization of the Islamic Conference insisted, as reported by the *Washington Post*, "that anti-Israeli militants be exempted."[27]

- In 1975 the General Assembly gave "permanent representative status to the PLO" and later approved Resolution 3379, which labeled Zionism as a "form of racism."[28] It wasn't until 1991 that that resolution was finally repealed. But even then not a single Arab country voted for the repeal.[29]

- Also in 1975 the aforementioned bloc voting ensured the creation of the "pro-PLO 'Committee on the Inalienable Rights of the Palestinian People,'" which became an important part of the PLO propaganda machine.[30]

- In 1986, with the continued prompting of the Arab states, the General Assembly declared that Israel "is not a peace-loving Member State and that it has not carried out its obligations under the Charter of the United Nations."[31]

  For all practical purposes, this was tantamount to a threat to expel Israel from the United Nations. Worse, it called for an international campaign for all member states to cease their dealings with Israel.[32]. Of course the United Nations could not enforce such statements. Yet the weight of those words undoubtedly reinforced the Arabs' belief that they were in the right and that Israel was inherently evil.

- On December 11, 1991, the General Assembly mandated "a UN-sponsored peace conference that would include the PLO."[33]

- On December 16, 1991, the General Assembly requested "Israel to rescind a Knesset resolution declaring Jerusalem its capital" and "demand[ed] Israel's withdrawal from 'occupied territories,'" including, of course, Jerusalem.[34]

- Another resolution (from a group of four resolutions approved in short order) supported the return of Palestinian refugees and Palestinian self-government.[35]

- Approximately twenty committees have been devoted to the Palestinian cause, with millions of dollars earmarked for the issue since 2004, plus $255,000 just to investigate "Israeli Practices Affecting the Human Rights of the Palestinian People and Other Arabs of the Occupied Territories."[36]

- The 1980s found the Arab states actually trying to deny Israel a seat in the General Assembly, and only the United States' persistent effort kept them from accomplishing this.[37]

- In 2003 the UN called for a total of three emergency sessions (unheard of)—all to discuss Israel. Two were to castigate Israel for its security fence and one because Israel was considering expelling Arafat.[38]

Then, again in 2003, the UN convened a two-day symposium, "International Conference of Civil Society in Support of the Palestinian People with the theme 'End the Occupation!'"[39]

End the occupation?

What was even worse was the statement made by Nasser al-Kidwa, Palestinian observer to the UN, that "violence in self-defense in the occupied Palestinian territories is not terrorism."[40]

Really? Sounds like legal carte blanche for terrorists to do whatever murderous acts they please. In other words, the idea that Palestinian terrorism against Israel is a legitimate form of protest was introduced at the United Nations.

If all of this were not enough, in 2005 (as Israel prepared to withdraw from the Gaza Strip) the Palestinian Authority celebrated with banners saying "Gaza Today. The West Bank and Jerusalem Tomorrow."[41] This egregious display was made worse by the fact that the banners were paid for with funds from the UN Development Program and actually bore the program's logo.[42] US Ambassador John Bolton was outraged and said, "Funding this kind of activity is inappropriate and unacceptable."[43]

Also in 2005 a Palestinian exhibition was on display at the UN to focus on "sympathy with the Palestinian people."[44] During the event a map of the Middle East was displayed that did not even show Israel.[45] Keep in mind that Israel is a UN member state, and it was totally ignored on the map of the Middle East, labeled instead as Palestine.

There can be no clearer indication of the intentions of the Arab peoples living in the region. They would prefer that Israel be wiped off the face of the map. And as far as I am concerned, allowing such anti-Israel demonstrations in the halls of the UN is unconscionable.

And I am not finished yet.

In November 2007, on the sixtieth anniversary of the General Assembly's vote to divide Palestine and create separate Jewish and Arab states, only two flags were flown in the room where the UN leaders gave their speeches to mark the occasion. The flags that were flown? "The UN flag and a Palestinian flag"; no Israeli flag was raised.[46]

You are no doubt beginning to see why Israel holds so much animosity against the United Nations. But some of the UN's worst displays of unfairness toward the State of Israel take place in the Human Rights Council—so much so that in March of 2013 the United States sent the following impassioned letter to the council:

> The United States remains extremely troubled by this Council's continued biased and disproportionate focus on Israel...the Human Rights Council must treat all countries by the same standards. This standing agenda item exemplifies the blatantly unfair treatment that one UN member state receives in this body.
>
> The legitimacy of this Council will remain in question as long as one country is unfairly and uniquely singled out under its own agenda item. The absurdity and hypocrisy of this agenda item is further amplified by the resolutions brought under it including, yet again, a resolution on the "human rights in the occupied Syrian Golan" motivated by the Syrian regime, at a time when that regime is murdering its own citizens by the tens of thousands. The United States implores Council members to eliminate these biased resolutions and permanent agenda item seven.[47]

In 2006 the Human Rights Council replaced the Commission on Human Rights, with the hopes that this new council would regain some of the United Nations' legitimacy on the subject.[48] Sadly, like its predecessor, the "new" commission has fallen far short of the mark. Time and again, it has singled out Israel as a violator of human rights and "health rights" while completely ignoring "health crises in Yemen, Saudi Arabia, Syria, Iran, Iraq, Libya and North Korea."[49] In fact, anti-Semitism is so rampant and obvious in the council that during the genocide in Darfur it spent its time writing reports castigating Israel instead of focusing on the tragedy and urgent needs in Darfur.[50]

Noting the council's fixation on Israel, UN Secretary-General Kofi Annan declared, "There are surely other situations, besides the one in the Middle East, which would merit scrutiny by a special session of this Council. I would suggest that Darfur is a glaring case in point."[51]

Year after year the Human Rights Council's hypocrisy has continued. As late as March of 2017 the United States boycotted a session about the Israeli-Palestinian conflict, "citing the council's 'long-standing bias against Israel.'" After attending the session, the UK decried its "disproportionate focus on Israel" and stated that members needed to "also recognize the continuing terrorism, incitement and violence that Israel faces."[52]

Yet that is something that the UN has repeatedly failed to do. Immediately following President Trump's announcement in December of 2017 that the United States would move its embassy from Tel Aviv to Jerusalem, the UN Security Council voted to reverse the move.[53]

Ban Ki-moon, general secretary of the United Nations, has admitted that the organization is biased against Israel. "Decades of political maneuvering have created a disproportionate number of resolutions, reports and committees against Israel," he said. Israel's ambassador to the UN, Danny Danon, agreed, saying: "The UN passed 223 resolutions condemning Israel, while only eight resolutions condemning the Syrian regime as it has massacred its citizens over the past six years. This is absurd."[54]

Here's a look at just a little of what the United Nations has done:

- Up until 2013 Israel had been condemned in forty-five resolutions by the UN Human Rights Council.[55] In 2017 alone the United Nations issued twenty-one resolutions or sanctions against Israel and six against the rest of the world.[56]

- In December of 2017 151 UN member states voted to disavow Israel's ties to Jerusalem, while 6 votes were cast against the resolution. This was during the period President Trump was considering a move of the US embassy to Jerusalem.[57]

- Thirty-six member nations of the United Nations don't even recognize Israel.[58]

- "EU states have failed to introduce a single [UN General Assembly] resolution on the human rights situation in China, Venezuela, Saudi Arabia, Belarus, Cuba, Turkey, Pakistan, Vietnam, Algeria, or on 175 other countries."[59]

- As of December 2017 the United States had used its veto power forty-three times to stop Security Council draft resolutions against Israel.[60]

It has become clear that anti-Semitism is not just rampant at the United Nations; it is alive, well, and broadly accepted. It is also shameful. Mitchell Bard and the Jewish Virtual Library have collected a sampling of the many comments that could be heard in the hallowed halls of the United Nations. All the examples below are from Bard's article, "United Nations: The U.N. Relationship With Israel":[61]

- Before the "1984 UN Human Rights Commission Conference on religious tolerance," Saudi Arabian delegate Marouf al-Dawalibi said the following: "The Talmud says that if a Jew does not drink every year the blood of a non-Jewish man, he will be damned for eternity."

- In 1991 the Syrian ambassador insisted that Jews killed Christian children and made matzos with their blood.

- In March of 1997 the Palestinian representative to the Human Rights Commission made the scurrilous claim that "the Israeli government had injected 300 Palestinian children with the HIV virus." Though the United States and Israel have tried to have this outrageous libel expunged from UN records, it is still there.

- In July 2005 the UN special rapporteur on the right to food, Jean Ziegler, "called the Gaza Strip 'an immense concentration camp' and compared Israelis to Nazis."

Peter Rough, a contributor to the *Hill*, visited Jerusalem in May 2017 and wrote afterward that no matter what pronouncements the United Nations makes or what resolutions it passes, the Israeli government will not give up either its settlements near the 1967 line or its access to Jerusalem.[62]

That being said, what can be done to help end the slaughter of innocent civilians on both sides and move the political discussion forward in a positive manner?

Because of the UN's history of bias against Israel, it has lost most, if not all, of its credibility with the Israelis. For there to be any progress, Mr. Rough suggests that the United Nations shift its focus from one-sided finger-pointing and instead cultivate "the most important prerequisite for peace," which is *trust*.[63]

Peace is crucial to any country's ability to thrive and prosper. Because Israel is the only democracy surrounded by autocratic regimes that desire to destroy it, Israel needs a new commitment from the United Nations to speak peace in its halls instead of promoting the voices of hate, anger, and violence. Unless that happens, Mr. Rough proposes that Israel will continue to distrust the UN, and Israeli citizens will continue to vote for "cautious leaders" who are less inclined to actively seek peaceful solutions to the problems they share with their neighbors.[64]

This responsibility is not solely in the hands of the UN. As Mr. Rough articulated in his article, if Palestinian leaders truly want peace, they must "prepare their people [and themselves] to accept a peace deal"[65]— and *any* peace deal will require compromise. Realistically the only way either side will ever accept compromise is through a revamping of the educational curriculum.[66] As long as hate is being taught and practiced, Palestinians will not be willing to live alongside the Israelis, and the Israelis in turn will not trust their Arab neighbors enough to refrain from building "walls and domes to defend themselves."[67]

According to Mr. Rough, the United Nations would do well to help the Palestinians with that undertaking rather than continuing to foment Israeli mistrust with anti-Israel proclamations.[68] Then perhaps there can be peace, not only between the Palestinians and Israelis but also between Israel and the United Nations.

CHAPTER 11

HEZBOLLAH, HAMAS, AND THE MUSLIM BROTHERHOOD

I am against any reconciliation with Israel.
—HASSAN NASRALLAH, HEZBOLLAH'S SECRETARY GENERAL

W E HAVE ALL heard of organizations such as Hezbollah, Hamas, and the Muslim Brotherhood. But who are they? What do they really want? Are they interchangeable? Are they all dedicated to Israel's annihilation?

In order to understand the situation in the Middle East today, we have to understand who the players are. That means we have to get beyond the propaganda and the public statements and get to know with whom we are really dealing.

Let's take them one by one.

WHAT IS HEZBOLLAH?

HEZBOLLAH IS A Shiite Muslim political (and military) group whose goal is to create an Islamic state in Lebanon that operates under Sharia law.[1] (Sound familiar?) The organization has strong ties to Iran and the late Ayatollah Ruhollah Khomeini in particular.[2]

The similarities to the Islamic State are obvious, but there are some major differences between the two. Hezbollah is a Shiite organization with strong ties to Iran, a 90 percent Shiite nation.[3] ISIS is a Sunni organization with ties to Iraq and Syria. Syria is a predominantly Sunni country. Iraq is majority Shiite, but Saddam Hussein was a Sunni, as were most of the officials in his government, which ruled Iraq for more than twenty years. (Because the Shiites were an "oppressed majority" in Iraq,[4] many Sunnis there continue to fear that Shiites will take revenge on them for the excesses of the Hussein regime. It is within these ranks that ISIS is likely to find many of its most dedicated supporters.)

It might be overstating it just a bit to say that Sunnis hate Shiites and Shiites hate Sunnis—but not by much. These two branches of Islam have been killing and maiming each other for centuries. As an example of the mistrust that exists between the groups, a 2010 poll in Lebanon revealed that 94 percent of Shiite Muslims had a favorable view of Hezbollah, while 84 percent of Sunni Muslims had an unfavorable view of the organization.[5]

Meanwhile both Sunnis and Shiites want to build an Islamic state here on earth from which the Mahdi (the Islamic version of the Messiah) will rule. In the final battle, which precedes the Mahdi's coming, the "other side" will either be converted or killed—it isn't really clear which.

I mentioned earlier that Hezbollah has strong ties to Iran's Ayatollah Khomeini. If you were around in the late 1970s and early 1980s, you certainly remember the ayatollah. He was the one who stirred up the Iranian Revolutionary Guard to take American diplomats hostage and then spent more than a year thumbing his nose at the United States while we tried to get them free. His disdain for American leadership and our inability to free the hostages was undoubtedly one of the biggest reasons why Jimmy Carter lost the 1980 election to Ronald Reagan.

Oddly enough, by today's standards I suppose that Khomeini might be considered a moderate. The hostages were not treated particularly well, but at least none of them were beheaded or killed while in captivity.

If you look in an encyclopedia, you will probably read that Hezbollah was formed in reaction to an Israeli invasion of Lebanon in 1982.[6] Once again, it sounds as if the Israelis were the aggressors, invading their "peaceful" neighbor next door. In fact, the move into Lebanon was an attempt not to overthrow the Lebanese government but to stop PLO terrorist attacks on Israel.[7]

PLO raiders had been coming across the border to launch attacks on innocent Israelis and then fleeing back to safety in Lebanon. In one of these attacks, known as the Coastal Road massacre, terrorists hijacked a bus and began killing everyone on board. Thirty-eight people were murdered, including thirty-seven Israelis, one American, and thirteen children.[8]

Imagine if one of our neighbors, Canada or Mexico, harbored terrorists who constantly made attacks on the United States. In fact, when Pancho Villa attacked a small New Mexico town in 1916, American troops poured into Mexico to track him down. A strong military response was considered absolutely necessary.[9] Yet Israel is roundly criticized for defending itself.

Moreover, Israel was not the only country with soldiers in Lebanon at the time Hezbollah was founded. Syria had thirty thousand troops there as part of an Arab "peace-keeping force."[10] Those troops entered Lebanon in 1976 and stayed for twenty-nine years, effectively controlling the Lebanese government for much of that time.

Bear in mind that Lebanon is not a solidly Muslim country. Although somewhere around 54 percent of Lebanese are Muslims, just over 40 percent are Christians, and almost 6 percent are Druze[11] (a religion that originated in Egypt during the eleventh century). Other reasons for Israel's presence in Lebanon included protecting Christians there and supporting the South Lebanon Army, a largely Christian organization.[12]

Since Hezbollah's beginning in the mid-1980s its primary goal has been the destruction of Israel. The organization's manifesto says, "Our struggle will end only when this entity [Israel] is obliterated."[13] Hezbollah's Deputy-General Na'im Qasim says that the struggle against Israel is a core belief of Hezbollah and a primary reason for the organization's existence.[14]

In a 2002 interview Hezbollah spokesperson Hassan Ezzeddin reiterated that Hezbollah will never stop fighting the Jews:

> "Our goal is to liberate the 1948 borders of Palestine," he added, referring to the year of Israel's founding. The Jews who survive this war of liberation, Ezzeddin said, "can go back to Germany, or wherever they came from." He added, however, that the Jews

who lived in Palestine before 1948 will be "allowed to live as a minority and they will be cared for by the Muslim majority."[15]

Hezbollah's leadership has consistently denied that the Holocaust ever took place, and they also claim that Israel has deliberately spread AIDS throughout the Middle East in an attempt to kill Arabs.[16]

Robert S. Wistrich, a historian specializing in the study of anti-Semitism, says that "Hezbollah has relied on the endless vilification of Jews as 'enemies of mankind,' 'conspiratorial, obstinate, and conceited' adversaries full of 'satanic plans' to enslave the Arabs."[17]

Where does Hezbollah get money to fund its war against the Jews? According to reports, the organization receives somewhere between $60 million and $100 million in financial assistance from Iran each year.[18] American law enforcement officials also believe that Hezbollah receives millions of dollars annually from drug and cigarette smuggling operations based in South America,[19] although Hezbollah denies this.

According to an investigation by NBC News and Telemundo:

> The Iranian-backed Hezbollah militia has taken root in South America, fostering a well-financed force of Islamist radicals boiling with hatred for the United States and ready to die to prove it, according to militia members, US officials and police agencies across the continent.
>
> From its Western base in a remote region divided by the borders of Paraguay, Brazil and Argentina known as the Tri-border, or the Triple Frontier, Hezbollah has mined the frustrations of many Muslims among about 25,000 Arab residents whose families immigrated mainly from Lebanon, in two waves after the 1948 Arab-Israeli war and after the 1985 Lebanese civil war.
>
> An investigation by Telemundo and NBC News has uncovered details of an extensive smuggling network run by Hezbollah, a Shiite Muslim group founded in Lebanon in 1982.... The operation funnels large sums of money to militia leaders in the Middle East and finances training camps, propaganda operations and bomb attacks in South America, according to US and South American officials.[20]

The article goes on to say that it would be fairly easy for Hezbollah terrorists to reach the United States from this "poorly patrolled" area of Latin America, "simply by posing as tourists."[21]

The United States classifies Hezbollah as a terrorist organization, as do several other countries around the world, including Canada, France, and Japan. Russia considers Hezbollah to be a "legitimate sociopolitical force."[22] Ties between Russia and Hezbollah have grown closer in recent months as Hezbollah fighters have poured into Syria to fight alongside Russian troops defending dictator Bashar al-Assad.[23] North Korea is one of two countries that officially support Hezbollah.[24] The other is Cuba, where Hezbollah has a base.[25]

Yes, you read that right. Hezbollah has a base in Cuba.

The existence of the base was revealed in emails released from former Secretary of State Hillary Clinton's files.[26] According to reports, the Israeli intelligence agency Mossad believed Israeli interests "in South America and the Caribbean" were targets, although Hezbollah has also been "casing facilities associated with the United States and the United Kingdom, including diplomatic missions, major banks, and businesses."[27]

This is one more reason why Americans can't afford to ignore the situation in the Middle East. It seems that whether or not we like it, Israel's problems are our problems.

One other thing you should know about Hezbollah is that the organization is very well armed, with a stockpile of thousands of sophisticated missiles and rockets, allegedly supplied by Syria and Iran. Robert Gates, who served as secretary of defense under George W. Bush and Barack Obama, said that Hezbollah had far more missiles and rockets than most countries.[28] The Israeli government estimates that there may be as many as 150,000 rockets stockpiled along the border between Lebanon and Israel.[29]

WHAT IS HAMAS?

In the opening chapter of this book we talked about the thousands of rockets that have been fired into Israel over the past twenty-five years. The vast majority have been launched from the Gaza Strip by members of Hamas, a Sunni Muslim organization that began operating in 1987, just a few years after Hezbollah formed in Lebanon.

Like other militant Islamic groups, Hamas (which stands for Islamic

Resistance Movement) is committed to the destruction of Israel. According to the BBC, "In May 2017, the group published a new policy document for the first time since its founding. It declared a willingness to accept an interim Palestinian state within pre-1967 boundaries, without recognising Israel, and did not repeat the anti-Jewish language of its charter. The text was seen as an effort by Hamas to soften its image, though the group made clear it did not replace the charter."[30]

The BBC also explains that after a "stunning victory" in the Palestinian Legislative Council elections in 2007, "tensions with the rival Fatah faction of Palestinian Authority (PA) President Mahmoud Abbas heightened. Deadly clashes between Fatah and Hamas erupted in Gaza in June 2007, after which Hamas set up a rival government, leaving Fatah and the PA running parts of the West Bank not under Israeli control."[31]

In some ways Hamas sprang up as a replacement for the PLO. Many younger Palestinians had grown tired of listening to the PLO's rhetoric and empty promises. As far as they were concerned, the PLO raged and ranted, but nothing changed. They also saw that revolution was big business for the PLO leadership. Why would the PLO really want to change something that had put countless millions of dollars into their coffers?

For the next few years Hamas and the PLO were rivals in revolution. They both wanted the same thing—the complete eradication of Israel. Even though the PLO continued to carry out terrorist attacks against Israeli citizens, it somehow came to be seen as more of a diplomatic organization. It just goes to show what a good public relations department can do.

Like Hezbollah, Hamas has stockpiled thousands of rockets to be used in its fight against Israel.[32] A problem for Israel, and for thousands of innocent Palestinians, is that the rockets are hidden in public buildings. In fact, many are hidden in the basements of schools, hospitals, and apartment buildings right in the middle of Gaza City,[33] an urban center with a population of more than half a million. In other words, Hamas is using its own people as hostages, as human shields to protect Hamas from Israel's retaliation against its attacks.

Israel has engaged in three brief "wars" against Hamas: Operation Cast Lead (2008–2009), Operation Pillar of Defense (2012), and Operation Protective Edge (2014). The most recent conflict lasted for fifty-one days, during which as many as twenty-three hundred Palestinians were killed and another ten thousand wounded. Some sixty-six Israeli soldiers lost their lives, as did six Israeli citizens. In addition, an estimated seventy-five thousand Gazans were driven from their homes.[34] But despite their losses, Hamas fighters are prepared for another conflict and insist there can be no long-term peace with Israel.[35]

During its battles with Hamas the Israeli government has taken the unprecedented step of dropping leaflets, sending texts, and making phone calls to tell Palestinians to evacuate buildings that are suspected of housing Hamas rockets. Tragically despite these precautions civilian casualties continue, and Israel is blamed for not doing enough to protect innocent civilians.[36]

Meanwhile Israeli citizens in towns such as Sderot have as little as fifteen-second warnings to get into bomb shelters where they are protected from Hamas' rockets.[37] Sderot, by the way, is nicknamed "Rocket Town" because it has been hit so many times.[38]

When it comes to Hamas, however, Israeli citizens are worried about more than attacks from the sky. They also fear invasions from beneath the ground. Hamas has dug at least thirty-six tunnels to provide access for its soldiers from Gaza to travel underneath the border and into Israel.[39] The tunnels are wide and deep enough for soldiers to comfortably walk through, are "equipped with electricity," and are stocked with "enough cookies, yogurt and other provisions to last its occupants several months."[40] The tunnels cost millions to build and provide a means of launching surprise attacks on unsuspecting Israeli soldiers and civilians. Israel estimates that the two-year tunnel project cost Hamas $10 million and used eight hundred tons of concrete.[41]

The *Washington Post* tells the story of one of those tunnels. The story begins with kibbutz residents hearing "strange sounds" and discovering their surprising source: they "weren't coming from above ground—but beneath it."[42]

What Israel Defense Forces (IDF) discovered was an "'extremely advanced and well prepared' tunnel…1.5 miles long and 66 feet underground."[43] In what the *Post* called an "audacious attack," Hamas fighters in Israeli army uniforms used the tunnels, "slipped from central Gaza into Israel," and "attacked an Israeli army patrol, killing two soldiers."[44]

Hamas attempted a second attack that day but was thwarted, and two militants were killed. That same day, a militant emerged from a tunnel and fired on Israeli soldiers.[45] Two days later terrorists "infiltrated Israel through a tunnel from northern Gaza. Israeli aircraft hit one group; the second fired an antitank missile at an army vehicle before ten of the operatives were killed by return fire."[46]

The article also explains that while much of Gaza remains desperately poor, with an annual per capita income of $1,165 in 2011, each of the thirty-six tunnels cost at least a million dollars to build and maintain[47]— one more indication of Hamas' commitment to the destruction of Israel.

Israel must always be prepared to defend itself. As a result, a higher percentage of the country's budget must be poured into defense spending. Of course you cannot increase spending somewhere without making cuts somewhere else, and Israel has been forced to slash spending on social programs for the poor.[48] Because of the constant threat of attacks by Hamas, Hezbollah, and other Islamic terrorist organizations, thousands of Israeli families have fallen into poverty.

Today it is estimated that almost one-third of Israeli children and about 20 percent of the elderly are living beneath the poverty line.[49] Some of those who are suffering are survivors (among them, no doubt, many widows and widowers) who endured the pain and terror of the Holocaust.[50] Now, in the last days of their lives, when all they want is to live in peace and freedom, they must endure more pain inflicted by those who cannot let go of their hatred of the Jews.

This is an important and tragic lesson. There cannot be a lasting peace in the Middle East until racial hatred has been overcome and there is mutual respect among Arabs, Jews, Christians, and all others who live in the region.

THE MUSLIM BROTHERHOOD

The third Islamic extremist group you need to know about is the Muslim Brotherhood. This group is generally considered to be the least radical of the three, taking positions that "seem to make them moderates."[51] But it is no stranger to terrorism and violence. It is also the "oldest political Islamist group in the Arab World,"[52] and although it is particularly strong in Egypt, there are also branches in countries across the Middle East, North and East Africa, and the United States.[53]

While Hezbollah is headquartered in Lebanon and Hamas is based primarily in Gaza and the West Bank, members of the Muslim Brotherhood are found in more than seventy countries, including the United Kingdom, France, and the United States.[54]

You might think of the Brotherhood as the elder brother and role model for Hamas, Hezbollah, and other extremist groups. Founded in Egypt in 1928 (after the fall of the Ottoman Empire following World War I), the Brotherhood works very hard to spread its message through a network of social and charitable organizations. It is a strong presence in elementary and secondary schools, universities, mosques, and professional organizations throughout the Arab world.[55]

Here is some of what this radical group has to say about the Jews and Israel:

> Israel is a Zionist entity occupying holy Arab and Islamic lands...and we will get rid of it no matter how long it takes.[56]
>
> —Former Muslim Brotherhood Supreme Guide Muhammad Mahdi 'Akef

> Today the Jews are not the Israelites praised by Allah, but the descendants of the Israelites who defied His word. Allah was angry with them and turned them into monkeys and pigs....There is no doubt that the battle in which the Muslims overcome the Jews [will come]....In that battle the Muslims will fight the Jews and kill them.[57]
>
> —Muslim Brotherhood Spiritual Leader Yusuf al Qaradawi

> Every Muslim must act to save Jerusalem from the usurpers and to [liberate] Palestine from the claws of occupation. This is a personal duty for all Muslims. They must participate in *jihad* by [donating] money or [sacrificing] their life.[58]
>
> —Brotherhood General Guide Muhammed Badi'

> "There is no dialogue between us [Muslims and Jews] except by the sword and rifle. [We pray to Allah] to take this oppressive Jewish, Zionist band of people...do not spare a single one of

them…count their numbers and kill them down to the very last one."[59]

—Muslim Brotherhood's Current Spiritual Head, Yusuf
al Qaradawi

So much for the perception of the Muslim Brotherhood as being less radical than some other groups engineering terrorist attacks on Israel. In fact, according to the Jewish Virtual Library, "The Brotherhood is also viewed by many in the Middle East and the West as the root source for Islamic terrorism."[60]

Early Nazi Assistance

When it was founded in the early twentieth century, the Muslim Brotherhood was more of a social than a political organization—one that reportedly accepted funding from an apparent Nazi-connected "German journalist affiliated with the German legation in Cairo. The Nazi money was used to establish the Brotherhood's quasi-military 'Special Apparatus,'" which its founder, Hassan al-Banna, seemed to find compatible with its overall mission.[61]

Al-Banna embraced anti-Semitism but "could not accept all Nazi ideas, especially not the concept that the Germans were a master race. But Nazi agents supported him, and anti-Semitism formed a key part of his political activity."[62]

As Hitler rose to power, the focus of the Brotherhood became more political and grew rapidly. In 1936, eight years after its founding, it had only eight hundred members. Two years later it had two hundred thousand. By 1948 the number stood at nearly two million.[63] Over time the organization began providing military training to its members[64] and then became involved in terrorist acts against Coptic Christians and the Egyptian government.[65]

In November of 1948 a number of the Brotherhood's leaders were arrested, and the organization was banned. Several months later Egypt's Prime Minister Mahmud Fahmi al-Nuqrashi was assassinated,[66] allegedly by a member of the Muslim Brotherhood. The following year al-Banna himself was shot and killed, reportedly by King Farouk's secret police.[67]

Today Muslims around the world continue to hail al-Banna as a great leader who devoted himself to peace and the struggle against poverty in the Middle East. They vigorously deny reports that he admired Hitler and fascism. The truth nonetheless is that he hated Jews and advocated their destruction. He said, "Degradation and dishonor are the results of the love of this world and the fear of death. Therefore prepare for jihad and be the lovers of death."[68] He also said, "Death is an art, and the most exquisite of arts when practiced by the skillful artist."[69]

Dr. Harold Brackman of the Simon Wiesenthal Center writes, "The roots of Hassan al-Banna's anti-Semitism were his selective reading of the Quran emphasizing the negative conflicts between Muhammad and seventh-century Jewish tribes in Arabia as personifying Jewish perfidy and malevolence, everywhere and for all time.... The more favourable passages about Jews as 'people of the Book' to be treated with respect were ignored."[70]

"As we shall see, the Brotherhood's hatred, not merely of Zionists but of Jews worldwide...took on a whole new dimension of apocalyptic conspiracy mongering when al-Banna's movement absorbed strains of Hitler's genocidal anti-Semitism as mediated through the influence of Mohammad Amin al-Husayni, the Grand Mufti of Jerusalem."[71]

The Grand Mufti himself went to Berlin during the war to meet with Hitler and got assurances from the führer that he would "carry on the battle" until the Jewish presence in Europe had been destroyed.[72] The Mufti reportedly toured Auschwitz and was disappointed that the killings weren't happening fast enough. He urged the Nazis to speed up the process and dreamed of the day when similar death camps would purge the Jews from the Middle East.[73]

Reporting back to Palestine through a radio show, the Mufti praised Hitler's Final Solution:

> The Germans know how to get rid of the Jews.... The Germans have never harmed any Muslim, and they are again fighting our common enemy who persecuted Arabs and Muslims. But most of all, they have definitely solved the Jewish problem. Arabs! Rise as one to protect your sacred rights. Kill the Jews wherever you find them.... God is with you.[74]

When the Mufti returned to Cairo after the war, the Muslim Brotherhood newspaper gave thanks for his return:

> Thank you, our Lord, for your mercy....The Arab hero and symbol of Al Jihad and patience and struggle is here in Egypt. The Mufti is among his friends....The Mufti is here, oh Palestine! Do not worry. The lion is safe among his brethren and he will draw plans of Al Jihad and struggle for you. We, here, shall be his soldiers and we shall not stop fighting for you until you rid yourself of Zionism....Germany and Hitler are gone, but Amin al-Husseini will continue the struggle....One hair of the Mufti's is worth more than the Jews of the whole world....Should one hair of the Mufti's be touched, every Jew in the world would be killed without mercy.[75]

So much for a peace-loving, nonviolent organization.

FIRE IN CAIRO

In 1952 Muslim Brotherhood members "took part in arson that destroyed some seven hundred and fifty buildings—mainly night clubs, theaters, hotels, and restaurants" frequented by the British and other foreigners.[76]

The "fire" on January 26, 1952, was the product of a riot resulting from escalating tensions between Britain and Egypt over control of the Suez Canal, among other issues. Rioters poured into the streets of Cairo, throwing containers full of gasoline and setting structures ablaze.[77] Twenty-six people died, and more than five hundred were injured.[78]

This tragedy set the stage for revolution in Egypt, as the monarchy seemed completely unable to stop the rioting or respond to the fire as it spread through the city. On July 23, 1952, the monarchy was overthrown in a coup led by soldiers calling themselves the Free Officers Movement, and Muhammad Naguib was installed as Egypt's first president.[79] The Free Officers Movement was led by men such as Gamal Abdel Nasser and Anwar Sadat, both of whom would later become presidents of Egypt.

Naguib served for less than two years before he was deposed and placed under house arrest by Nasser, who declared himself to be Egypt's new prime minister. Two years later he was elected president, receiving a suspiciously spectacular 99.948 percent of the popular vote.[80] Shortly thereafter, when an attempt on Nasser's life was blamed on the Muslim Brotherhood, he turned against his old friends with a vengeance.[81] Thousands of its members were imprisoned, and many were tortured and held for years in prisons and concentration camps.[82]

But the Brotherhood lived on.

SADAT ASSASSINATION AND THE MUSLIM BROTHERHOOD

THE MEN WHO killed Egyptian President Anwar Sadat on October 6, 1981, "plotted the attack with Al Gamaa al-Islamiyya, a Muslim Brotherhood offshoot."[83] Three years earlier Sadat had shared the Nobel Prize with Israeli Prime Minister Menachem Begin after the two men signed a historic peace treaty between their two countries.[84] Ironically Sadat was killed during an annual parade commemorating a victory over Israeli forces at the start of the Yom Kippur War in 1973. When assassins in military uniforms approached the reviewing stand where Sadat was seated, he stood up, thinking they were coming to salute him. Instead, they shot him dead.[85]

The Muslim Brotherhood does not want peace with Israel; it wants Israel to be destroyed.

Today the Brotherhood is alive, well, and active around the world, especially in Egypt, where the organization is accused of burning scores of Christian churches[86] and killing hundreds of Christians. All of this comes in the aftermath of the revolution that was supposed to remove the dictator Hosni Mubarak from power and usher in a new day of freedom and democracy in Egypt.

Members of the Muslim Brotherhood were deeply involved in the revolution, but I believe their intent was never to bring about a democratic Egypt. As is true of Hamas, Hezbollah, and the Islamic State, the Brotherhood seeks to install a fundamentalist Muslim government where Sharia law is the rule of the land. They want, in other words, a country where sins such as adultery and homosexuality are punishable by death, where thieves will have hands cut off, and where women can be jailed for not keeping every inch of their bodies covered or even for driving.

What a contrast to our God, who promises forgiveness to all who seek Him earnestly, no matter what they may have done!

As I sat at my computer today, I decided to google "Muslim Brotherhood" and see what popped up. Here are just a few of the headlines I saw: "The Muslim Brotherhood's War on Coptic Christians," "Muslim Brotherhood Incites More Terror Attacks Targeting Egypt's Coptic Christians," "28 Killed in Attack on Bus Carrying Coptic Christians in Egypt," "Why Does the Muslim Brotherhood Attack Churches?" And on and on it goes.

This is not at all surprising, because for years the Muslim Brotherhood has made a "joke" out of its desire to eliminate Christians and Jews. If you travel in the Middle East, you may see graffiti splashed on the sides of buildings that reads, "First the Saturday people, then the Sunday people."[87] What does it mean? Basically this: "Today is Saturday, so we're killing Jews. Tomorrow is Sunday, so we'll kill the Christians."

The problem is that it's not a joke. As we have seen far too many times in recent years, they mean it. In 2017 the Saudi Arabian newspaper *Arab News* (which bills itself as "The Middle East's Leading English Daily") published an article by Abdellatif el-Menawy titled, "Have No Illusions About the Muslim Brotherhood."[88] After an "inconclusive and unsatisfactory" British assessment of the organization, el-Menawy was encouraged to see the British government taking a closer look and asking whether the Muslim Brotherhood should be classified as a terrorist organization.[89]

El-Menawy explained that while the extremists have been adept at concealing their true nature, "there is new evidence that, in Britain at least, it no longer works."[90] He added that "Britain and many other European countries have begun to realize the danger they face, and have begun to take many measures to protect their borders, and their very societies."[91] El-Menawy urged these nations not to delay but to seize the opportunity and "work together to achieve a common goal."[92]

May his message be heeded.

CHAPTER 12

TROUBLE IN IRAN

*Iran is the land where Queen Esther saved the Jews and God
closed the mouths of vicious lions after Daniel was thrown
into the lions' den. It was also from Iran that Nehemiah
returned to Jerusalem to rebuild the city's broken walls.*

—JONATHAN BERNIS

OVER THE NEXT few chapters I want to talk briefly about a few of the countries that will have a huge bearing on whether there will be war or peace in the Middle East. Most, if not all, of these countries might rightly be called enemies of Israel, or are moving rapidly in that direction. We must pray for them and for the protection of their Christian communities. We need to be praying for the salvation of their leaders and for revival among their vast Muslim populations.

Also, please remember that I am not attempting to chronicle a comprehensive history of these nations. If I were, I could write thousands of pages about each of them, all of which have a long and complex history. Even Jordan, which did not exist as a country until the twentieth century, has a history that stretches back thousands of years.

Let's start with Iran, which is undoubtedly one of the world's biggest exporters of terror. As I discussed earlier, the Iranian government is the primary supporter of Hezbollah and supplies many of that terrorist group's weapons. In fact, Hezbollah is a proxy of Iran, and according to the *Military Times*, "At least 500 US military deaths in Iraq and Afghanistan were directly linked to Iran and its support for anti-American militants."[1] The newspaper adds that "scores of American personnel were killed or maimed by highly lethal bombs, known as explosively formed penetrators, or EFPs, that Iran manufactured and supplied to Shiite militias across the border in Iraq. Many EFPs were powerful enough to destroy US Humvees and breach tank hulls."[2]

In recent years Iran has been an outspoken enemy of Israel. The official government printing house has even published editions of the infamous *Protocols of the Elders of Zion*.[3] This anti-Semitic work, first published in Russia toward the end of the nineteenth century, "purports to be the minutes of meetings held secretly by Jewish wise men plotting to control the world."[4] The book is full of lies and slanders that have been shown again and again to be false. But it remains one of the favorite texts of Jew haters everywhere, including those in the top echelons of the Iranian government.

Former Iranian President Mahmoud Ahmadinejad, who left office in 2013, was also noted for vehemently denying that the Holocaust ever took place and for claiming that Israel "should be 'wiped off the map.'"[5] His successor, Hassan Rouhani, has been much more moderate in his public expressions. However, in a 2013 interview with the *Jerusalem Post*, Israel's then intelligence minister, Yuval Steinitz, encouraged circumspection where Rouhani's "moderation" is concerned, saying, "His message was 'Ahmadinejad was stupid enough to be a wolf in wolf's clothing, to expose his teeth and nails and alert the West. I can be a wolf in sheep's clothing. I have all the diplomatic and rhetoric skills to do so.'"[6]

The bottom line is that Iran is yet another Middle Eastern country that wants to see Israel destroyed. But it hasn't always been that way. Let's back up for just a minute and take a closer look.

NOT ARABS BUT PERSIANS

Most people don't realize that Iran is not really an Arab country. Iranians are Persians. In fact, the country was known as Persia until 1935, when the government requested the name change to Iran. The fact is that for over two thousand years the people who lived there referred to their homeland as Iran, which means "Land of the Aryans." But as far as the rest of the world was concerned, the name was Persia.

Some sources say changing the official name of the country to Iran was first suggested by the country's ambassador to Nazi Germany and was influenced by the Germans.[7] That doesn't mean there is anything intrinsically evil about the name. I just mention it because I think it is an interesting bit of Iran's history.

As we have already seen, most Americans think of Iran as the country that caused the United States great grief in the late 1970s and early 1980s by holding Americans hostage in our embassy in Tehran. It has been nearly forty years since Islamic revolutionaries stormed the embassy and filled our television screens with angry faces shouting, "Death to America!" but those of us who are old enough remember it clearly. For many of us, it came as a shock to see how much the Iranians hated us, and we didn't really understand why.

That was also when the Ayatollah Khomeini introduced us to Muslim radicalism. Most of us had never seen anything like him and had trouble believing that anyone took him seriously. He was so strange to our Western eyes.

Four decades later Iran is just as dangerous as it was then—even more so, in fact. The radical theocracy that has ruled Iran since the Islamic revolution of 1979 is Israel's sworn enemy and has pledged itself to Israel's destruction. One thing Israel has working in its favor is that Arab countries in the Middle East are "increasingly wary of Iran's policies and nuclear ambitions"[8] and do not want it to have a stronger influence in the region.

Before the revolution Iran was ruled by Mohammad Reza Pahlavi, the shah of Iran, who had always been friendly to Israel. In fact, in 1950, two years after Israel's founding, Iran recognized Israel's sovereignty.[9] At the time, Iran was home to the largest Jewish community in the Middle East.[10]

In 1948 there were one hundred thousand Jews in Iran.[11] Today the number is under nine thousand, and Jews face pervasive discrimination, "particularly in the areas of employment, education, and public accommodations."[12]

The shah was a forward-looking man who was not blinded by hatred of Israel. He saw Israel as a trading partner that could benefit Iran as the country moved forward.[13]

With the help of the United States, he instituted a program called the White Revolution.[14] His goal was to build a modern network of roads, railroads, and air routes that would connect communities throughout Iran. He sought to eradicate diseases such as malaria, undertake a number of dam and irrigation projects, and encourage the growth of industries.[15] He also "established literacy and health corps to benefit Iran's rural areas."[16]

Unfortunately for the shah, not everyone in Iran liked what he was doing. Some thought his reforms were not moving fast enough. Others resented his efforts to Westernize Iran because they felt this was not compatible with Islam. And still others hated the shah because of his close ties with the United States[17]—even though during his later years in power he strengthened his relationship with the Soviet Union.[18]

Another problem for the shah was that even though he seemed to be determined to improve the life of the average Iranian citizen, he was an autocratic ruler whose secret police, SAVAK, suppressed any dissent or opposition to his rule.[19] SAVAK was notorious for its use of torture and other brutal methods.[20]

After the shah was overthrown, Jews in Iran believed their lives were at risk. When prominent Jewish businessman Habib Elghanian was executed, they became even more fearful that a bloodbath was coming. "Two rabbis and four young intellectuals"[21] were chosen for a sit-down with Iran's new leader, Ayatollah Khomeini. "After the group congratulated the Ayatollah on his victory over the Shah in the recent revolution, the Ayatollah gave a long monologue," in which he said that Christianity, Islam, and Judaism "are the only religions that are truly descended from heaven."[22] The discussion concluded with Ayatollah Khomeini claiming, "We recognize our Jews as separate from those godless, bloodsucking Zionists."[23] For the time being it seemed that Jews in Iran were safe.[24]

But it was a fragile peace. Thousands of Jews fled Iran through Pakistan or Turkey after being unable to obtain passports from the government, and many left everything behind.[25] They were understandably eager to get to Israel or some other country where they would be safe.

According to the Jewish Virtual Library, twenty or so Jewish schools were operating before the revolution, most of which no longer exist. Jewish principals of the remaining schools "have been replaced by Muslims."[26] Jewish student majorities exist in only three schools in Tehran, but they are taught from an Islamic curriculum. Jewish studies cannot be taught in Persian; "the Orthodox Otzar ha-Torah organization...is responsible for Jewish religious education"[27] and provides Hebrew lessons every Friday. Jewish students must attend school on Saturdays, as the Saturday sabbath is "no longer officially recognized."[28] Finally, three synagogues remain in Tehran, but there have been no rabbis in the nation since 1994.[29]

WHAT IF IRAN GETS THE BOMB?

On July 14, 2015, President Barack Obama made a major announcement from the White House. The following excerpt is from the official text of his remarks posted in the White House archives:

> Today, after two years of negotiations, the United States—together with our international partners—has achieved what decades of animosity has not: a comprehensive, long-term deal that will verifiably prevent Iran from obtaining a nuclear weapon.... This deal is not built on trust—it's built on verification.[30]

This agreement, called the Joint Comprehensive Plan of Action (JCPOA), created much controversy and was seen by many supporters of Israel as a huge threat. The deal dropped billions of dollars in sanctions in exchange for Iran's promise not to pursue nuclear weapons—a promise many feared they would not keep.

According to Israel's former defense minister Ehud Barak, on three occasions between 2010 and 2012 Israel came very close to launching air strikes on Iran's nuclear laboratories. He said attack plans had been drawn up and approved, but approval could not be obtained from Prime Minister Netanyahu's so-called Forum of Eight cabinet ministers, which was necessary before the matter could be taken to the entire cabinet.[31]

Another serious problem with the deal was that it produced no softening of Iran's hard-line stance against Israel. In fact, several Iranian leaders seemed more belligerent than ever. Iran's foreign minister, Mohammad Javad Zarif, one of the chief negotiators for Iran, said "after meeting the head of Hezbollah, Hassan Nasrallah, that the nuclear deal has provided an historic opportunity to stand against the Zionist entity."[32] It is almost as if he found the name Israel so repulsive that he could not even mention it. Hussein Sheikholeslam, a high-level advisor at the time, said, "Our positions against the usurper Zionist regime have not changed at all; Israel should be annihilated and this is our ultimate slogan."[33] Benjamin Netanyahu reported, "The ruler of Iran, Khamenei, said...'We will take measures to support all those who fight against Israel.'"[34]

To be fair, Zarif later said that when Iranian officials talk about Israel being annihilated, they aren't really referring to the country as a whole but rather to Netanyahu's government, which they accuse of numerous acts of hostility against Arab states. In fact, Zarif told Ann Curry of NBC news, "We don't want to annihilate anybody."[35]

If this is true—and I'll leave it up to you to make your own decision—then it marks a turning point in Iran-Israeli relations, especially since Supreme Leader Khamenei once called Israel "a cancerous tumor...that has to be removed."[36] The cancer analogy is not new. Benjamin Netanyahu writes that he first heard it in 1984 by an Iranian representative to the United Nations.[37]

Thankfully as I was preparing the final manuscript of this book for publishing, President Trump announced that he would nullify this treaty and reimpose sanctions against Iran. Sanctions have been imposed, and in May 2018 the United States withdrew from the deal. As far as most people who love Israel are concerned, this is most definitely a step in the right direction.

CHAPTER 13

CATASTROPHE IN SYRIA

We don't kill our people...no government in the world kills its people, unless it's led by a crazy person.

—Bashar al-Assad, President of Syria

THE STORY OF Syria is one of the greatest tragedies to date in the twenty-first century. When Bashar al-Assad inherited power from his father in 2000, new hope was ignited. Even the United States government believed that a fairer, more just Syria was on the way. After all, one of Assad's first acts as president of Syria was to shut down the infamous Mezzeh penitentiary and free many of the political prisoners held there, including members of the Muslim Brotherhood, an organization that had been banned in Syria for more than fifteen years.

Most observers saw Assad as a reformer. He was young and well educated, and he surrounded himself with people like himself, moderates who wanted to build a bright future for all the people of Syria. He was not seen as an autocrat like his father, Hafez, an ironfisted ruler who in 1982 killed as many as twenty-five thousand people during a failed coup attempt led by the Muslim Brotherhood.[1]

Assad was an articulate man with an advanced degree in ophthalmology. His wife spoke out on issues such as women's rights. Clearly the Assad family was not made up of barbarians. In fact, after a visit to Syria in 2009 Sen. John Kerry, who went on to serve as Secretary of State under Barack Obama, said, "My judgment is that Syria will move; Syria will change, as it embraces a legitimate relationship with the United States and the West and economic opportunity that comes with it."[2]

Still there were signals that all was not as hoped. For one thing, Assad had a quick temper that sometimes raged out of control. Robert Ford was named the US ambassador to Syria in December of 2010. Before Ford's appointment the United States had broken off diplomatic relations with Syria in 2005 because of Assad's support for terrorism around the world. Because so many in Congress were opposed to the resumption of normal relations with Syria, President Obama waited until Congress was adjourned for Christmas before appointing Ford the US ambassador to that country.

During Ford's first meeting with Assad, all was going well until the ambassador brought up the subject of human rights. Assad was livid.

> "The last country in the world that I'm going to take advice from is the United States," he said in a low snarl. "Not on human rights. Not after what you've done in Guantánamo, Abu Ghraib, and Afghanistan."[3]

Despite the high hopes at the beginning of his regime, Bashar al-Assad led his country into a brutal civil war that tore Syria apart and left its major cities in ruins. He has relentlessly bombed his own people, killing hundreds of thousands of men, women, and children in the process and driving millions more from their homes. He has even resorted to using deadly chemical weapons, which are forbidden by international law.

More evidence seems to be surfacing every day that this educated doctor is actually a brutal and sadistic man in the mold of his father and other ruthless dictators such as Saddam Hussein and Muammar Gaddafi. According to the *Los Angeles Times*, the United States has even "accused Syria's government of hanging hundreds of political opponents and other prisoners and burning their bodies at a military prison near Damascus."[4] The *Times* quoted the State Department as calling the executions "an egregious pattern of atrocities by Syrian President Bashar Assad."[5]

The article reported that as many as thirteen thousand prisoners may have been "killed at the prison" between March 2011, when the war began, and December of 2015.[6]

Nicolette Waldman, a researcher for Amnesty International who wrote a forty-eight-page report on the situation in Syria, believes the death toll may be significantly higher and added that "there is no reason to think the executions have stopped."[7]

What a terrible price the people of Syria have paid for Assad's lust for power. Here are some more examples:

- **According to PBS**, 470,000 people had been killed, directly or indirectly, in Syria by 2016.[8]

- **Another eleven million people** have been driven from their homes. More than five million have fled Syria, and another six million are displaced inside the country.[9]

- **All together, more than 11.5 percent** of Syria's people have been wounded or killed in the fighting, which rages on without an end in sight.[10]

ASSAD DID NOT FOOL THE ISRAELIS

Although many people around the world thought that Bashar al-Assad could lead Syria to a new day, the people of Israel were not fooled. They knew that nothing changed when he took power. Rather, it was business as usual—and that wasn't good. Syria continued to be a major supporter of weapons and training for Hezbollah. In 2005, when Lebanon's former prime minister Rafik Hariri called for his country to be set free from Syria's control, he was killed in a car bomb attack that left another twenty-one people dead.[11] Although Assad was never formally charged in the murder, it has always been suspected that he was involved.[12]

Syria has been run for decades by dictators, and it seemed unlikely that would change no matter who was in power. Thus, there was no surprise in Israel when Assad turned to military might to put down protests in Syria. He was not going to let what had happened to Egypt's Hosni Mubarak happen to him.

ASSAD CHOOSES VIOLENCE

There were many reasons for the uprising that began in Syria in 2011. Assad's government was perceived as corrupt and oppressive. The Arab Spring was in full flower throughout the Middle East, and Syria had just been through the worst drought in the country's modern history. The drought had lasted for more than four years, killing livestock, leaving fields empty and barren, and putting many families at risk of starvation. Hundreds of thousands of farming families were forced to flee to urban areas looking for work, which was not always available.[13]

It was in the drought-stricken rural province of Daraa in southern Syria that the first major protests occurred.[14] As mentioned in chapter 9, schoolchildren were arrested and reportedly tortured by the authorities for writing anti-government graffiti. Local citizens took to the streets to support the children and to call for government reforms.

The government responded with mass arrests and beatings and in some instances even fired on protesters. As word spread, similar protests began to erupt in other parts of the country. The violent response of the Assad regime was captured on cell phone videos that were circulated around the country and smuggled out to foreign media outlets.

After years of waiting for the reforms that he had promised them, it seemed that most of the country was against Assad. His downfall appeared certain, and it was expected to happen soon. Very few people believed that the dictator was so desperate to stay in power that he would destroy his country to do it. But they overestimated the man's humanity.

His troops encircled cities and neighborhoods where the major protests had taken place, and then they bombarded them, using tanks, heavy artillery, and attack helicopters. Entire neighborhoods were obliterated, and refugees were sent fleeing for their lives. In response, many protesters took up arms and fought back against the government. Soon civil war was raging throughout Syria. There were so many factions and countries involved in the fighting that it was almost impossible to keep it all straight. The United States, the European Union, and Turkey called on Assad to resign, as did Qatar and Saudi Arabia. The Russians and Iranians supported him, and when a resolution condemning Assad's crackdown came before the Security Council of the United Nations, Russia and China vetoed it.[15]

Here, mostly courtesy of CNN, is a look at who was, or still is, fighting whom in Syria:[16]

- **For a time, ISIS controlled a big chunk of the country**, but it has now been all but defeated and is in retreat.

- **The Kurdish continue to fight ISIS**, as do rebel groups such as the Free Syrian Army and the Syrian Democratic Forces. "And there are also competing Islamist groups like Jabhat Fateh al Sham."[17]

- **The Iranian-supported Hezbollah militia is backing Assad**, while the US is backing the Kurdish YPG. Turkey hates the YPG because it fears Kurdish separatism.

- **Russia supports Assad** and is helping to keep him in power.

- **The US led the attack on ISIS** and stepped up military action under the Trump administration in 2017 to wipe out ISIS. The US also has bombed Syrian military targets in retaliation for a chemical attack on civilians.

All of this is very confusing and will likely get more confusing as things continue to unravel.

What Does the Future Hold for Syria?

As I write these words, the conflict in Syria is nearing the completion of its eighth year, and there is no end in sight. Assad still insists the war is between his legitimate government and Islamic extremists. He says this to make himself look like the "better" choice, but choosing Bashar al-Assad over the Islamic State is a little like choosing Adolf Hitler over Joseph Stalin. Either way you can't win.

It is true that many of Syria's people are caught between the bombs and bullets of Assad's military and the swords of the Islamic State. In other words, they must choose between being shot or beheaded. No wonder half the population has fled from their homes.

The United States has insisted that any solution to the crisis in Syria must include the removal of Assad from power and the implementation of democratic reforms. Yet the US also admits that Assad's removal might take some time.[18] Russia, on the other hand, is standing by a longtime ally, insisting that the Assad government must be preserved because only it is strong enough to hold the country together and to protect the people from Islamic radicals and thereby give them the peace and security for which they yearn.

It is unlikely that the fighting will end anytime soon. And when it finally does, whoever prevails will face a rebuilding challenge that will take decades to complete, if it is possible at all.

Currently this is the most unstable region in the Middle East, and it poses a huge threat to the security of Israel and stability in the Middle East. Tensions between the United States and Russia are growing as no-fly zones are established and enforced. This has also created a very unstable border for Israel in the north. Iran has had free rein to operate military bases in Syria and has repeatedly launched missile attacks into Israel. Of course Israel has responded immediately by bombing military targets and destroying the launch sites.[19] The likelihood of engagement with Russian planes in the region is escalating, and it may be just a matter of time before Israel shoots down a Russian fighter or something worse.

The situation is a powder keg waiting to explode.

CHAPTER 14

BETRAYAL IN EGYPT

Studying Hebrew is a popular option for thousands of Egyptian university students.... Nine of Egypt's 23 state-run universities have Hebrew language departments. About 2,000 students enroll in their classes each year and the number is rising.
—THE ARAB WEEKLY, JULY 17, 2016

GYPT PLAYS A prominent role in the history of the Jewish people, and it will most certainly play a significant role in Israel's future. For 430 years Egypt was home to the children of Israel. First, they were among the nation's most favored people due to God's blessing on their ancestor Joseph. Later, however, they were slaves, until God sent Moses to lead them out of Egypt and back to their Promised Land.

The story of Joseph takes up thirteen chapters of Genesis (chapters 37 and 39–50), so it would take more space than I have here to retell it in its entirety. Briefly, for those who may not know the story, Joseph's brothers were so jealous of him that they sold him into slavery. He wound up in Egypt, where he remained faithful to God despite enduring many trials, including being thrown into prison on false charges. There, he was able to correctly interpret the dreams of two of his fellow prisoners, one of whom was Pharaoh's cupbearer.

After he released the cupbearer from prison and restored him to service, Pharaoh had a troubling dream that no one could interpret. That's when the cupbearer remembered how Joseph had interpreted his dream and suggested that he be summoned. Of course God revealed the meaning of Pharaoh's dream, which was that a terrible famine was coming to Egypt. Joseph also suggested a plan of action that would save the Egyptian people. He told Pharaoh that for the next seven prosperous years, one-fifth of all the crops grown in Egypt should be stored and saved to feed the people during the seven years of famine that were to follow.

Pharaoh was so impressed with Joseph that he elevated him to be his second in command and put him in charge of preparations for the famine, which arrived just as Joseph said it would. When Joseph's brothers came to Egypt to buy food, he was miraculously reunited with them, forgave them for what they had done to him, and brought them and his father to Egypt to live.

This is the thumbnail version of an exciting story that has many twists and turns and teaches a wonderful lesson about trusting God in all circumstances. As Joseph told his brothers when they feared he would take revenge on them, "You intended to harm me, but God intended it for good to accomplish what is now being done, the saving of many lives" (Gen. 50:20).

Archaeologists are divided in their opinions of whether there is evidence to support the story of Joseph and the long stay of the Israelites in the country of Egypt. A lack of evidence would not be surprising, "given the relative paucity of information about Egyptian officials before the New Kingdom and the lack of consensus regarding Joseph's Egyptian name."[1]

But on January 28, 2016, the Associates for Biblical Research published an article titled "The Sons of Jacob: New Evidence for the Presence of Israelites in Egypt."[2] It tells of the discovery of a villa in the Egyptian city of Rameses on the eastern Nile Delta, an area where scholars believe Joseph and his family would have lived. The villa is extraordinary, in part because it is much larger and more solidly built than the smaller, hut-like structures otherwise found throughout the area. It was obviously the residence of an important person. The home includes six rooms around an open courtyard.

Also, the most striking thing about the house, according to the report, "is that the floor plan is identical to the Israelite 'four-room house' of the later Iron Age in Palestine."[3] Several smaller, two-room homes were arranged in a semicircle around the larger home, and the article suggests that these may have been the dwellings of Joseph's father and brothers. The article also states that about 20 percent of the pottery found in these houses was of "Palestinian Middle Bronze Age type."[4]

Archaeologists found the most compelling evidence in a small cemetery: fragments of a large statue (one-and-a-half-times-life-size) that had been sculpted in honor of an important person, most likely the man who lived in the villa. Numerous aspects of the statue seemed to indicate that the man was a foreigner in Egypt.[5] The cemetery also contained several tombs that "still had weapons of Palestinian type in them. Typically, the deceased males were equipped with two javelins, battle-axes and daggers. Tomb 8 contained a fine example of a duckbill-ax and an embossed belt of bronze."[6]

Whether or not this is the home of Joseph, it is an indication that Israelites were in Egypt at a very early point in history, just as the Bible says.

Centuries later, as the tribes of Israel and Judah were scattered around the globe, many found their way back to Egypt. Thousands came to Egypt during the reign of Alexander the Great and during the next few centuries, where they were, for the most part, accepted and welcomed by the Ptolemies.[7] Several synagogues were built in Egypt at this time, and many Jews prospered in Egypt as "tradesmen, farmers, mercenaries, and government officials."[8] In fact, the commanders of Cleopatra III's army were two Jewish brothers named Ananias and Helkias. According to the Jewish Virtual Library, by AD 100 Jews made up one-eighth of the population of Egypt.[9]

We also know from the Gospels that Joseph and Mary fled to Egypt with their child to escape the wrath of King Herod, who sought to protect his throne by slaughtering all the male children under two years of age who had been born in Bethlehem. They returned to Nazareth only after hearing of Herod's death, which means they were in Egypt for several years before returning home.

Move forward to the late 1940s, and there were more than seventy thousand Jews in Egypt.[10] Although they were generally prosperous, life was more difficult for them than it had been for previous generations. In fact, after the fall of the Third Reich hundreds of former Nazis found refuge in Egypt, and many were given government positions. One example is Leopold Gleim, who headed up the Gestapo in Poland and had been sentenced to death in absentia. At war's end he fled to Egypt, where he controlled the Egyptian secret police.[11]

Still, Egypt's Jewish community was strong and thriving until Israel was founded in 1948. Between June and November of that year bombings in Cairo's "Jewish Quarter killed more than 70 Jews and wounded nearly 200."[12] Then, in 1956, following the Sinai Campaign (the war that began when Egypt nationalized the Suez Canal and "closed the Strait of Tiran and the Gulf of Aqaba—both international waterways—to Israeli shipping"),[13] an estimated twenty-five thousand Jews were expelled from Egypt and had their property confiscated by the Egyptian government, while another thousand or so Jews were arrested and placed in "prisons and detention camps."[14]

On November 23, 1956, Egypt's Minister of Religious Affairs signed a proclamation that was "read aloud in mosques throughout Egypt," declaring all Jews to be "Zionists and enemies of the state" who would soon be expelled.[15] "Thousands of Jews," including many who had lived in Egypt for generations, "were ordered to leave the country...[with] only one suitcase and a small sum of cash" and were forced to "donate" their property to Egyptian authorities.[16] Jews who stayed in Egypt were reportedly "taken hostage" so that "those forced to leave did not speak out against the Egyptian government."[17]

Things are different in Egypt now since the peace treaty with Israel initiated by Anwar Sadat was signed in 1979. Israel has an embassy in Cairo and vice versa. The Egyptian government has publicly "condemned anti-Semitism," although wild allegations against Jews still find their way into newspapers and magazines, including the accusation that Israel was responsible for the September 11, 2001, attacks on the United States.[18]

A BREAKTHROUGH AT THE UNITED NATIONS

A breakthrough of sorts occurred in 2015 when the Egyptian representative to the United Nations voted in favor of Israel. The issue up for debate was not a very dramatic one. It concerned whether Israel should be invited to join the Committee on the Peaceful Uses of Outer Space. Egypt was one of 117 countries voting in favor.[19] As I said, the vote was historic because it marked the first time Egypt had ever voted in favor of Israel on any issue coming before the United Nations.

And so it would seem that things are much better for Jews in Egypt than they were seventy or seventy-five years ago. There's only one thing wrong with saying something like that—and it is the fact that almost no Jews remain in Egypt. By some accounts there are fifty of them. Other sources claim there are "perhaps 18 souls."[20] Although there are a number of synagogues in Egypt, only one "functioning synagogue" remains in Cairo and one in Alexandria.[21] Egypt's once-thriving Jewish community has become a nostalgic curiosity, a relic of a bygone era. Now that Egyptian Jews are almost extinct, it is as if they have become a protected species. Jews can be tolerated now that they are clearly not a threat to the Egyptian government or its Muslim people.

EGYPT TODAY

After Anwar Sadat was assassinated in 1981, Hosni Mubarak took over as president of Egypt, and he ruled for the next thirty years. Mubarak, the former Egyptian Air Force commander appointed by President Anwar Sadat,[22] headed a military cabal that governed Egypt with an iron hand. It is believed that during his time as Egypt's leader thousands of people were arrested, tortured, and executed (some without trial) because they were suspected of opposing the government.[23]

The protests that began in Tunisia during the spring of 2011 quickly spread to Egypt, as tens of thousands of people took to the streets in Cairo and Alexandria, and then in other cities, to demand free elections and other rights. The protesters were putting their lives at risk, and many of them paid the ultimate price. In three weeks of protests against the Mubarak regime, an estimated eight hundred people were killed.[24]

Mubarak realized that the protesters were not going to be intimidated, so he tried to appease them by making concessions to some of their demands. But it was much too little far too late. It seemed that the people of Egypt would settle for nothing less than the dictator's resignation.[25] In fact, many eventually called for his execution.

At first, Mubarak sought to bring peace by promising that he would not run for reelection but only finish out his current term.[26] When that plan touched off more protests, Mubarak decided to step down. On

February 11, 2011, Egypt's vice president announced Mubarak's resignation and said that power would be turned over to the Egyptian military[27]—the same military that had killed hundreds of protesters in the first weeks of the upheaval.

To Western observers it seemed that all the protesters in Egypt were on the same page and all wanted the same things: freedom and democracy. But that was not true. Many were radical Islamists who wanted to see the implementation of Sharia law in Egypt. In fact, the Egyptian constitution says that the country's legal system is partly based on Sharia law.[28] However, this is not interpreted as strictly as in other countries such as Saudi Arabia. The radicals wanted to see Egypt rid itself of infidels and "polytheists," the Muslim name for Christians.

Some opposed Mubarak because they perceived him as being too friendly to Israel. They wanted to review the peace treaty that had been negotiated between Egypt and Israel in 1979, with an eye toward overturning it.[29] Many also accused Mubarak of being a traitor for selling gasoline to Israel.

Although Mubarak and his family were placed under house arrest at a presidential palace on the Red Sea,[30] it seemed that Egypt's new military leaders were more sympathetic to the former president than they were to the goals of the Arab Spring revolution. To be sure, Mubarak was now an old man in his eighties and was experiencing health problems. He reportedly suffered a heart attack and soon after was diagnosed with stomach cancer. Put on trial for ordering the murder of protesters and a variety of other charges, Mubarak was brought to court on a hospital bed, and charges against him were dismissed.

In March of 2017 Mubarak, then eighty-eight, was released from prison after six years and returned to his home in a suburb of Cairo. What happened after Mubarak was removed from power? Did things change for the better in Egypt?

Hardly.

A man named Mohamed Morsi was chosen to become Egypt's next president. Morsi was a member of the Muslim Brotherhood who had spent time in prison, but he promised to move the country toward stability and development.[31] Morsi espoused other, more controversial views about such subjects as 9/11, publicly stating that the World Trade Center's twin towers were taken down "from the inside" and insisting that the

United States lacked sufficient evidence to prove Muslim involvement in the attacks.[32] In online interviews from 2010 he also denied Israel's right to exist:

> There is no place for [Zionists] on the land of Palestine. What they took before 1947–[1948], constitutes plunder, and what they are doing now is a continuation of this plundering. By no means do we recognize their Green Line. The land of Palestine belongs to the Palestinians, not to the Zionists.[33]

Morsi also called Israelis "blood-suckers…warmongers, the descendants of apes and pigs."[34] He later insisted that his words were taken out of context.[35]

During Morsi's brief time in power the Muslim Brotherhood stirred up a huge demonstration against Israel in Cairo.[36] Thousands of people took to the streets, waving Palestinian flags and urging that the treaty between Israel and Egypt be overturned.

One of the early actions Morsi undertook as president was to pass a temporary constitutional declaration that greatly expanded his powers.[37] The declaration, which said that his decisions were "final and unchallengeable by any individual or body until a new constitution has been ratified and a new parliament has been elected," touched off new outrage and protests throughout Egypt.[38]

Morsi's attempt to hastily approve a new draft of the constitution was slammed by the Coptic Christian Church for representing only the Islamists who drafted it.[39] Mohamed ElBaradei, a former United Nations diplomat and a leading liberal politician in Egypt, said the revised constitution would end up in "the dustbin of history."[40]

Morsi spoke often of being fair and impartial, but it seemed that he favored the Muslim Brotherhood in almost everything he did. Writing in the newspaper *El-Tahir*, Ibrahim Eissa said angrily, "We got rid of Mubarak's National Democratic Party (NDP), and replaced it with the Brotherhood."[41]

The end result of all this was more protests and deaths. *The Guardian* said:

As many as 14 million people in the country of 84 million took part in the demonstrations....."The scenes of protests are unprecedented in size and scope, and seemingly surpass those during the 18-day uprising that toppled Mubarak," said Michael Hanna, a fellow at the Century Foundation and a longtime Egypt analyst.[42]

The unrest caused concern as "senior members of the Muslim Brotherhood spent the day travelling, fearing for their safety. Morsi himself moved from Itahadiya to...a state building in a safer part of Cairo."[43] The man formerly seen as "a consensus candidate for Islamist and secular voters" was now criticized for having "alienated secular politicians and failed to achieve the unity he was elected to build."[44] Morsi, however, blamed his opposition for "failing to meet him halfway."[45]

As protesters hurled stones at a Morsi poster, government critic Hassan Shanab admitted that Morsi was democratically elected but claimed that the nation became polarized under his presidency. "All of a sudden," Shanab said, "we see ourselves part of an Islamic regime like Iran. Morsi's answerable to the Brotherhood, but they are not answerable to us."[46]

After about a year in power Morsi was removed from office by a military coup, imprisoned, and sentenced to death. His death sentence was later overturned, but a life sentence still stands.[47] Morsi remains behind bars, waiting for a retrial that he hopes will set him free. Meanwhile the presidency passed to Abdel Fattah el-Sisi, who had served as Morsi's Minister of Defense.

Under Sisi it seems little has changed in Egypt. Peter Hessler, writing in the *New Yorker*, describes the situation:

> Human-rights violations have become much worse than they were under Mubarak, and the economy is dangerously weak. During the past year and a half, a plane crash in Sinai, the murder of a foreign graduate student in Cairo, and public protests over the sovereignty of two Red Sea islands have illustrated the tragedy of a failed political movement. Everything that it took for a man like Sisi to rise in revolutionary Egypt—secrecy, silence, and commitment to the system—has also made it impossible for him to enact real change.[48]

For the most part, it seems to be a case of "business as usual" in Egypt, except that, as we noted previously, there is growing hostility toward Egypt's Coptic Christian community.

Clearly Egypt stands at a crossroads. According to the *Jerusalem Post*, a high-ranking Egyptian official said that relations between Israel and Egypt are currently better than they have ever been.[49] Israeli Prime Minister Netanyahu applauded Egypt's President Sisi for saying that he would like to see other Arab countries make peace with Israel, as Egypt has done.[50] At the same time, however, a poll of Egyptian citizens showed that they see Israel as the world's most hostile country and the United States as the second–most hostile nation.[51]

Egypt is by far the world's largest Arab country,[52] with a population of close to one hundred million. It has the sixth-largest Muslim population, ranking behind such giants as Indonesia, India, and Pakistan.[53] It has more than twice as many people as Algeria, the second–most populous Arab country.[54] What happens in Egypt will have a tremendous impact on the rest of the Muslim world. Egypt also has the largest military in the Arab world—and a hostile Egypt would present a challenge that Israel has not had to face in more than thirty years.[55]

GOOD NEWS FROM EGYPT

In the meantime, official relations between Egypt and Israel are better than they have been in decades. In September of 2017 the leaders of the two countries met in New York City, where both were attending the General Assembly of the United Nations. Netanyahu and Sisi talked for more than an hour and a half and, according to the *Times of Israel*, had "a comprehensive discussion about the problems of the region."[56] The *Times* also reported that Sisi told Netanyahu, "It's a great pleasure to have this meeting with you."[57]

In addition to the thawing of relations between the two countries, it is also reported that the Muslim Brotherhood is splintered and in disarray. In 2017 Al Jazeera asked, "What happened to Egypt's Muslim Brotherhood?" and answered that "the current crisis within the Brotherhood is likely to continue and escalate given the current circumstances....The critical question now is not whether it will break apart or not, but rather when."[58]

Still with an estimated 2.5 million Muslim Brotherhood members in Egypt,[59] the organization is not likely to vanish overnight. And as recent history shows, things can change quickly in Egypt. Conditions are a bit better for Christians there right now, primarily because President Sisi has cracked down on some freedoms that were granted by previous administrations.

It remains to be seen whether his autocratic style of leadership will be able to maintain control. Besides, it is far too early to be talking about lasting peace between Israel and Egypt, especially while persecution of Coptic Christians continues. Of course Copts are not Jews, but they are being persecuted simply because they are not Muslims. If there is to be any talk of a lasting peace, there has to be an understanding that someone is not the enemy just because he or she has beliefs that are different from yours.

Writing for *Forbes*, human rights activist Ewelina U. Ochab tells of attacks on two churches that took place in Egypt in 2017.[60] The first attack occurred on Palm Sunday, when two Coptic churches were targeted by terrorists. Twenty-seven people were believed to be killed in one church; seventeen people perished in the second. More than one hundred people were injured in both. Within hours Daesh (ISIS) claimed responsibility. Its brutal handiwork extended "the legacy of international terror that is at an increase in the recent months. It also adds to the legacy of the terrorist attacks specifically targeting Christian communities."[61]

Ochab describes the response to such persecution and attacks as being "predominately reactive and not preventive," focusing on the single attack and failing to consider "reoccurring incidents of violence" in order to "prevent further attacks."[62] Ochab reports that Egyptian President Sisi "introduced a state of emergency for the next three months…deployed the military…announced three days of mourning…[and] will also establish a new body to counter extremism and terrorism."[63] According to Ochab, "The response of the Egyptian government is a positive one. However, it may be too little too late."[64]

The future political stability of Egypt is uncertain, as is its relationship with Israel. But there is an interesting prophecy in the Book of Isaiah that speaks of a time of unity between Egypt and Israel in the last days. The prophet writes:

In that day there will be an altar to *ADONAI* in the middle of the land of Egypt, and next to the border a pillar to *ADONAI*. It will be as a sign and a witness to *ADONAI-TZVA'OT* in the land of Egypt....*ADONAI* will make Himself known to Egypt, and the Egyptians will know *ADONAI*....In that day there will be a highway from Egypt to Assyria, and the Assyrians will come to Egypt, and the Egyptians to Assyria, and the Egyptians will worship with the Assyrians. In that day Israel will be the third, along with Egypt and Assyria—a blessing in the midst of the earth. For *ADONAI-TZVA'OT* has blessed, saying: "Blessed is Egypt My people, and Assyria My handiwork, and Israel My inheritance."

—ISAIAH 19:19–21, 23–25, TLV

In these early years of the twenty-first century, Egypt is clearly passing through a time of turmoil. But as far as the long-range future is concerned, with God's help it will be absolutely glorious.

CHAPTER 15

JORDAN: FRIEND OR FOE?

The Arab world is writing a new future; the pen is in our own hands.
—KING ABDULLAH II OF JORDAN

JORDAN IS MOST definitely a friend to Israel, at least as far as the official government is concerned. But it is hard to say what lies beneath the surface or to know what would happen if there were a sudden change in Jordan's leadership.

Jordan is Israel's eastern neighbor and shares a border with Israel that stretches for more than 140 miles across deserts and valleys and even through the middle of the Dead Sea. There are three legal crossing points where travelers may pass from one country to the other. And although Jordan and Israel are officially at peace with each other, Israel recently began building an eighteen-mile security fence along the southern part of the border.[1]

Israel has constructed similar security fences along its borders with Egypt and Syria. The main purpose, of course, is to keep terrorists from sneaking into Israel to launch attacks on its citizens. The government of Jordan most certainly understands Israel's caution and desire for protection because Jordan itself has suffered numerous terrorist attacks since signing a peace treaty with Israel in 1994. Al Qaeda bombed three hotels in the capital city of Amman in 2005, killing nearly sixty people and wounding more than one hundred others.

The same wave of unrest that touched off the Arab Spring in 2011 also

139

came to Jordan. Protesters took to the streets at the start of that year, calling for the prime minister to step down[2] and the parliament to be dissolved.[3] Much of the discontent centered on Jordan's difficult economic situation. High employment coupled with rapidly rising prices for food and fuel created widespread unrest and opposition to the government's policies.[4] The king reacted swiftly, enacting economic and political reforms that quieted the protests and restored peace to the country.[5] As difficult as things may have been in Jordan in 2011, the country still had one of the better economies in the Middle East. It is classified by the World Bank as "an upper middle income country."[6]

Today, although King Abdullah is generally regarded as a popular leader, his perceived pro-Israel stance is not shared by a significant portion of the population. Jordan is a largely Muslim country, with some 92 percent of its people identifying themselves as Sunnis.[7] Jews cannot forget (and neither should the rest of the world) that the founder of the Islamic State, Abu Musab al-Zarqawi, was a Jordanian citizen. Apparently he was radicalized in a Jordanian prison. Clearly Jordan is not free of Islamic radicalism—an important reason why Israel is building a fence along that border.

Zarqawi, by the way, was released from prison in March of 1999, when several hundred prisoners were given amnesty to honor King Abdullah's ascension to the throne. Apparently, Zarqawi's name was mistakenly placed on the list of prisoners to be released, though royal pardons were granted to those convicted of nonviolent crimes or political offenses. By the time the error was discovered, it was too late. He was already free.

We don't know how many Jordanians may be radical Islamists, but we do know that another 6 percent of the population are Christians,[8] an estimated 500,000 people. In fact, Jordan has some of the world's oldest Christian communities, dating back to the first century.[9]

King Abdullah, who inherited the throne when his father died in 1999, was educated in the West and has positioned his nation as an ally of Israel. The king has said that because Jordan and Egypt have a special relationship with Israel, they can be the leaders in helping Israel and other Arab nations come together.[10] At the same time, Abdullah has been sharply critical of expanded Israeli settlements in the West Bank. He recently made a rare visit to the Gaza Strip to show his support for Palestinians there, and in an interview with the *Washington Post* he said, "If we can solve the Palestinian problem, then this is a new era of stability in our area, where Israelis are truly a part of the neighborhood."[11]

King Abdullah claims to be a forty-second-generation direct descendent of Muhammad and as such is a member of the Hashemite dynasty.[12] The Hashemites, who trace their ancestry back to Muhammad's great-grandfather Hashem,[13] ruled Mecca for centuries until it was taken by the House of Saud in the 1920s.[14]

In Jordan today you will not hear the same type of statements you often hear from other leaders in the Arab world, such as calls for Israel to be obliterated or claims that the Holocaust is a Jewish hoax. As you can imagine, Islamic extremists revile Jordan because of the country's peaceful relationship with Israel, and although there have been no major terrorist attacks in recent months, Jordan must always anticipate and guard against them.

JORDAN FOR THE JEWS?

One of the most interesting things about Jordan is that it originally was intended to be part of the Jewish homeland as described in the Balfour Declaration.[15] The Jewish people were to be given all of Palestine, east and west of the Jordan River, as their homeland. Many Jews owned property in Jordan, and in biblical times three of Israel's twelve tribes were allotted land in what is today Jordan. The tribes of Reuben, Gad, and Manasseh all lived east of the Jordan River Valley.[16]

Before World War I, Jordan (then known as Transjordan) was not a single country but a collection of districts and provinces of the Ottoman Empire, each with its own governor or director.[17] It was a mostly rural and quiet region, sparsely settled, with little in the way of an economy that would support a larger population. For this reason it wasn't considered particularly important until World War I erupted on the world stage.

The Ottoman Empire, which ruled Palestine from Turkey, sided with the Germans in the conflict. Naturally the British wanted the Arabs to help by rising up against the Turks. To this end, the British High Commissioner in Egypt, Sir Henry McMahon, wrote a letter to the Hashemite King Hussein, Sharif of Mecca. Although McMahon's letter was purposefully vague, it seemed to promise the Arabs their own country, stretching from Damascus to the Arabian Peninsula, if they would help defeat the Ottomans.[18]

But when King Hussein declared a revolt against the Ottoman Empire in 1916, very few responded. For the most part, the Arabs did not seem interested in rebellion. The British had backed a man who was not a dynamic military leader by any means.[19]

Meanwhile, even as the British promised the Arabs a country of their own, they also entered into an agreement with the French and Russians to divide up the Middle East among themselves,[20] promising that this arrangement would only be in place until the newly liberated peoples there could learn to stand on their own.

This was the Sykes-Picot agreement of 1916.[21] No matter how benign the British, French, and Russians made it sound, it was in direct contradiction to what McMahon had promised the Arabs for fighting the Turks. And the following year the British also promised the establishment of a Jewish homeland in the Middle East. Of course it wasn't just difficult to do all these things at the same time; it was impossible.

Sir Mark Sykes of Britain and Francois Georges-Picot of France set to work carving up the Middle East. Syria and Lebanon were grouped together into the French sphere of influence, while much of the area that is now Jordan, southern Palestine, and Iraq was part of the British sphere of influence.

RUSSIA SPILLS THE BEANS

The authors of the Sykes-Picot agreement intended to keep it a secret for as long as possible. That changed in 1917, when the czar was overthrown and the Bolsheviks came to power in Russia. The new government printed and published the entire text of the agreement,[22] hoping to show the world that these three powers were fighting a war not because they wanted to see justice and right prevail but because they sought to enlarge their own empires.

The Russian revelation of Sykes-Picot had no impact on the fighting, which raged on. When the long, devastating war finally ended, in 1918, the Mandates of Palestine and Iraq were awarded to the British. Two and a half years later, following a conference in Cairo, the British government announced that Transjordan would be an Arab country separate from Palestine and would not be part of the Jewish National Home as originally promised.[23] In September of 1922 the League of Nations approved a memorandum that spelled out and made official the exclusion of Transjordan from the Jewish homeland provision.

Colonel Richard Meinertzhagen, as mentioned earlier, served as British chief of intelligence in the Middle East. He wrote that he "exploded" upon hearing that Transjordan was no longer to be included as part of the Jewish homeland. He wrote:

> This reduces the Jewish National Home to one-third of Biblical Palestine. The Colonial Office and the Palestine Administration have now declared that the articles of the mandate relating to the Jewish Home are not applicable to Transjordan....This discovery was not made until it became necessary to appease an Arab Emir....
>
> I went [to see Winston Churchill] foaming at the mouth with anger and indignation. Churchill heard me out; I told him it was grossly unfair to the Jews, that it was yet another promise broken and that it was a most dishonest act, that the Balfour Declaration was being torn up by degrees and that the official policy of His Majesty's Government to establish a Home for the Jews in Biblical Palestine was being sabotaged.[24]

Churchill listened, and although he appeared to agree with much of what he was hearing, he didn't seem to think there was anything he could do. "I'm thoroughly disgusted," said Meinertzhagen.[25]

The colonel wasn't the only one to feel that way. Lord Sydney Arnold, British Under-Secretary for the Colonies, said, "During the war we recognized Arab independence, within certain border limits. There were discussions as to what territories these borders should take in. But there was no dispute as to Transjordan. There is no doubt about the fact that Transjordan is within the boundaries to which the [Balfour] Declaration during the war refers."[26]

BRITAIN PULLS OUT OF PALESTINE

It was not until 1947, two years after the end of World War II, that Britain finally announced its withdrawal from the Middle East altogether. After sustaining massive losses during the war, there was simply no way to maintain a large military force in Palestine.

The withdrawal was also prompted by a number of attacks on British installations by Jewish paramilitary organizations such as Irgun and Lehi.[27] These groups blew up bridges, attacked British military installations, and generally waged guerrilla war. Irgun had split off from Haganah,[28] which had been organized in the early 1920s to protect Jewish citizens and farms and had the backing of the Jewish leadership. Haganah's purpose was to defend rather than attack, and as I mentioned earlier, it operated under the policy of *havlaga* (restraint).[29]

Other Jews, tired of continuous attacks on Jews by Arabs—attacks that the British army seemed incapable of stopping (or was, perhaps, disinterested in stopping)—decided that the time had come to go on the offensive. One of the largest and most deadly attacks occurred on July 22, 1946, at the King David Hotel in Jerusalem, which was being used as British military headquarters. The blast killed ninety-one people.[30]

Lehi was a more radical group that split off from Irgun. During World War II, Lehi actually tried to enlist Nazi Germany and Fascist Italy to help them in their fight against Britain.[31] Lehi's leaders apparently believed that Britain was more of an enemy to the Jews than the Nazis were. They also hoped, foolishly, that they could save the Jews of Europe by getting the Nazis to ship them all to the Middle East.[32] That way Europe would be free from Jews and their influence, which was exactly what the Nazis wanted—wasn't it? The problem was that the leadership of Lehi had completely underestimated the depth of the Nazis' hatred of the Jews.

Lehi's overture to the Nazis is just one indication of how bad the relationship between Israel and Great Britain had become. The Jews wanted the British out of Palestine for a number of reasons, one of the most important being that they wanted to open Palestine to Jewish immigration after the British had cut it back to almost nothing. In 1939 the British government, under the direction of Neville Chamberlain, issued a White Paper that severely restricted Jewish immigration to Palestine,[33] touching off anger throughout the region. David Ben-Gurion, who then headed the Jewish Agency, responded, "We shall fight side by side with the British in our war against Hitler as if there were no White Paper, and we shall fight the White Paper as if there were no war."[34]

Benjamin Netanyahu writes, "For over ten years the British shut the doors of the Jewish National Home to Jews fleeing their deaths. In so doing they not only worked to destroy the Jewish National Home, which no one believed could survive without immigrants, but made themselves accomplices in the destruction of European Jewry."[35]

When news of Hitler's mass murder of the Jews reached the ears of British officials in Palestine, they would not change their position. John Shuckburgh, a deputy secretary of the British Colonial Office, described the news as "unscrupulous Zionist sobstuff" and added that "we cannot be deterred [from our policies] by the kind of perverse, pre-war humanitarianism that prevailed in 1939."[36]

With attitudes like these gaining the upper hand in Great Britain, it is easy to understand why there was rejoicing among Palestinian Jews when Britain pulled its troops from the region.

But there was trepidation too. Palestine was a tiny land surrounded on all sides by enemies who opposed a homeland for the Jews. The Arab countries were bigger and stronger and would undoubtedly attack if and when the Jews declared statehood. The Jews of Palestine were also uncertain if any other nation would help them if war broke out. If their efforts failed, the world could wash its hands of them and say, "Well, they tried to create a Jewish homeland. It just didn't work."

Of course it did work. Although outnumbered and outgunned, the newly formed State of Israel prevailed against its enemies. It not only prevailed but also grew, as portions of Arab land were absorbed through victories in wars that Israel did not start or want.

Now, I realize that I have spent quite a bit of time talking about history in this chapter, but it is necessary to understand the history of the region in order to have a clear picture of the relationship that Israel and Jordan have today. Jordan's history is especially important when we hear all the talk about carving out a homeland for Palestinians in the Middle East. We have heard over and over again that the establishment of such a homeland is a vitally important key to peace in the region. But the reality is that such a homeland already exists, and Jordan is its name.

Again, keep in mind that the land that is today Jordan was once included in a territory that had been set aside for a Jewish homeland. Both Jews and Arabs lived there. Now there are no Jews in Jordan, but hundreds of thousands of Palestinians have become Jordanian citizens. It is true that Jordan's royal family is not Palestinian. Rather, the Hashemites came from Mecca, which became part of Saudi Arabia when it was conquered by the House of Saud in 1924. But half of all Jordanians have Palestinian roots.[37] I also want to repeat here that the area known as the West Bank (often referred to as "occupied territory," as if it had been taken from an independent Palestinian people) was part of Jordan until Jordan's defeat in the Six-Day War of 1967.

Benjamin Netanyahu puts it this way:

> The land of Palestine comprises the modern states of Jordan and Israel. It is large enough to accommodate both a small Jewish state, Israel, and a substantially larger state for the Arabs of Palestine, which is today called Jordan. This is a two-state solution to resolve a conflict between two peoples: a Jewish state for the Jewish people of Palestine, an Arab state for the Arab people of Palestine.[38]

Netanyahu recognizes that King Abdullah is not of Palestinian origin but explains the irrelevance of the fact:

> That Palestinian Jordan is ruled by a monarch of Bedouin extraction no more justifies the creation of an additional Palestinian state than the election of a Hispanic-American president in the United States would justify the creation of a separate country for Americans of, say, Anglo-Saxon extraction. The fact remains that Jordan is a state that encompasses the overwhelming majority of Palestine's territory and that has a majority of Palestinian Arabs.[39]

Mr. Netanyahu's point is well taken.

CHAPTER 16

UPHEAVAL IN TURKEY

Turkey may well be at the head of a restored Islamic confederacy in the days ahead. It was always the seat of power for the caliphate and is once again striving to regain that power. Once a friend of Israel, it has, in recent years, become increasingly hostile to Israel and the West and is a growing threat in the region.

—JONATHAN BERNIS

O N JULY 15, 2016, everything changed in Turkey. It was on that date that a military coup was staged to topple the government of President Recep Tayyip Erdogan. By all accounts the coup was clumsy and amateurish. Certainly it was poorly planned and quickly crushed—but not before nearly three hundred Turkish citizens had been killed.

In the first year after the failed coup, more than fifty thousand people were arrested and imprisoned. In addition, an estimated one hundred fifty thousand public officials have been fired from their jobs,[1] as have almost six thousand university professors.[2] Turkey does not have a death penalty, but there were demonstrations calling for its restoration after the coup, and Erdogan publicly said that he was open to reinstating it.[3]

Erdogan blamed the coup on a then seventy-five-year-old cleric named Fethullah Gülen, who currently resides in Pennsylvania. He is described as a "moderate" Muslim who believes that education is the key to a better future for Muslims.[4] To help bring this about, Gülen and his organization have founded hundreds of schools in Turkey and around the world, including many here in the United States.[5]

Gülen and Erdogan were once allies. That ended after Erdogan accused Gülen of instigating corruption charges that nearly brought his government down.[6] After the coup Erdogan demanded that Gülen be extradited from the United States to Turkey, but the Obama administration refused.[7] Erdogan also charged that several United States generals were involved in planning the coup, a charge the US has denied.[8] Currently Gülen is "Number One" on Turkey's list of most-wanted criminals.[9]

Before the coup Turkey was seen by many as a model of democracy in the Middle East. A devout Muslim, Erdogan was "proof" that a Muslim leader could uphold democratic standards and strive for freedom for his people. Since the coup, however, the Turkish people have experienced a continual deterioration of personal freedoms and a tightening of government power.

Ostensibly those changes were designed to protect the Turkish government in a time of crisis. But many observers believe the coup was perhaps encouraged or even staged by Erdogan's government in order to justify crackdowns that were already planned.[10] One example of the suspected staging involves the airplanes commandeered by rebels that attacked Turkey's parliament on a Friday night when no one was there. In addition, the bombs that fell on government buildings inflicted minimal damage, almost as if the bombers were trying to avoid hitting crucial targets.[11]

That being said, Gülen has millions of followers in Turkey. To think that they would try to bring down Erdogan is entirely plausible. Clearly, though Gülen describes himself as a moderate, he distrusts and hates Israel the way many more "extreme" Muslims do.[12]

DID THE COUP REALLY HAPPEN?

Relations between Turkey and the United States have deteriorated in the two years since the failed coup. Although the government tried not to let too much information get out, details reported by the *Washington Post* point to anti-Western tendencies *before* the coup.

> Fewer than 9,000 soldiers were out on the street that night, most
> of them unaware of what was going on. Yet, almost immediately,

the government fired some 149 generals and admirals representing 46 percent of the general staff of the Turkish military.
In addition, many colonels and majors, most of them staff-level
officers, were also purged.... The speed with which these officers
were dismissed and the absence of any due process indicate that
lists had been readied well before the coup attempt.[13]

The *Washington Post* goes on to say that most of the officers who were
dismissed shared a pro-Western viewpoint. Many were actually serving
abroad in NATO installations when the coup attempt was made. Those
officers were arrested upon their return home, and those arrests turned
into jail sentences because few have been indicted or seen a judge.[14]

Writing in the *Huffington Post*, Stanley Weiss, founding chairman of
Business Executives for National Security, notes, "Turkey…has moved so
far away from its NATO allies that it is widely acknowledged to be defiantly
supporting the Islamic State in Syria in its war against the West." Weiss
points out Turkey's "authoritarian turn," its favor toward "Islamic terrorists of every stripe," and its battle against the Kurds, who are fighting ISIS.[15]

Weiss calls for Turkey to be booted out of NATO, contends that
Erdogan "is Islamist to the core," and quotes Erdogan's Islamist declaration: "The mosques are our barracks, the domes our helmets, the
minarets our bayonets, and the faithful our soldiers."[16] Weiss claims
that Erdogan dreams of leading "a post-Arab-Spring Muslim world."[17]
So far, Weiss claims, Erdogan has stripped Turkey of its "secular and
democratic" distinctives and molded it into what Caroline Glick of the
Center for Security Policy says is a combination Putin-style autocracy
and Iranian theocracy. Weiss added that Erdogan has even praised the
extreme powers Adolf Hitler enjoyed.[18]

Weiss notes some of Erdogan's anti-democratic moves,[19] saying he

- "**arrested** more journalists than China";
- "**jailed** thousands of students for the crime of free speech";
- "**replaced** secular schools with Islamic-focused madrassas";
- "**flaunted** his support for Hamas and the Muslim
  Brotherhood";

- **accused** Israel of "crimes against humanity";

- **denied** the United States "use of its own air base to conduct strikes…against Islamic terrorists in Syria";

- **allowed** jihadists to reach Syria via Turkey;

- **enabled** ISIS to market Syrian oil by way of Turkey; and

- **allowed** supply trucks to reach ISIS via Turkey.

In the past, Turkey and Israel have enjoyed a somewhat friendly relationship. It has steadily deteriorated, however, especially since the volatility that followed the 2016 "revolt." For example, the two countries had been active trading partners, but trade has declined since 2016.[20] In 2000, when Israel suffered a severe drought, Turkey and Israel signed an agreement allowing Israel to purchase up to 50 million cubic meters (13,208,602,618 gallons) of water from Turkey annually for the next decade.[21] Also, Turkey was a favorite destination for many Israelis[22] who took advantage of the inexpensive vacation opportunities there.

For the past several years Turkey has seemed to move away from its ties with Israel and identified itself more closely with other Islamic states. Some observers have even suggested that President Erdogan would like to revive the Ottoman Empire,[23] with Turkey leading an alliance of Islamic nations. After Erdogan attacked Israel in a speech before the Turkish parliament, "Israeli Foreign Ministry spokesperson Emmanuel Nahshon said the days of the Ottoman Empire are over."[24]

Erdogan has even compared Israeli government actions to those of Adolf Hitler, saying he cannot decide which are "more barbarous."[25] These are not the words one expects from an ally wanting to build a closer relationship.

BACKLASH AGAINST CHRISTIANS

Although Turkey plays an important role in Christian history, there are few Christians in Turkey today. Estimates vary between 120,000 and 160,000, or about two-tenths of a percent of the total population of approximately eighty million.[26]

In the aftermath of the 2016 coup Turkey experienced a shift toward radical Islam, with many Turks obviously equating patriotism with religious fervor. This affected not only Turkey's small number of Jews but churches as well.[27] Some were attacked by angry mobs, and deaths were reported.[28]

On April 22, 2016, a headline in the British newspaper *Express* reported, "Islamist Turkey Seizes ALL Christian Churches in City and Declares Them 'State Property.'"[29] The article explained that Erdogan took over six churches representing a variety of Christian sects (one of the churches has existed for seventeen centuries) and claims that Erdogan's goal was "to squash freedom of speech and religious movement," even as he negotiated with the EU for Turks to gain free travel.[30] In effect, the churches became state property in a country known for its poor human rights record—a nation that is about 98 percent Muslim.[31]

Meanwhile Erdogan also blames Israel for some of the troubles his country is facing. According to *Newsweek*, Turkish media outlets have claimed that a secret agreement exists between Kurds and Israel to obtain Kurdish independence by "resettling Jews to the region."[32] *Newsweek* claims these reports, which appeared in Turkish newspapers such as *Yenia Akit*, *Aksam*, and *Al-Monitor*, are "apparently false."[33] Yet Turkish newspapers claimed that Mahmoud Barzani, the Kurds' regional leader, entered an agreement to receive "200,000 Israeli Jews of Kurdish origin" to Kurdistan in exchange for Israeli support for "Barzani's bid for Kurdish statehood."[34]

As you may know, Kurdistan is not a nation but a large region, primarily in northern Iraq, with a population of more than twenty-eight million. The Kurds have been valuable allies in the fight against the Islamic State. They were badly mistreated and discriminated against by the government of Saddam Hussein. In the closing days of the Iran-Iraq War, Hussein used chemical weapons in Kurdistan, killing an estimated five thousand civilians and injuring thousands more.[35]

For years the Kurds have been seeking their independence from Iraq, and more than 92 percent of them voted for independence in a nonbinding referendum held in September of 2017. There is only one country in the Middle East that supports the Kurds in their fight for freedom, and that is Israel.

Turkey has been vocal in its opposition to an independent Kurdistan and considers the PKK, the Kurdish nationalist party within Turkey, a terrorist organization. The Turkish government has even staged military drills along its border with Kurdistan to show its opposition to the Kurdish independence movement.

Why does Turkey hate the Kurds? Basically for the same reason the pharaohs of ancient Egypt turned against the Israelites. There are too many of them, and they are militarily strong. They have proved their bravery and skill by slowing and then reversing the Islamic State's march across the Middle East.

For more than one hundred years the Kurds have been fighting for a country of their own. In fact, the Allies promised them their own country at the conclusion of World War I, but the promise was broken.[36] The Kurds' push for independence has led to armed clashes with Turkish troops. Turkey is not about to willingly give up huge chunks of its territory so the Kurds can have their own country.

Yet if not for the Kurds, ISIS may very well have taken control of Baghdad. In some instances, when Kurds advanced against the Islamic State's invaders, they also had to deal with bombs and bullets from Turkish planes.

In his book *ISIS, Iran and Israel,* newsman Chris Mitchell describes his trip to Kurdistan and meeting with high-ranking military officers there. He reports that the Kurds "love" the United States and are "totally pro-American."[37] Although more than 99 percent of them are Muslim, they are deeply opposed to the brutality of the Islamic State. They are our best hope of defeating and eradicating ISIS once and for all.

DEATH ON BOARD THE *MAVI MARMARA*

One of the low points in the relationship between Turkey and Israel occurred in 2010, when a gun battle took place on a Turkish ship, the *Mavi Marmara,* resulting in the death of ten Turkish activists.[38]

The *Mavi Marmara* was the largest vessel in a flotilla of six Turkish ships delivering aid to the Gaza Strip, which was being blockaded through a joint operation conducted by Israel and Egypt. The Turkish activists claimed the ships were filled with humanitarian supplies, but the Israeli government feared that weapons were also being sent to Hamas fighters in Gaza. The Turkish government claimed the ships were under the control of a registered charity, but Israeli officials suspected that the "charity" in question was a front for terrorist activity.[39]

The flotilla was ordered by the Israeli Navy to proceed to an Israeli port where the ships could be searched.[40] Once that had been done, beneficial supplies would be transported overland to Gaza. When this order was rejected, Israeli commandos boarded the *Mavi Marmara*, descending on ropes from helicopters, about 130 miles from the Israeli coast. As soon as the commandos hit the deck, gunfire reportedly erupted. By the time the shooting stopped, nine crew members were dead. A tenth crew member died later.[41]

In the aftermath of the tragic incident, Turkey withdrew its ambassador from Tel Aviv and expelled the Israeli ambassador in Ankara.[42] President Erdogan called for Israel to be punished for its "bloody massacre,"[43] and Turkey's foreign minister, Ahmet Davutoglu, said that because of what happened, "Israel is going to be devoid of Turkey's friendship."[44]

Tensions remained high until March of 2013, when Israel's Prime Minister Netanyahu called Erdogan, and the two men decided to take steps toward normalizing the relationship between the two countries.[45]

THE TRAGIC STORY OF THE STRUMA

Another tragedy at sea—this one on a much larger scale—plagued the relationship between Turkey and Israel for years but dates all the way back to December 1941. That was when the *Struma*, a ship packed full of Jewish refugees from Europe, steamed into Istanbul while on its way to Palestine but was turned away.

The *Struma* was an old, leaky vessel built in 1867[46] and designed to carry 150 crew passengers.[47] When it limped into port in Turkey, more than 750 refugees were on board, many of them children.

The refugees had come from Romania, where, according to the US minister in Bucharest, Jews were being killed in great numbers and their corpses displayed on butcher's hooks.[48] If anyone ever deserved sanctuary and safety, it was these poor refugees, who would most certainly be murdered if they returned to their native land. Yet the Turkish government said no. Or did it? More about this in just a moment.

One thing is certain: the ship was turned away and towed ten kilometers out into the Black Sea by the Turkish Navy.[49] Suddenly the ancient ship burst into flames. It had been struck by a torpedo fired by a Soviet submarine.[50] There were two survivors, one of them a pregnant woman who was brought back to Istanbul. She survived, but her baby died. The other survivor was a young man of nineteen.[51]

The Turkish government was blamed for the massive loss of life. But who was really to blame? According to author Joan Peters, subsequent research has revealed that the Turkish government was not really to blame for the loss of the *Struma*; the British were.

Peters writes:

> Regarding the Turkish government's reactions...more fully documented accounts of the *Struma* catastrophe show that the Turks were willing to allow "and even assist" the ship to Palestine, but the British Ambassador in Ankara said that his government "did not want these people in Palestine."[52]

The ambassador also expressed his concern that "if they [the refugees] reached Palestine, they might despite their illegality receive humane treatment."[53]

In other words, he apparently felt that they should be made to suffer because they were illegal aliens! It was also suggested that the refugees should be turned away because Nazi spies might be hiding among them—although, according to Peters, there was never one case of this happening.[54] Another reason for denying the refugees entry into Palestine was that most of them were "professionals." They wouldn't know how to dig ditches, build houses, plow fields, and engage in other manual labor, which was what was needed in Palestine at that time.[55]

Unfortunately there is more to this sad story. It was suggested that the British government bring in a ship to rescue the children who were aboard the *Struma*; they would apparently be welcomed into Palestine. Yet the British made excuses: They couldn't find a ship. They were afraid that the parents would object when they tried to remove their children from the ship. One official asked, "Has the possibility of the adults refusing to let the children go been considered?"[56]

And so the *Struma* sank into the Black Sea with all 750 passengers aboard, including many children.[57]

You may be wondering why I bring up this story. After all, it is really "ancient" history now, and there were many other such tragedies during the days of Nazi Germany. This is true, of course, and pointing the finger at the British is not my intention. Instead, my point is to show that the Jewish people, quite understandably, haven't always known whom to trust. There are Jew haters everywhere, including in Britain, Turkey, and the United States. Tragically, for Israel and the Jewish people, you never know who your friends are—or, for that matter, who your enemies are.

JEWISH HISTORY IN TURKEY

According to the World Jewish Congress, there are an estimated eighteen thousand Jews in Turkey, most of them in Istanbul.[58] Although the Jewish population has dwindled in recent years, with nearly fifty thousand Jews leaving Turkey for Israel since its founding in 1948, many of Turkey's Jews have stayed put.[59] Who can blame them? Their roots in Turkey are strong and deep, going back centuries. Archaeologists have found remnants of Jewish settlements in Turkey that date back to the fourth century BC,[60] making them some of the oldest in the world.

The World Jewish Congress explains that Ottomans who captured Bursa in the fourteenth century found Jews who had suffered for centuries under Byzantine rule. "In the liberal atmosphere of Ottoman rule,"[61] Turkey became a safe haven for Jews who were oppressed or expelled from European nations "including Hungary, France, Spain, Sicily, Salonika, and Bavaria." Jews prospered, and Constantinople became "the home of great rabbis and scholars and was a Hebrew book-printing center."[62]

The World Jewish Congress further explains that after World War I, Turkey vehemently opposed religious instruction and banned Hebrew until Kemal Atatürk died in 1938. Hit with oppressive taxation, Jews suffered financially. Many left Turkey and started new lives elsewhere, including "North and Latin America and...Israel."[63]

TURKEY IN THE BIBLE

Turkey is often referred to as "the other Holy Land" because so many of the cities and other locations mentioned in the Scriptures are located in present-day Turkey. I think this is worth talking about because it shows us that God's gracious hand has rested upon Turkey in the past. I believe

His hand is still upon the Turkish people today. He loves them and wants them to come to Him so they can partake of His blessings. Whether they respond is entirely up to them.

Here are just a few Scripture references to Turkey:

- Genesis 8:4 tells us that when the waters subsided after the great flood, the ark landed on **Mount Ararat**. Reaching up over sixteen thousand feet, the mountain towers above the landscape of eastern Turkey.

- **Haran**, a city in eastern Turkey, was once home to the great patriarch Abraham and his family. Genesis 11:31 says, "Terah took Abram his son and Lot, Haran's son, his grandson, and Sarai his daughter-in-law, his son Abram's wife, and he took them out of Ur of the Chaldeans to go to the land of Canaan. But when they came to Haran, they settled there" (TLV).

- **Ephesus**, where the apostle Paul lived for about three years, is located in Turkey. The epistle to the Ephesians was written to the Believers in Ephesus, and it was here that Paul had a show-down with those who worshipped the goddess Diana. It is also believed that the apostle John is buried in Ephesus. In the time of Jesus, Ephesus was the fourth–most important city in the world, after Rome, Alexandria, and Antioch. It was also an important seaport, although the coastline has shifted over the centuries and the city's ancient docks are now six miles inland.

- Paul himself was born in **Tarsus**, which is an ancient Turkish city near the Mediterranean coast. With a history that stretches back for thousands of years, Tarsus was a wealthy and important community of perhaps half a million inhabitants when the apostle was born there.

- **Antioch** is another important Turkish city. It was here that the followers of Jesus the Messiah were first called Christians. The Cave Church of St. Peter, located just outside the city, was supposedly built by the apostle himself and is considered to be the oldest Christian church in the world.[64] It was also the church at Antioch that sent Paul and Barnabas out on their missionary journeys, which are recorded in the Book of Acts.

- **The Isle of Patmos**, where the apostle John was exiled in the latter days of his life and where he was inspired to write the Book of Revelation, is off the coast of Turkey. The seven churches of Asia mentioned in the Book of Revelation are located in Turkey.

Obviously God has had His hand on Turkey in the past. He alone holds the key to Turkey's future.

CHAPTER 17

RUSSIA'S PLANS FOR THE MIDDLE EAST

*Nobody should have any illusion about the possibility of gaining
military superiority over Russia. We will never allow this to happen.*

—VLADIMIR PUTIN

RUSSIA HAS A special place in my heart. Having lived in St. Petersburg, Russia, for several years, I have fond memories of the wonderful people I met there, particularly among the Jewish population that was so hungry for spiritual truth.

Although memories of my time in Russia have been made gentler and happier by the passage of time, the truth is that life in what was, when I first arrived, the Soviet Union, was not easy. Russia was cold, drab, and in many ways depressing. You never knew when someone might be listening in on your conversations or watching you, and you never knew who might be a government agent. Fear and uncertainty were always in the air.

It was in Russia that I saw some of the worst anti-Semitism I have ever encountered. I told about it in my book *A Rabbi Looks at the Last Days*. When we were out doing street ministry, sharing our faith, people spit at us, shoved us, called us pigs, screamed that they hated Jews, and hurled other insults at us. The hateful looks on the faces of ordinary Russian citizens were truly terrifying. It was disturbing to think that people could hate other people with such intensity, simply because of their ethnicity.

But then, anti-Semitism in Russia goes back a long time. Thousands of Jews were killed in pogroms in Russia during the late 1880s and early 1900s.[1] The outrageous *Protocols of the Elders of Zion* was written in Russia during the time of these pogroms to justify the persecution of Jews.[2] It has been widely read in Russia—*and believed*—even though it has been proved to be complete fiction.

The hard truth is that for centuries Jews in Russia were oppressed and persecuted—beaten, discriminated against, forced to live in squalor in ghettos, raped, and killed. Many Jews saved their own lives by converting to the Russian Orthodox Church. (This is not unique to Russia, of course. Throughout history many thousands of Jews have been converted at sword-point, which is one of the reasons so many Jews are hostile to Christianity, especially when so many have never encountered the real thing.)

If I seem to be too hard on Russia, let me say that I have met many fine people there, Jews and non-Jews alike. But the truth is that the Soviet Union has not been a friend of Israel. The Soviets did support the Jewish state in the beginning but only because they thought it would become a Communist nation; that support evaporated as soon as they discovered this was not going to happen.[3] For decades they did everything within their power to destroy Israel. They poured weapons into the hands of its enemies and then encouraged them to attack it, and they consistently opposed Israel in the United Nations.

The Soviet Union has long since vanished from the scene. And even though Vladimir Putin says that because more than 1.5 million Russian Jews have emigrated to Israel, Russia has a "special relationship" with the Jewish state, Russia is still not a true friend to Israel.

RUSSIA HAS PLANS FOR THE MIDDLE EAST

You might think that based on its past experiences in the Middle East, Russia would keep its troops out of the region. From 1979 to 1989 Russian soldiers were involved in an unwinnable, highly unpopular war in Afghanistan that resulted in an estimated thirty-five thousand casualties among Soviet troops, including as many as fifteen thousand deaths.[4]

Well over a million Afghani civilians also died during that conflict before Soviet troops were finally brought home.[5]

Today Russian soldiers are again dodging bombs and bullets in the Middle East, this time in Syria, where they are fighting to prop up the regime of their longtime ally Bashar al-Assad.

Although Russia ostensibly sent troops into Syria to fight the Islamic State, it quickly became clear that it is more interested in helping Assad stay in power. Vladimir Putin has even come up with excuses for Assad's atrocities. For instance, when the Assad regime used chemical weapons in northern Syria (in an attack that killed eighty-three people and injured at least one hundred fifty more), the Russians had an explanation. They said the chemicals had been released when a Syrian attack blew up a rebel warehouse. The rebels, they claimed, had been stockpiling chemical weapons that were to be shipped to Islamic fighters in Iraq.[6]

The Russian version of the situation was quickly refuted by a number of military experts around the world. For one thing, they said, an attack on a warehouse would be unlikely to spread the deadly gas to the extent it dispersed during this incident.[7] For another, Hasan Haj Ali, commander of the Free Idlib Army rebel brigade, told Reuters that "everyone saw the plane while it was bombing with gas."[8]

Furthermore, the Assad regime has been accused of using chemical weapons before, most notably in 2013, when a chemical attack on the outskirts of Damascus killed an estimated fourteen hundred people.[9] Assad still denies responsibility for that attack.

British Foreign Secretary Boris Johnson refuted the denials, saying, "All the evidence I have seen suggests this was the Assad regime…using chemical weapons on their own people."[10]

What can we learn from Russia's defense of Assad's heinous attack on innocent civilians? First, that the Russian government has no regard for the truth and is still employing the misinformation tactics used so frequently during the days of the Soviet Union. And second, that the Russians are deeply interested in what happens in the Middle East and will continue to be heavily involved there.

I understand that many Americans admire Vladimir Putin for what he has done in Russia. They see him as a strong leader who brought the country together when it seemed to be on the verge of collapse. He has established strong ties with the Russian Orthodox Church after years of militant atheism under Communist rule. But when it comes to Russia, extreme caution and skepticism must be exercised.

WHAT THE BIBLE SAYS ABOUT RUSSIA

Although this is not really a book about Bible prophecy, I think it is important to take a look at what the Bible has to say about Russia's role in the Middle East. Let's take a quick look at some of what God says in Ezekiel chapter 38:

> The word of ADONAI came to me saying: "Son of man, set your face toward Gog of the land of Magog, chief prince of Meshech and Tubal. Prophesy against him and say, thus says ADONAI Elohim: 'Behold, I am against you, Gog, chief prince of Meshech and Tubal.'"
>
> —EZEKIEL 38:1–3, TLV

> In the latter years, you will come against the land that has been brought back from the sword and regathered from many peoples on the mountains of Israel. . . . When all of them are dwelling securely, you will come up, you will come like a storm, you will be like a cloud covering the land—you and all your troops and many peoples with you.
>
> —EZEKIEL 38:8–9, TLV

> In that day when My people Israel dwell safely, will you not know? You will come from your place out of the extreme north— you and many peoples with you, all of them riding on horses, a great company and mighty army. You will come up against My people Israel like a cloud covering the land. It will happen in the last days. I will bring you against My land, so that the nations may know Me—when I am sanctified through you, Gog, before their eyes.
>
> —EZEKIEL 38:14–16, TLV

> "In that day, when Gog comes against the land of Israel"—it is a declaration of ADONAI—"My fury will rise up in My nostrils. In

> My jealousy and the fire of My wrath I have spoken!...I will call for a sword against him throughout all my mountains"—it is a declaration of *ADONAI*—"every man's sword will be against his brother. I will punish him with pestilence and blood. I will pour out rain on him, on his troops and on the many peoples with him, a torrential rain, with hailstones, fire and brimstone. So I will magnify and sanctify Myself. I will make Myself known in the eyes of many nations, and they will know that I am *ADONAI*."
> —EZEKIEL 38:18–19, 21–23, TLV

Who are Gog and Magog, the ones who will come against Israel in the last days? There has been a great deal of speculation, but many end-time prophecy experts have concluded that the Bible is referring to what is today Russia.

The late John F. Walvoord, who served for years as the president of Dallas Theological Seminary, wrote:

> In Ezekiel 38 and 39, a description is given of a war between Israel and a nation which many have identified as Russia....The Scriptures are plain that this is a military invasion and reveal many details about the situation existing at the time of that invasion. The dramatic outcome of the battle is the utter destruction of the army that invades the land of Israel. Written by the prophet Ezekiel, who himself was in exile from the land of Israel, this prophecy was inspired by the Spirit of God. A natural question can be raised, however, inasmuch as this was written some twenty-five hundred years ago, whether this passage has already been fulfilled.
>
> The land of Israel has been the scene of many wars, and invasions have come from various parts of the world, north, east, and south.... [However,] there never has been a war with Israel which fulfills the prophecies of Ezekiel 38 and 39. If one believes that the Bible is the Word of God and that it is infallible and must be fulfilled, the only logical conclusion is that this portion of Scripture, like many others, is still due a future fulfillment.[11]

My friend Joel Rosenberg, a well-known Bible teacher who has taught extensively on the Book of Ezekiel, was asked by CBN's Chris Mitchell whether he saw current events in the Middle East as a fulfillment of Ezekiel's prophecies about Gog and Magog. Rosenberg replied in a live interview that is quoted in Mitchell's book *ISIS, Iran and Israel*:

> Now does this mean the prophecies about Gog and Magog will happen soon, or even in our lifetime? No. This could be decades or theoretically centuries off. However, when you actually have [longtime enemies like] Russia and Iran fighting on the same side...I think it's an incredibly dangerous situation for the United States; it's an incredibly dangerous situation for Israel.[12]

At the beginning of this book we talked about the many thousands of missiles that have been fired into Israel since 2001. Most of them are Scud rockets from Russia. In fact, the Middle East is full of weapons made in Russia or the former Soviet Union—and a majority of them are pointed at Israel. Syrian troops are using Russian weapons to destroy their own cities and kill their own people. Since Russia stepped into the Syrian war, it has shipped billions of dollars of newer, more advanced weapons into the country, weapons with an increased ability to inflict casualties and cause destruction.

Whatever Vladimir Putin may be, he is not a man of peace. Rather, he seems bent on restoring the former glory of the Russian empire. His actions in Ukraine, Georgia, and now Syria speak for themselves. It would be wonderful to think we could count on Russia as our ally against Iran, ISIS, and other terrorist groups and be sure that Russia had no other motives than to do the right thing.

But when it comes to Russia and Vladimir Putin, the utmost caution is absolutely necessary.

CHAPTER 18

RECOGNITION AT LAST

Break forth in joy, sing together, you ruins of Jerusalem, for
ADONAI has comforted His people. He has redeemed Jerusalem.
—ISAIAH 52:9, TLV

A S THIS BOOK neared publication, President Donald Trump made a decision that shocked the world and put the United States in position to receive great blessings from the hand of God. I also believe Mr. Trump took a big step toward initiating a real and lasting peace plan by laying a foundation of truth.

The president did what several of his predecessors had promised to do during their election campaigns but failed to do once elected: he moved the US embassy from Tel Aviv to Jerusalem. In doing so, he acknowledged what many Jews and evangelical Christians have always said: that the city of Jerusalem belongs to Israel and is the legitimate and rightful capital of the Jewish state.

Although the United States Congress voted in 1995 to move the embassy to Jerusalem,[1] three presidents had already refused to make the move: Bill Clinton, George W. Bush, and Barack Obama. They changed their minds because they were warned by the US State Department that moving the embassy would anger Muslims around the world—especially in the Palestine territories—and cause them to turn against the United States. It was also anticipated that the move would likely trigger violent protests and perhaps terrorist attacks against Israel and the United States.

Admittedly this escalation might be hard to spot since violent terror attacks have been almost a daily fact of life for Israelis.

The United States was attempting to be a good friend to Israel, the Palestinians, and the Arab world. The problem is that it's not at all easy to play all sides in a situation like this one. In fact, it's impossible.

As you can imagine, most Jewish people in Israel, in the United States, and around the world joyfully welcomed the president's decision to move the embassy. But as you would also expect, the decision was not well received in the West Bank, Gaza Strip, or other Muslim countries around the world. Many Arab leaders denounced the move and promised a bloodbath to follow. Although there were some violent protests, particularly in Gaza, the most dire predictions of violence never materialized.

Israel's Prime Minister Benjamin Netanyahu said that Trump's announcement regarding the embassy came on a "historic day" for the nation of Israel.[2] He said, "It's rare to be able to speak of new and genuine milestones in the glorious history of this city. Yet today's pronouncement by President Trump is such an occasion. We are profoundly grateful for the president for his courageous and just decision to recognize Jerusalem as the capital of Israel and to prepare for the opening of the US Embassy here."[3] Netanyahu also reassured the world that Jerusalem's holy sites would remain open to people of all religious faiths.[4]

Jerusalem's Israeli mayor, Nir Barkat, was also elated. "On behalf of the city of Jerusalem, the beating heart and soul of the Jewish people for more than 3,000 years, I thank you from the bottom of my heart for your commitment and intention to officially recognize Jerusalem as the capital of Israel."[5] Barkat added, "This historic step will send a very clear message to the world that the United States stands with the Jewish people and the State of Israel."[6]

As you would expect, representatives of Muslim countries and organizations did not feel the same way. According to Al Jazeera, Egyptian President Abdel Fattah el-Sisi said the move "would undermine the chances of peace in the Middle East."[7] His words were echoed in a statement delivered on behalf of Palestinian President Mahmoud Abbas, who warned of "the dangerous consequences such a decision would have to the peace process and to the peace, security and stability of the region and of the world."[8]

Jordan's King Abdullah II said that Jerusalem is central to "achieving peace and stability in the region and the world" and warned the move would "inflame" feelings for Christians and Muslims.[9] Saudi King Salman agreed that "such a dangerous step is likely to inflame the passions of Muslims around the world due to the great status of Jerusalem and the al-Aqsa mosque."[10]

I understand that passions may be inflamed for a while. But recognizing the sovereign right of a nation to choose its own capital—not to mention recognizing the three thousand–year history of Jerusalem as the place God chose as the seat of power for this nation—will only lead to greater stability in the long run.

Another reason why this move will further rather than hinder the peace process is that it provides clarity regarding where the United States stands. No longer can anyone criticize America for being wishy-washy or easily manipulated to change its position. Stability is exactly what the Middle East needs. I loved what Vice President Mike Pence stated in a speech he made while visiting Jerusalem after the announcement to move the US embassy: "By finally recognizing Jerusalem as Israel's capital, the United States has chosen fact over fiction. And fact is the only true foundation for a just and lasting peace."[11]

A LONG TIME COMING

As I mentioned earlier, the move of the embassy was first planned twenty-three years ago, when the Jerusalem Embassy Act of 1995 was passed by the 104th Congress. The proposed law was approved by a whopping margin of 93 to 5 in the Senate and 374 to 37 in the House.[12] The Act became law *without* a presidential signature on November 8, 1995.[13]

The Act recognizes Jerusalem as the capital of the State of Israel and calls for Jerusalem to remain an undivided city. Its purpose was to set aside funds for the relocation of the Embassy of the United States in Israel from Tel Aviv to Jerusalem by May 31, 1999.[14] The law also allowed the president to invoke a six-month waiver of the application of the law and reissue the waiver every six months on "national security" grounds. Waivers have been signed every six months since that time. After signing one waiver, President Trump decided not to sign any more of them and finally carried out the law.

JUST COINCIDENCES?

Although I don't see the movement of the embassy as a fulfillment of any specific Bible prophecy, it is interesting to note that this decision was made in December of 2017, on the one hundredth anniversary of the Balfour Declaration, which opened the doors to the creation of the modern State of Israel.

As I touched on in chapter 3, the Balfour Declaration was written by Arthur Balfour, a former British prime minister who was serving as Britain's foreign minister in 1917. He was a lifelong statesman and a Bible-believing Christian who saw that the return of the Jews to Israel was related to the Messiah's return.[15]

At the time when the declaration was issued, all of what is today Israel was under British control. Thirty-one years passed before the Balfour Declaration was finally implemented and Israel became an actual country instead of an abstract idea.

It is also interesting to note that 2017 marked the fiftieth anniversary of Israel's reunification of the Old City of Jerusalem in the Six-Day War, another Arab attack on Israel that went awry. In that short war Israel was once again vastly outnumbered by its enemies. But the Arab effort to "push Israel into the sea" actually expanded the country's borders and united the city of Jerusalem under the Israeli flag. Since that day many Arab officials have continually demanded the return of the Old City of Jerusalem to Palestinian control.

Their demands seem disingenuous since control of the city was lost through their aggression. I also want to mention again that Jerusalem was not part of an autonomous Palestinian nation before 1967 but was under the control of Jordan. And since 1967 Jordan has never asked for this land back.[16]

As I write these words, I am just returning from Jerusalem, where I had the privilege of witnessing the opening of the new US embassy. It is only a temporary facility; a new embassy will be built over the next few years. It is interesting to note that the move took place on May 14, 2018, to coincide with the seventieth anniversary of the formation of Israel in 1948. I can't think of a better gift for the United States to give Israel on its seventieth anniversary as a nation than opening up a new embassy in Jerusalem.

Furthermore, 2017 marked the five hundredth anniversary of Israel's fall to the Ottoman Empire and the one hundredth year since Britain defeated the Turks and assumed complete control of Palestine.

Perhaps it's easy to dismiss all these anniversaries as coincidences, but I know that our God pays attention to numbers and often speaks to His people through them. Even the casual Bible reader will see how often God uses numbers such as forty, twelve, and seven. I also believe that coincidences are rare. What we call "coincidences" are more often what I call "God-incidences."

BLESSINGS FOR THE US

At the beginning of this chapter I said that I believed President Trump's decision to move the American embassy would bring blessings upon the United States. Why is this? Because God declared to Abraham that those who blessed his descendants would be blessed in return, while those who cursed them would be cursed (Gen. 12:3).

In moving the embassy, the American government has blessed Israel by aligning with its sovereign and biblical right to reestablish Jerusalem as its capital. It actually goes further than that: it acknowledges that the *current* government of Israel is also sovereign and has rightful claim to the land and the city of Jerusalem.

Sadly there are few other countries in the world today that are willing to support Israel in this way. Yet I am convinced that God will bless every one of them. As I write these words, only one other country has followed the lead of the United States in moving its embassy to Jerusalem, and that is Guatemala. However, at least four other nations have announced that they will soon move their embassies—the Czech Republic, Honduras, Paraguay, and Romania.[17]

Jerusalem has been the capital of Israel since the reign of King David over three thousand years ago. Jerusalem is where the temple stood. Jesus died for our sins there, and He will return and rule from Jerusalem during the Messianic Age.

No wonder this city is so important to God.

The Scriptures are full of passages that show God's love for and commitment to Jerusalem. And He calls His people to support that commitment:

- Psalm 122:6 tells us, "Pray for the peace of Jerusalem," and then adds, "May those who love you be at peace!" (TLV).

- Isaiah 2:3 says that in the days to come "many peoples will go and say: 'Come, let us go up to the mountain of ADONAI, to the House of the God of Jacob! Then He will teach us His ways, and we will walk in His paths.' For *Torah* will go forth from Zion and the word of ADONAI from Jerusalem" (TLV).

- Isaiah 62:6–7 declares, "I have posted watchmen on your walls, Jerusalem; they will never be silent day or night." Then we are exhorted, "You who call on the LORD, give yourselves no rest, and give him no rest till he establishes Jerusalem and makes her the praise of the earth."

A HISTORY OF VIOLENCE AND BLOODSHED

In her long history Jerusalem has been attacked fifty-two times, besieged twenty-three times, and completely destroyed twice,[18] yet it still stands strong today.

On November 29, 1947, while Jews throughout Israel were celebrating the United Nations' approval of a Jewish state, Arab discontent over the decision brewed. By December 1 Arab mobs attacked the Jewish commercial center near Jerusalem's Jaffa Gate.[19] This began the Israeli War of Independence. Jerusalem was cut off from other Jewish settlement centers and surrounded by Arab towns and villages.

War raged for over six months, with many casualties in and around the city. It seemed inevitable that Arab forces would conquer Jerusalem, especially because the British authorities, though ostensibly neutral, actually supported the Arab cause.[20] Jewish fighters defended the city valiantly, as their ancestors had done many times throughout history. Many assaults against the city from the east and south were eventually repelled, and Jerusalem remained in Jewish hands.

Over the past seventy years Jerusalem has grown rapidly, becoming one of the largest and most progressive cities in the Middle East. In 1948 its population was estimated at 165,000, with 100,000 of those residents being Jews and 40,000 Muslims.[21] By 2012 there were just under a million people in Jerusalem—some 660,000 Jews and 310,000 Muslims.[22] There is no city in the Arab world with a comparatively high percentage of Jews. Jerusalem is a multiethnic city with a diverse population.

BLESS ISRAEL AND BE BLESSED

In my book *A Rabbi Looks at the Last Days*, I quoted from an article by radio personality Dennis Prager, who wrote:

> Look at who most blesses the Jews and who most curses them....It is the Arab world that curses the Jews....Look at its state....[It] lags behind the rest of humanity...in virtually every social, moral and intellectual indicator....Its half-century long preoccupation with destroying Israel has only increased the Arab world's woes.[23]

In chapter 5 I talked about Bill Koenig's book *Eye to Eye*,[24] which tells how the fortunes of the United States are directly tied to our treatment of Israel. Specifically every time our government pressures Israel to give up land in exchange for peace with its neighbors, catastrophe strikes the United States. For example:

- **On October 30, 1991**, President George H. W. Bush opened the Madrid Conference, in which Israel would be asked to exchange land for the sake of peace. A huge storm developed in the North Atlantic, sending thirty-five-foot waves crashing onto the New England coast, including Kennebunkport, Maine, site of the president's home.[25]

- **Ten months later**, "when the Madrid Conference moved to Washington, DC," Hurricane Andrew slammed into Florida, causing an estimated $30 billion in damage.[26]

- **On January 16, 1994**, President Bill Clinton sat down with Syria's President Hafez el-Assad (father of the current dictator, who has presided over a horrendous civil war and is accused of using deadly chemical attacks on his own people) to discuss Israel's surrender of the Golan Heights to Palestinian control. The following day the Northridge Earthquake struck Southern California. At the time, it was the "second most destructive natural disaster" in America's history.[27]

- **On September 28, 1998**, as American officials worked out the details of a peace agreement that would ask Israel to "give up 13 percent of [Judea] and Samaria," Hurricane Georges inflicted $1 billion of destruction on the US Gulf Coast.[28]

- **On May 3, 1999**, as Yasser Arafat prepared "to declare a Palestinian state with Jerusalem as the capital," the most powerful tornadoes on record lashed Oklahoma and Texas. President Clinton asked Arafat to postpone his speech until December.[29]

- **In August of 2005**, as Jewish families were being evicted from their homes in the Gaza Strip (as part of Prime Minister Ariel Sharon's Disengagement Plan for the Region), a hurricane named Katrina began "forming in the Atlantic."[30]

Again, these are just some incidents from a long list that goes on for hundreds of pages in Bill's book and are recorded elsewhere, including online, as noted here. I honestly believe that there is a natural law in place that revolves around the safety, security, and peace of Jerusalem. Anyone who ignores a law that God has decreed will pay the price. For example, no one can ignore the law of gravity. If you jump off the roof of your house to prove that you can fly, you will be seriously injured. I believe that in the same way, any person or country that turns against Israel will pay the price. God cannot revoke the promise He made to Abraham.

To sum up what I have said in this chapter, the United States of America cannot go wrong by moving its embassy to Jerusalem. We have nothing to lose and everything to gain by showing our support for Israel in this way.

CHAPTER 19

WHERE DO WE GO FROM HERE?

The kingdom of this world has become the kingdom of our Lord and of His Anointed One. And He shall reign forever and ever!
—REVELATION 11:15, TLV

WE STARTED THIS journey together by asking a simple question: Is lasting peace in the Middle East possible?

After all we have examined, it would seem that the answer to that question is a resounding no. But we must not forget that with God all things are possible—even peace between Arabs and Jews. I have seen this firsthand in Israel, where Israeli Jews and Arab Palestinians who love the Lord worship together and love each other because Jesus has changed their hearts.

There is no doubt in my mind that the day is coming when the Messiah will return to Jerusalem to reign over all the earth. He will bring judgment on His enemies, after which the whole world will live together in peace.

But until that day comes, abundant mercy and peace are available for people of all nations—Arabs and Jews alike. God is not willing that any should perish, but that all should receive eternal life through faith in His Son. Together we can bring this peace to individuals, families, communities, and nations! The only solution is the gospel. It is the gospel that transforms lives and hearts and replaces anger, hostility, and violence with peace, love, and forgiveness.

I've raised a lot of very difficult and concerning subjects. Clearly we live in a world that is tainted by sin and is therefore not the way God intended it to be. When sin came into the world, it was like a virus that corrupted everything. Sin brought hate, greed, lust, unbridled ambition, thirst for power—all of the evil things we find in the world today.

Admittedly much of what we have talked about in this book is distressing. Anyone who has human feelings is bound to feel anger, disgust, and perhaps fear when hearing about the savagery taking place in the world today and especially in the Middle East. It can be difficult to remember that vengeance and judgment belong to the Lord and not to us.

Yes, the world is unpredictable, unstable, and getting worse. But in the midst of these difficult times, I have some very good news for you: God is still on His throne. He is still in control. He is watching over and caring for His people, and it is still true that any troubles we go through on this side of paradise are as nothing when compared with the glories that await us!

Now, when I say that vengeance and judgment belong to the Lord, that doesn't mean that we should sit by passively with the attitude that "whatever will be, will be." As Believers we have an important role to play. Following are some things we can and should do:

We can stay informed by getting involved with and supporting organizations that keep track of Christian persecution around the world. We cannot stick our heads in the sand and pretend it isn't happening. When we really know what is going on around the world, we will have the passion and strength to fight back. There are many good organizations really helping our brothers and sisters in need and sharing the good news around the world.

We can pray for our persecuted brothers and sisters around the world. It is good to pray for our families and friends—our children, spouses, and coworkers. But our prayers need to be bigger, wider, and deeper than that. I guarantee you that there are Believers in terrible trouble right now, and they desperately need our prayers. Our prayers *do* make a difference. And don't forget to pray daily for the peace of Jerusalem (Ps. 122:6). Israel needs our prayers, and this is a command from the Lord.

We can make our voices heard by writing letters to your members of Congress, telling them how we feel and that we want to see the United States stand up for the rights of Christians and Jews around the world.

Our country should not be engaging in "business as usual" with countries that (1) look the other way while Christians and Jews are being persecuted, or (2) use their criminal justice systems to jail those who refuse to renounce their faith in the Messiah. Continue to stand in support of Israel. The US embassy was moved to Jerusalem in large part due to the outspoken support of the evangelical community.

We can spread the word about what's going on through Facebook, Twitter, and other social media platforms. Share links from Voice of the Martyrs or other organizations. There is strength in numbers, so shout it from the housetops (Matt. 10:27). Remember what Edmund Burke said: "All that is necessary for evil to triumph is for good men to do nothing."[1] Don't delay. Do something.

We can make sure our pastors and other church leaders are aware of the persecution taking place around the world. Far too many people don't know what's going on. Some may not want to know because their lives are comfortable. They have been sailing on smooth seas, and they don't want anything to rock the boat. But ignorance is not bliss. Our God calls us to stand up for His people around the world. As Hebrews 13:3 says, "Remember the prisoners as if you were fellow prisoners, and those who are mistreated as if you also were suffering bodily" (TLV).

I am so grateful to you for the time you have spent with me in this book. May God bless you for your concern about the things of His kingdom and for your determination to be on His side as His will unfolds in these last days. Your attitude reminds me of the words often attributed to Abraham Lincoln: "Sir, my concern is not whether God is on our side; my greatest concern is to be on God's side, for God is always right."[2]

In closing, no matter what the future brings, may these words from the Book of Numbers be true in your life—today, tomorrow, and always:

> *Adonai* bless you and keep you! *Adonai* make His face to shine on you and be gracious to you! *Adonai* turn His face toward you and grant you *shalom*!
>
> —Numbers 6:24–26, TLV

NOTES

CHAPTER 1
BLOODSHED IN ISRAEL

1. "Israel Has Been Rocket Free for…," October 29, 2018, http://israelhasbeenrocketfreefor.com. This is the rocket count as of October 29, 2018.
2. "Israel Under Fire—IDF Responds," Embassy of Israel in Cameroon, October 7, 2014, http://embassies.gov.il/yaounde/NewsAndEvents/Pages/Israel-under-fire-IDF-responds.aspx.
3. William Booth and Ruth Eglash, "Israelis Are Calling Attacks a 'New Kind of Palestinian Terrorism,'" *Washington Post*, December 25, 2015, https://www.washingtonpost.com/world/middle_east/israelis-are-calling-attacks-a-new-kind-of-palestinian-terror/2015/12/24/e162e088-0953-4de5-992e-adb2126f1dcc_story.html?utm_term=.4a636f96fd6f.
4. Booth and Eglash, "Israelis Are Calling Attacks a 'New Kind of Palestinian Terrorism.'"
5. Booth and Eglash, "Israelis Are Calling Attacks a 'New Kind of Palestinian Terrorism.'"
6. Booth and Eglash, "Israelis Are Calling Attacks a 'New Kind of Palestinian Terrorism.'"
7. Booth and Eglash, "Israelis Are Calling Attacks a 'New Kind of Palestinian Terrorism.'"
8. Booth and Eglash, "Israelis Are Calling Attacks a 'New Kind of Palestinian Terrorism.'"
9. Booth and Eglash, "Israelis Are Calling Attacks a 'New Kind of Palestinian Terrorism.'"
10. Anna Ahronheim, "IDF Soldier Wounded in Car Ramming Attack, Assailant Killed," *Jerusalem Post*, July 10, 2017, http://b2.jpost.com/Arab-Israeli-Conflict/Soldier-moderately-injured-in-car-ramming-attacker-neutralized-499267?.
11. "Wave of Terror 2015–2018," Israel Ministry of Foreign Affairs, August 14, 2018, http://mfa.gov.il/MFA/ForeignPolicy/Terrorism/Palestinian/Pages/Wave-of-terror-October-2015.aspx.
12. Ahronheim, "IDF Soldier Wounded in Car Ramming Attack, Assailant Killed."
13. "Is It True That Israel Stole Palestinian Land?," Israel Advocacy Movement, accessed July 23, 2018, http://www.israeladvocacy.net/

knowledge/the-truth-of-how-israel-was-created/israel-stole-palestinian-land/.

14. Benjamin Netanyahu, *A Durable Peace* (New York: Bantam Books, 2000), xii–xiii.

15. Netanyahu, *A Durable Peace*, xi.

16. Netanyahu, *A Durable Peace*, xi–xii.

17. Netanyahu, *A Durable Peace*, xii.

18. Rushfan, "10 Attempts at Arab-Israeli Peace," Listverse, August 29, 2008, http://listverse.com/2008/08/29/10-attempts-at-arab-israeli-peace/.

19. Rushfan, "10 Attempts at Arab-Israeli Peace."

20. Rushfan, "10 Attempts at Arab-Israeli Peace."

21. Rushfan, "10 Attempts at Arab-Israeli Peace."

22. Rushfan, "10 Attempts at Arab-Israeli Peace."

23. Rushfan, "10 Attempts at Arab-Israeli Peace."

24. Rushfan, "10 Attempts at Arab-Israeli Peace."

25. Rushfan, "10 Attempts at Arab-Israeli Peace."

26. Ari Soffer, "The 'Secret Jews' of Ethiopia Emerge From the Shadows," Arutz Sheva, December 20, 2015, http://www.israelnationalnews.com/News/News.aspx/205081.

27. United Nations, *Universal Declaration of Human Rights* (Paris: United Nations General Assembly, December 10, 1948), http://www.un.org/en/universal-declaration-human-rights/.

Chapter 2
The Growing Conflict

1. Eliza Mackintosh and Kara Fox, "Manchester Attack: What We Know and Don't Know," CNN.com, May 23, 2017, https://www.cnn.com/2017/05/23/europe/manchester-arena-what-we-know/index.html.

2. Helena Horton, Barney Henderson, and Robert Midgley, "Everything We Know About the Barcelona Terror Attack," *The Telegraph*, August 18, 2017, https://www.telegraph.co.uk/news/2017/08/17/everything-know-barcelona-terror-attack/.

3. Will Worley, "9/11 Anniversary: Rare Images Show the Aftermath of World Trade Center Attack That Killed 2,997," *Independent*, September 11, 2017, https://www.independent.co.uk/news/world/americas/9-11-anniversary-images-aftermath-world-trade-center-terror-attack-responders-emergency-al-qaeda-a7940256.html.

4. "How Much Did the September 11 Terrorist Attack Cost America?," Institute for the Analysis of Global Security, accessed July 9, 2018, http://www.iags.org/costof911.html.
5. Josephus, *Bellum Judaicum VI*, 4.6, quoted in Peter Schäfer, *The History of the Jews in Antiquity* (New York: Routledge, 1995), 127–128.
6. "Second Jewish Revolt," *Encyclopaedia Britannica*, July 22, 2010, https://www.britannica.com/event/Second-Jewish-Revolt.
7. "Blood Libel: A False, Incendiary Claim Against Jews," Anti-Defamation League (ADL), accessed July 23, 2018, https://www.adl.org/education/resources/glossary-terms/blood-libel.
8. Joan Peters, *From Time Immemorial: The Origins of the Arab-Jewish Conflict Over Palestine* (Chicago: JKAP Publications, 1984), 176.
9. Peters, *From Time Immemorial*, 177.
10. Peters, *From Time Immemorial*, 501.
11. "Immigration to Israel: The First Aliyah (1882–1903)," Jewish Virtual Library, accessed July 9, 2018, https://www.jewishvirtuallibrary.org/the-first-aliyah-1882-1903.
12. Daniel Bensadoun, "This Week in History: Revival of the Hebrew Language," *Jerusalem Post*, October 15, 2010, https://www.jpost.com/Jewish-World/Jewish-News/This-week-in-history-Revival-of-the-Hebrew-language.
13. Bensadoun, "This Week in History."
14. "Immigration to Israel," Jewish Virtual Library. For more on Walter Rothschild's contributions to Israel, see http://www.balfour100.com/biography/lionel-walter-rothschild/.
15. Mitchell G. Bard, *Myths and Facts: A Guide to the Arab-Israeli Conflict* (Chevy Chase, MD: American Israeli Cooperative Enterprise, 2017), 6–7.
16. Dawood Barakat as quoted in Neville J. Mandel, *The Arabs and Zionism Before World War I* (Berkeley, CA: University of California Press, 1976), 150.

CHAPTER 3
THE BIRTH OF ZIONISM

1. Jonathan Bernis, *Unlocking the Prophetic Mysteries of Israel* (Lake Mary, FL: Charisma House, 2017), 79.
2. "Theodore Herzl (1860–1904)," Knesset.gov, accessed August 7, 2017, https://www.knesset.gov.il/vip/herzl/eng/Herz_Zion_eng.html.
3. Bernis, *Unlocking the Prophetic Mysteries of Israel*, 79–80; "Theodor (Binyamin, Ze'ev) Herzl (1860–1904)," Jewish Virtual Library, accessed July

9, 2018, https://www.jewishvirtuallibrary.org/theodor-binyamin-ze-rsquo -ev-herzl.

4. Bernis, *Unlocking the Prophetic Mysteries of Israel*, 80.

5. Arthur James Balfour, "Balfour Declaration 1917," The Avalon Project, accessed July 9, 2018, http://avalon.law.yale.edu/20th_century/balfour.asp.

6. Balfour, "Balfour Declaration 1917."

7. Netanyahu, *A Durable Peace*, 53.

8. Netanyahu, *A Durable Peace*, 36.

9. Alexander Scholch, "The Demographic Development of Palestine," *International Journal of Middle East Studies* 17, no. 4 (1985): 488; Netanyahu, *A Durable Peace*, 44.

10. Marvin Lowenthal, ed., *The Diaries of Theodor Herzl* (New York: Dial, 1956), 292; Netanyahu, *A Durable Peace*, 44.

11. Eugène Victor Félix Bovet, *Egypt, Palestine, and Phoenicia: A Visit to Sacred Lands*, trans. W. H. Lyttelton (London: Hodder and Stoughton, 1882), 379.

12. 2nd British Royal Commission Report (1937), ch. 1, p. 6, quoted in Gudrun Krämer, *A History of Palestine: From the Ottoman Conquest to the Founding of the State of Israel* (Princeton, NJ: Princeton University Press, 2008), 166.

13. David Fromkin, *A Peace to End All Peace: The Fall of the Ottoman Empire and the Creation of the Modern Middle East* (New York: Henry Holt and Company, 1989), 401.

14. Jan Smuts, *Selections From the Smuts Papers: Volume 7, August 1945– October 1950*, ed. Jean van der Poel (Cambridge, MA: Cambridge University Press, 2007), 29.

15. "The Great Depression," *Holocaust Encyclopedia*, United States Holocaust Memorial Museum, accessed July 23, 2018, https://www.ushmm.org/wlc/ en/article.php?ModuleId=10008291.

16. Netanyahu, *A Durable Peace*, 40.

17. Anna Isaacs, "How the First World War Changed Jewish History," *Moment*, June 16, 2015, https://www.momentmag.com/how-the-first- world-war-changed-jewish-history/.

18. Eli Barnavi, "World War I and the Jews," My Jewish Learning, accessed July 23, 2018, https://www.myjewishlearning.com/article/wwi-and-the- jews/.

19. Isaacs, "How the First World War Changed Jewish History."

20. Barnavi, "World War I and the Jews." The Jews fought with their respective nations but were accused on all sides.

21. Isaacs, "How the First World War Changed Jewish History."
22. Isaacs, "How the First World War Changed Jewish History."
23. Netanyahu, *A Durable Peace*, 55.
24. Netanyahu, *A Durable Peace*, 55.
25. Peter Grose, *Israel in the Mind of America* (New York: Alfred A. Knopf, 1983), 134.
26. Netanyahu, *A Durable Peace*, 59.
27. Netanyahu, *A Durable Peace*, 59.
28. Netanyahu, *A Durable Peace*, 59; William Bernard Ziff, *The Rape of Palestine* (London: St. Botolph's, 1948), 14; Ronald Sanders, *The High Walls of Jerusalem: A History of the Balfour Declaration and the Birth of the British Mandate for Palestine* (New York: Holt, Rinehart and Winston, 1983), 653.
29. Netanyahu, *A Durable Peace*, 59.
30. Netanyahu, *A Durable Peace*, 60.
31. Jabotinsky, quoted in Sanders, *The High Walls of Jerusalem*, 653.
32. Netanyahu, *A Durable Peace*, 62.
33. Richard Meinertzhagen, *Middle East Diary, 1917–1956* (London: Cresset, 1959), 82.
34. Netanyahu, *A Durable Peace*, 63.
35. Netanyahu, *A Durable Peace*, 63.
36. Netanyahu, *A Durable Peace*, 97.
37. Ami Isseroff, "Sheikh Izz ad-Din al-Qassam," *Encyclopedia of the Middle East*, November 12, 2008, http://www.mideastweb.org/Middle-East-Encyclopedia/sheikh_izz_ad-din_al-qassam.htm.
38. Isseroff, "Sheikh Izz ad-Din al-Qassam."
39. Wikipedia, s.v. "1936–1939 Arab Revolt in Palestine," last modified July 17, 2018, 01:03, https://en.wikipedia.org/wiki/1936–1939_Arab_revolt_in_Palestine.
40. Isseroff, "Sheikh Izz ad-Din al-Qassam."
41. Beverley Milton-Edwards, *Islamic Politics in Palestine* (London: I.B. Tauris, 1999), 19.
42. Charles Townshend, "Palestine: The First Intifada Rebellion," *Welcome to Repositioning Mindset*, accessed July 10, 2018, http://dipoolatade.blogspot.com/2017_05_04_archive.html.
43. Townshend, "Palestine."
44. Townshend, "Palestine."
45. Milton-Edwards, *Islamic Politics in Palestine*, 22.

46. "Arab Higher Committee (Palestine)," Encyclopedia.com, accessed September 12, 2018, https://www.encyclopedia.com/humanities/ encyclopedias-almanacs-transcripts-and-maps/arab-higher-committee-palestine.

47. "Pre-State Israel: The Arab Revolt (1936–1939)," Jewish Virtual Library, accessed July 10, 2018, https://www.jewishvirtuallibrary.org/the-1936-arab-riots.

48. Martin Gilbert, *Israel: A History* (New York: Harper Perennial, 2008), 80.

49. "Pre-State Israel," Jewish Virtual Library.

50. Wikipedia, s.v. "Havlagah," last modified May 23, 2018, https:// en.wikipedia.org/wiki/Havlagah.

51. Spencer C. Tucker and Priscilla Roberts, eds., *The Encyclopedia of the Arab-Israeli Conflict: A Political, Social, and Military History* (Santa Barbara, CA: ABC-CLIO, 2008), 433.

Chapter 4
Who Really "Owns" the Land of Israel?

1. "Vital Statistics: Latest Population Statistics for Israel," Jewish Virtual Library, accessed July 10, 2018, https://www.jewishvirtuallibrary.org/ latest-population-statistics-for-israel. These figures are quoted as of April 2018.

2. "Jews in Islamic Countries: Lebanon," Jewish Virtual Library, accessed July 10, 2018, https://www.jewishvirtuallibrary.org/jews-of-lebanon; David Singer and Lawrence Grossman, eds., *American Jewish Year Book 2003* (New York: American Jewish Committee, 2003).

3. "Jews in Islamic Countries: Syria," Jewish Virtual Library, accessed September 12, 2018, https://www.jewishvirtuallibrary.org/jews-of-syria.

4. "Jews in Islamic Countries: Syria," Jewish Virtual Library; Howard Sachar, *A History of Israel: From the Rise of Zionism to Our Time* (New York: Alfred A. Knopf, 1979), 400; Maurice Roumani, *The Case of the Jews From Arab Countries: A Neglected Issue* (Tel Aviv: World Organization of Jews from Arab Countries, 1977), 31; Norman Stillman, *The Jews of Arab Lands in Modern Times* (New York: Jewish Publication Society, 1991), 146.

5. "Jews in Islamic Countries: Syria," Jewish Virtual Library.

6. "Jews in Islamic Countries: Syria," Jewish Virtual Library.

7. Peters, *From Time Immemorial*, 81–82.

8. James Parkes, *Whose Land? A History of the Peoples of Palestine* (Harmondswoth, Great Britain: Penguin Books, 1970), 72; Peters, *From Time Immemorial*, 82–83.
9. Peters, *From Time Immemorial*, 84.
10. "1322 The Temple Mount—Jewish Guides From Gaza, Ramleh and Safed," Center for Online Judaic Studies, accessed July 10, 2018, http://cojs.org/1322-temple-mount-jewish-guides-gaza-ramleh-safed/.
11. Martin Gilbert, *Exile and Return: The Struggle for a Jewish Homeland* (Philadelphia: Brown Book Company, 1978), 17, quoted in Peters, *From Time Immemorial*, 85.
12. Peters, *From Time Immemorial*, 85.
13. Peters, *From Time Immemorial*, 85.
14. Peters, *From Time Immemorial*, 85, 90.
15. Peters, *From Time Immemorial*, 85.
16. James Finn, *Stirring Times: Or, Records From Jerusalem Consular Chronicles of 1853 to 1856, Volume 1* (London: C. Keegan, Paul & Co., 1878), 127–128; Peters, *From Time Immemorial*, 90.
17. Mitchell Bard, "Pre-State Israel: The Arabs in Palestine," Jewish Virtual Library, accessed July 10, 2018, https://www.jewishvirtuallibrary.org/the-arabs-in-palestine.
18. Bard, "Pre-State Israel."
19. Shabtai Teveth, *Ben-Gurion and the Palestinian Arabs: From Peace to War* (Oxford: Oxford University Press, 1985), 32.
20. Bard, "Pre-State Israel."
21. Bard, "Pre-State Israel."
22. Bard, "Pre-State Israel."
23. J. B. Barron, Superintendent of the Census, "Palestine: Report and General Abstracts of the Census of 1922," October 23, 1922, accessed July 11, 2018, https://archive.org/details/PalestineCensus1922.
24. Peters, *From Time Immemorial*, 222.
25. Peters, *From Time Immemorial*, 223.
26. Peters, *From Time Immemorial*, 223.
27. Peters, *From Time Immemorial*, 223.
28. "Demographics of Israel: Population of Israel/Palestine (1553–Present)," Jewish Virtual Library, accessed July 11, 2018, https://www.jewishvirtuallibrary.org/population-of-israel-palestine-1553-present. Note the near doubling of Palestine's Muslim population between 1922 and 1945.

29. See Netanyahu, *A Durable Peace*, 36, and Peters, *From Time Immemorial*, 223–224.

30. Robert Rhodes, ed., *Churchill Speaks, 1897–1963: Collected Speeches in Peace and War* (New York: Chelsea House, 1980), 686; David Patterson, "'A Crime Without a Name'—Churchill, Zionism, and the Holocaust," *Finest Hour* 170 (Fall 2015): 6, accessed July 11, 2018, https://winstonchurchill.org/publications/finest-hour/finest-hour-170/churchill-and-the-jews/.

31. Peters, *From Time Immemorial*, 226.

32. Peters, *From Time Immemorial*, 227–228.

33. Eli E. Hertz, "'Mandate for Palestine': The Legal Aspects of Jewish Rights," Myths and Facts, accessed July 11, 2018, http://www.mythsandfacts.org/conflict/mandate_for_palestine/mandate_for_palestine.htm.

34. Netanyahu, *A Durable Peace*, 84–85.

35. Benjamin Welles, "Travel Power: The Story Behind the Mexico Boycott," *New York Times*, June 27, 1976, https://www.nytimes.com/1976/06/27/archives/travel-power-the-story-behind-the-mexico-boycott-travel-power-the.html.

36. "Kristallnacht," History.com, accessed July 11, 2018, https://www.history.com/topics/kristallnacht.

37. "Daniel Patrick Moynihan: Response to United Nations Resolution 3379" (speech, United Nations, November 10, 1975), American Rhetoric, accessed July 11, 2018, http://www.americanrhetoric.com/speeches/danielpatrickmoynihanun3379.htm.

38. Paul Lewis, "UN Repeals Its '75 Resolution Equating Zionism With Racism," *New York Times*, December 17, 1991, https://www.nytimes.com/1991/12/17/world/un-repeals-its-75-resolution-equating-zionism-with-racism.html.

39. Adam Kredo, "Columbia University Hosts 'Zionists Are Racists' Forum," *Washington Free Beacon*, February 27, 2017, http://freebeacon.com/culture/columbia-university-hosts-zionists-racists-forum/.

40. Netanyahu, *A Durable Peace*, 86–87.

CHAPTER 5
THE HOLOCAUST AND BEYOND

1. "Jewish Population of Europe Before the Holocaust Map," Jewish Virtual Library, accessed July 11, 2018, https://www.jewishvirtuallibrary.org/jewish-population-of-europe-before-the-holocaust-map.

2. "The Final Solution," *Holocaust Encyclopedia*, United States Holocaust Memorial Museum, accessed July 11, 2018, https://www.ushmm.org/outreach/en/article.php?ModuleId=10007704.
3. "The Miracle of Israel—1945–1948," JewishHistory.org, accessed July 23, 2018, https://www.jewishhistory.org/the-miracle-of-israel/.
4. "Cyprus Detention Camps," Shoah Resource Center, The International School for Holocaust Studies, Yadvashem.org, accessed July 11, 2018, https://www.yadvashem.org/odot_pdf/Microsoft%20Word%20-%20727.pdf.
5. Netanyahu, *A Durable Peace*, 75.
6. Richard Meinertzhagen, *Middle East Diary, 1917–1956* (London: Cresset, 1959), 171, as quoted in Netanyahu, *A Durable Peace*, 75.
7. George Santayana, *The Life of Reason* (New York: Open Road Media, 2017), chapter 12, https://books.google.com/books?id=EH13DgAAQBAJ&vq.
8. Bill Koenig, *Eye to Eye: Facing the Consequences of Dividing Israel* (McLean, VA: Christian Publications, 2017), 406.
9. Koenig, *Eye to Eye*, 293–294, as quoted in Jonathan Bernis, *A Rabbi Looks at the Last Days* (Bloomington, MN: Chosen Books, 2013), 177–178.
10. Carma Hassan, Faith Karimi, and Ralph Ellis, "Joplin, Missouri, Tornado: 5 Years Later," updated May 22, 2016, https://www.cnn.com/2016/05/22/us/joplin-tornado-anniversary/index.html.
11. Hassan, Karimi, and Ellis, "Joplin, Missouri, Tornado."
12. Avery Stone, "Looking Back: 10 Things to Know About Hurricane Irene," *Coastal Living*, accessed July 11, 2018, https://www.coastalliving.com/lifestyle/the-environment/hurricane-irene-facts.
13. Bernis, *A Rabbi Looks at the Last Days*," 143.
14. Amy Tikkanen, "MS St. Louis, German Ocean Liner," *Encyclopaedia Britannica*, September 15, 2017, https://www.britannica.com/topic/MS-St-Louis-German-ship.
15. Daniel A. Gross, "The US Government Turned Away Thousands of Jewish Refugees, Fearing That They Were Nazi Spies," *Smithsonian*, November 18, 2015, https://www.smithsonianmag.com/history/us-government-turned-away-thousands-jewish-refugees-fearing-they-were-nazi-spies-180957324/.
16. Gross, "The US Government Turned Away Thousands of Jewish Refugees, Fearing That They Were Nazi Spies."
17. Peters, *From Time Immemorial*, 7.

18. Peters, *From Time Immemorial*, 12–13.

19. Peters, *From Time Immemorial*, 13.

20. Joseph B. Schechtman, *The Arab Refugee Problem* (New York: Philosophical Library, 1952), 8–9; Jeffrey, *The Next World War*, 28.

21. Peters, *From Time Immemorial*, 13.

22. Peters, *From Time Immemorial*, 11.

23. Khalid al-Azm, *Memoirs* [Arabic] (Al-Dar al Muttahida lil-Nashr, 1972), 386–387, cited by Maurice M. Roumani, *The Case of the Jews From Arab Countries: A Neglected Issue*, preliminary edition (Jerusalem: World Organization of Jews From Arab Countries, 1975), 61, as quoted in Peters, *From Time Immemorial*, 16.

24. Roumani, *The Case of the Jews From Arab Countries* (1977), 82; Joseph E. Katz, "Exchange of Populations," EretzYisroel.org, accessed July 12, 2018, http://www.eretzyisroel.org/~peters/exchange.html.

25. William Dalrymple, "The Great Divide," *New Yorker*, June 29, 2015, https://www.newyorker.com/magazine/2015/06/29/the-great-divide-books-dalrymple.

26. "The Great Population Exchange Between Turkey and Greece," Al Jazeera, February 28, 2018, https://www.aljazeera.com/programmes/aljazeeraworld/2018/02/great-population-exchange-turkey-greece-180220111122516.html.

27. Mojli Amin, "Exchange of Populations," transmission to Elialm Sasson, Political Department, Palestine, May 16, 1939 CZA-525/5630 (Central Zionist Archives), quoted in Katz, "Exchange of Populations."

28. Amin, "Exchange of Populations," quoted in Katz, "Exchange of Populations."

29. "The Morality of Transfer—Part 2," Arutz Sheva, January 31, 2002, http://www.israelnationalnews.com/Articles/Article.aspx/828.

Chapter 6
Yasser Arafat and the PLO

1. "Palestine Liberation Organization: The Original Palestine National Charter (1964)," Jewish Virtual Library, accessed July 12, 2018, https://www.jewishvirtuallibrary.org/the-original-palestine-national-charter-1964; "Palestine Liberation Organization: Analysis of the Palestine National Charter," Jewish Virtual Library, accessed September 12, 2018, https://www.jewishvirtuallibrary.org/analysis-of-the-palestine-national-charter.

2. "Palestine Liberation Organization: The Original Palestine National Charter (1964)," Jewish Virtual Library.

3. "Palestine Liberation Organization: The Original Palestine National Charter (1964)," Jewish Virtual Library.

4. "Palestine Liberation Organization: The Original Palestine National Charter (1964)," Jewish Virtual Library.

5. Tricia McDermott, "Arafat's Billions: One Man's Quest to Track Down Unaccounted-For Public Funds," *60 Minutes*, November 7, 2003, https://www.cbsnews.com/news/arafats-billions/.

6. David Brooks, "A Brief History of Yasir Arafat," *Atlantic Monthly*, July/August 2002, https://www.theatlantic.com/magazine/archive/2002/07/a-brief-history-of-yasir-arafat/302532/.

7. "Munich Massacre: Munich, Germany [1972]," *Encyclopaedia Britannica*, August 29, 2018, https://www.britannica.com/event/Munich-Massacre; see also Netanyahu, *A Durable Peace*, 20; and Aimee Lamoureux, "'Our Worst Fears Have Been Realized': The Story of Black September and the Munich Massacre," All Things Interesting, updated July 20, 2018, https://allthatsinteresting.com/black-september-munich.

8. Thomas L. Friedman, "Arafat Expelled After Saying Syria Aids PLO Revolt," *New York Times*, June 25, 1983, https://www.nytimes.com/1983/06/25/world/arafat-expelled-after-saying-syria-aids-plo-revolt.html.

9. Pierre Tristam, "Black September: The Jordanian-PLO Civil War of 1970," ThoughtCo, updated January 2, 2018, https://www.thoughtco.com/black-september-jordanian-plo-civil-war-2353168.

10. "1982 Lebanon Invasion," BBC News, updated May 6, 2008, http://news.bbc.co.uk/2/hi/middle_east/7381364.stm.

11. Rebecca Grant, "The Bekaa Valley War," *Air Force Magazine* 85, no. 6 (June 2002): 61, https://web.archive.org/web/20120614232948/http://www.airforce-magazine.com/MagazineArchive/Documents/2002/June%202002/0602bekaa.pdf.

12. "Yasser Arafat (1929–2004)," Jewish Virtual Library, accessed September 12, 2018, https://www.jewishvirtuallibrary.org/yasser-arafat.

13. Dan Fisher, "Israel Denies Raid's Aim Was to Kill Arafat; Officials Pleased by Reagan Reaction," *Los Angeles Times*, October 3, 1985, http://articles.latimes.com/1985-10-03/news/mn-660_1_yasser-arafat.

14. Fred Barbash, "Arafat, Rabin, Peres Awarded Peace Prize," *Washington Post*, October 15, 1994, https://www.washingtonpost.com/archive/

politics/1994/10/15/arafat-rabin-peres-awarded-peace-prize/400a7856
-dfae-4b26-9631-39ea284a50f8/?utm_term=.a3574f8101bf.

15. "The Oslo Accords and the Arab-Israeli Peace Process," United States Department of State, Office of the Historian, accessed July 12, 2018, https://history.state.gov/milestones/1993-2000/oslo.

16. Yaacov Bash, "Palestinian Corruption and Poverty," Aish Ha Torah, November 22, 2003, http://www.aish.com/jw/me/48901837.html.

17. Isabel Kershner, "PLO Extends President Mahmoud Abbas's Term," *New York Times*, December 16, 2009, https://www.nytimes.com/2009/12/17/world/middleeast/17mideast.html?mtrref=www.google.com&gwh=6593D572578659C922DDA3BA211297CD&gwt=pay.

18. Dictionary.com, s.v. "intifada," accessed July 12, 2018, http://www.dictionary.com/browse/intifada.

19. "Israel's Wars and Operations: First Intifada (1987–1993)," Jewish Virtual Library, accessed July 12, 2018, https://www.jewishvirtuallibrary.org/first-intifada.

20. "Israel's Wars and Operations: First Intifada," Jewish Virtual Library.

21. Robert J. Brym and Bader Araj, "Intifadah: Palestinian-Israeli History," *Encyclopaedia Britannica*, May 2, 2018, https://www.britannica.com/topic/intifadah.

22. Netanyahu, *A Durable Peace*, 166.

23. Netanyahu, *A Durable Peace*, 166.

24. Melanie Lidman, "Bethlehem's Declining Christian Population Casts Shadow Over Christmas," *National Catholic Reporter*, December 19, 2016, https://www.ncronline.org/news/world/bethlehems-declining-christian-population-casts-shadow-over-christmas.

25. Lidman, "Bethlehem's Declining Christian Population Casts Shadow Over Christmas."

26. Lidman, "Bethlehem's Declining Christian Population Casts Shadow Over Christmas."

27. Ronald S. Lauder, "Who Will Stand Up for the Christians?" *New York Times*, August 19, 2014, https://www.nytimes.com/2014/08/20/opinion/ronald-lauder-who-will-stand-up-for-the-christians.html?smid=pl-share.

28. Lauder, "Who Will Stand Up for the Christians?"

29. "Casualty Comparison," Institute for Middle East Understanding, November 18, 2012, https://imeu.org/article/casualty-comparison.

30. Jeremy Pressman, "The Second Intifada: Background and Causes of the Israeli-Palestinian Conflict," *Journal of Conflict Studies* 23, no. 2 (Fall

2003), accessed July 13, 2018, https://journals.lib.unb.ca/index.php/jcs/article/view/220/378.

31. David Shyovitz, "2000 Camp David Summit: Background and Overview," Jewish Virtual Library, accessed July 13, 2018, https://www.jewishvirtuallibrary.org/background-and-overview-of-2000-camp-david-summit#_ftn1.

32. Shyovitz, "2000 Camp David Summit."

33. Judah Ari Gross, "Police Chief Confirms Two Officers Killed in Temple Mount Shooting," *Times of Israel*, July 14, 2017, https://www.timesofisrael.com/temple-mount-attack-victims-identified-as-police-officers/.

34. "Israel Removes Temple Mount Metal Detectors That Enraged the Muslim World," *Jerusalem Post*, July 25, 2017, https://www.jpost.com/Israel-News/Politics-And-Diplomacy/Israel-removes-Temple-Mount-metal-detectors-that-enraged-the-Muslim-world-500663.

35. Adam Rasgon, "Fatah Calls for 'Day of Rage,'" *Jerusalem Post*, July 18, 2017, https://www.jpost.com/Arab-Israeli-Conflict/Fatah-calls-for-day-of-rage-500064.

36. David Rosenberg, "Report: Mahmoud Abbas Funding Jerusalem Riots," Arutz Sheva, July 30, 2017, https://www.israelnationalnews.com/News/News.aspx/233175.

37. Rosenberg, "Report: Mahmoud Abbas Funding Jerusalem Riots."

38. Rosenberg, "Report: Mahmoud Abbas Funding Jerusalem Riots."

CHAPTER 7
A MONSTER CALLED ISIS

1. Dov Lieber, "ISIS Explains Why It Doesn't Attack Israel (Yet)," Times of Israel, March 24, 2016, http://www.timesofisrael.com/islamic-state-explains-why-it-doesnt-attack-israel-yet/; "ISIS Explains Why It's Not Attacking Israel—Yet," Jewish Telegraphic Agency, March 25, 2016, https://www.jta.org/2016/03/25/news-opinion/israel-middle-east/isis-article-fighting-israel-important-but-not-top-priority.

2. Lieber, "ISIS Explains Why It Doesn't Attack Israel (Yet)"; "ISIS Explains Why It's Not Attacking Israel—Yet," Jewish Telegraphic Agency.

3. "The Islamic State," Stanford University, accessed July 13, 2018, http://web.stanford.edu/group/mappingmilitants/cgi-bin/groups/view/1?.

4. "The Islamic State," Stanford University.

5. "The Islamic State," Stanford University.

6. William McCants, *The ISIS Apocalypse: The History, Strategy, and Doomsday Vision of the Islamic State* (New York: St. Martin's Press, 2015), 7.
7. "The Islamic State," Stanford University; Lee Teslik, "Profile: Abu Musab Al-Zarqawi," Council on Foreign Relations, June 8, 2006, https://www.cfr.org/backgrounder/profile-abu-musab-al-zarqawi; M. J. Kirdar, "Al Qaeda in Iraq," Center for Strategic and International Studies, June 2011, accessed July 13, 2018, https://csis-prod.s3.amazonaws.com/s3fs-public/legacy_files/files/publication/110614_Kirdar_AlQaedaIraq_Web.pdf.
8. Kirdar, "Al Qaeda in Iraq."
9. "The Islamic State," Stanford University.
10. "The Islamic State," Stanford University; Peter Bergen et al., "Bombers, Bank Accounts, and Bleedout: Al-Qa'ida's Road In and Out of Iraq," ed. Brian Fishman, Combatting Terrorism Center at West Point, July 22, 2008, https://www.hsdl.org/?view&did=487885.
11. Kirdar, "Al Qaeda in Iraq."
12. McCants, *The ISIS Apocalypse*, 10–13, 146.
13. McCants, *The ISIS Apocalypse*, 7.
14. Andrew Buncombe, "The Story of Nick Berg—A Tale That Haunts America," *The Independent*, May 13, 2004, https://www.independent.co.uk/news/world/americas/the-story-of-nick-berg-a-tale-that-haunts-america-563219.html.
15. Joby Warrick, *Black Flags: The Rise of ISIS* (New York: Anchor Books, 2016), 157.
16. Warrick, *Black Flags*, 157.
17. Warrick, *Black Flags*, 170.
18. McCants, *The ISIS Apocalypse*, 148.
19. Octavia Nasr, Henry Schuster, and David Ensor, "Voice on Tape: Jordanians Not Targeted," CNN.com, November 18, 2005, http://www.cnn.com/2005/WORLD/meast/11/18/zarqawi.jordan/. Zarqawi reportedly claimed that Jordanians were not targeted. However, the hotel was in Jordan, and Jordanians were slaughtered there.
20. "The Islamic State," Stanford University; see also Robert F. Worth, "Muslim Clerics Call for an End to Iraqi Rioting," *New York Times*, February 25, 2006, https://www.nytimes.com/2006/02/25/world/middleeast/muslim-clerics-call-for-an-end-to-iraqi-rioting.html; Robert F. Worth, "Blast at Shiite Shrine Sets Off Sectarian Fury in Iraq," *New York Times*, February 23, 2006, https://www.nytimes.com/2006/02/23/

world/middleeast/blast-at-shiite-shrine-sets-off-sectarian-fury-in-iraq.
html.

21. "The Islamic State," Stanford University; see also Worth, "Muslim Clerics Call for an End to Iraqi Rioting," and Worth, "Blast at Shiite Shrine Sets Off Sectarian Fury in Iraq."

22. "The Islamic State," Stanford University.

23. McCants, *The ISIS Apocalypse*, 13–14.

24. William McCants, "How ISIL Out-Terrorized Bin Laden," Politico, August 19, 2015, https://www.politico.com/magazine/story/2015/08/isis-jihad-121525; see also McCants, The ISIS Apocalypse, 28.

25. Warrick, *Black Flags*, 170.

26. Chris Mitchell, *ISIS, Iran and Israel: What You Need to Know About the Current Mideast Crisis and the Coming Mideast War* (Pleasantville, TN: C&L Publishing, 2016), 187.

27. Mitchell, *ISIS, Iran and Israel*, 187.

28. Ryan Mauro, interview on Jerusalem Dateline, CBN, October 10, 2014, quoted in Mitchell, *ISIS, Iran and Israel*, 187.

29. McCants, *The ISIS Apocalypse*, 175.

30. "The Islamic State," Stanford University.

31. "The Islamic State," Stanford University; Kirdar, "Al Qaeda in Iraq."

32. McCants, *The ISIS Apocalypse*, 10.

33. McCants, *The ISIS Apocalypse*, 28–29.

34. Robert Spencer, *The Complete Infidel's Guide to ISIS* (Washington, DC: Regnery, 2015), 167–168.

35. Spencer, *The Complete Infidel's Guide to ISIS*, 167–168.

36. Robert Spencer, interview by Chris Mitchell, "Obama Secures Support to Press On With Iran Nuke Deal—September 4, 2015," Jerusalem Dateline, CBN, accessed September 12, 2018, http://www1origin.cbn.com/video/jerusalem-dateline/2015/09/4/obama-secures-support-to-press-on-with-iran-nuke-deal-ndash-september-4-2015, quoted in Mitchell, *ISIS, Iran and Israel*.

37. John F. Burns, "US Strike Hits Insurgents at Safehouse," *New York Times*, June 9, 2006, https://archive.nytimes.com/www.nytimes.com/learning/teachers/featured_articles/20060609friday.html.

38. "The Islamic State," Stanford University.

39. "The Islamic State," Stanford University.

40. "The Islamic State," Stanford University.

41. "The Islamic State," Stanford University.

42. "The Islamic State," Stanford University; Thomas Joscelyn, "Al Qaeda's General Command Disowns the Islamic State of Iraq and the Sham," Long War Journal, Foundation for the Defense of Democracies, February 3, 2014, https://www.longwarjournal.org/archives/2014/02/al_qaedas_general_co.php.
43. "The Islamic State," Stanford University.
44. "What Is 'Islamic State'?," BBC News, December 2, 2015, https://www.bbc.com/news/world-middle-east-29052144; Greg Myre, "Americans in ISIS: Some 300 Tried to Join, 12 Have Returned to US," NPR, February 5, 2018, https://www.npr.org/sections/parallels/2018/02/05/583407221/americans-in-isis-some-300-tried-to-join-12-have-returned-to-u-s.
45. Kobi Michael and Udi Dekel, "ISIS Success in Iraq and Syria: Strategic Ramifications," Tel Aviv University Institute for National Security Studies Insight No. 563, June 24, 2014, http://www.inss.org.il/publication/isis-success-in-iraq-and-syria-strategic-ramifications/.
46. "What Is 'Islamic State'?," BBC News.
47. Colin Dwyer, "A Window Onto the 'Shocking' Final Days of ISIS in Mosul," NPR, November 2, 2017, https://www.npr.org/sections/thetwo-way/2017/11/02/561537779/a-window-onto-the-shocking-final-days-of-isis-in-mosul.
48. "The Islamic State," Stanford University; Michael Pizzi, "In Declaring a Caliphate, Islamic State Draws a Line in the Sand," Al Jazeera America, June 30, 2014, http://america.aljazeera.com/articles/2014/6/30/islamic-state-caliphate.html.
49. Stephen Kalin, "Mosul Mosque Where Islamic State Took World Stage Lies in Rubble," Reuters, July 1, 2017, https://www.reuters.com/article/us-mideast-crisis-iraq-mosque/mosul-mosque-where-islamic-state-took-world-stage-lies-in-rubble-idUSKBN19M3IB.
50. Chris Mitchell, *Destination Jerusalem: ISIS, Convert or Die, Christian Persecution and Preparing for the Days Ahead* (Pleasantville, TN: C&L Publishers, 2015), 70.
51. "What Did Abu Bakr al-Baghdadi Say?," Middle East Eye, July 5, 2014,
52. http://www.middleeasteye.net/news/what-did-baghdadi-say-320749010.
53. Mary Grace Lucas, "ISIS Nearly Made It to Baghdad Airport, Top US Military Leader Says," CNN, updated October 13, 2014, https://www.cnn.com/2014/10/12/politics/isis-baghdad-martin-dempsey/index.html.
54. Mitchell, *ISIS, Iran and Israel*, 62.
55. Mitchell, *ISIS, Iran and Israel*, 62.
56. Mitchell, *ISIS, Iran and Israel*, 62.

57. Mitchell, *ISIS, Iran and Israel*, 62. Mitchell cites James M. Arlandson, "The Quran and the Sword," Answering Islam, updated August 3, 2012, https://www.answering-islam.org/authors/arlandson/sword/05.html.

58. John Haltiwanger, "Trump Has Dropped Record Number of Bombs on Middle East," *Newsweek*, September 19, 2017, http://www.newsweek.com/trump-era-record-number-bombs-dropped-middle-east-667505.

59. "Abu Bakr al-Baghdadi: 'Alive but Wounded' in Syria," Al Jazeera, February 12, 2018, https://www.aljazeera.com/news/2018/02/abu-bakr-al-baghdadi-alive-wounded-north-syria-180212150123915.html.

60. "ISIS Forces Christians to Live Under Its Rules in Syrian Town After Release," *Newsweek*, September 4, 2015, http://www.newsweek.com/christians-syria-isisislamic-statemiddle-eastal-qaryatainal-qaryataynsyriaisis-600703.

61. Glenn Beck, "Would You Sign This Contract and Conform or Be Killed?," Glenn, September 6, 2015, https://www.glennbeck.com/2015/09/06/would-you-sign-this-contract-and-conform-or-be-killed/.

62. Beck, "Would You Sign This Contract and Conform or Be Killed?"

CHAPTER 8
THE WAR AGAINST CHRISTIANS

1. "Martin Niemöller: 'First They Came for the Socialists…,'" *Holocaust Encyclopedia*, United States Holocaust Memorial Museum, accessed July 14, 2018, https://www.ushmm.org/wlc/en/article.php?ModuleId=10007392.

2. Edward Malnick, "Christianity 'Close to Extinction' in Middle East," *The Telegraph*, December 23, 2012, https://www.telegraph.co.uk/news/religion/9762745/Christianity-close-to-extinction-in-Middle-East.html.

3. Malnick, "Christianity 'Close to Extinction' in Middle East."

4. Malnick, "Christianity 'Close to Extinction' in Middle East."

5. Malnick, "Christianity 'Close to Extinction' in Middle East."

6. Helene Cooper, Mark Landler, and Alissa J. Rubin, "Obama Allows Limited Airstrikes on ISIS," *New York Times*, August 7, 2014, https://www.nytimes.com/2014/08/08/world/middleeast/obama-weighs-military-strikes-to-aid-trapped-iraqis-officials-say.html.

7. Rami Ayyad's story draws from several sources, including firsthand reports as well as the following: "Wife of Martyred Gaza Bookstore Manager Chooses Not to Hate," Beliefnet, accessed July 14, 2018, http://www.beliefnet.com/columnists/pray_for_the_persecuted_church/2011/06/

wife-of-martyred-gaza-bookstore-manager-chooses-not-to-hate.html;
Eric Silver, "Gaza's Christian Bookseller Killed," *Independent*, October
8, 2007, https://www.independent.co.uk/news/world/middle-east/gazas-
christian-bookseller-killed-396283.html; Deann Alford, "Christian
Bookstore Manager Martyred in Gaza City," *Christianity Today*, October
8, 2007, https://www.christianitytoday.com/news/2007/october/141-
12.0.html; Timothy C. Morgan, "In Gaza, Is Love in the Land of Enmity
Still Possible?," *Christianity Today*, January 13, 2009, https://www.
christianitytoday.com/news/2009/january/in-gaza-is-love-in-land-of-
enmity-still-possible.html.

8. Luis Martinez, "What to Know About the Offensive to Take Raqqa,
De Facto Capital of ISIS," ABC News, June 6, 2017, https://abcnews.
go.com/International/upcoming-offensive-raqqah-de-facto-capital-isis/
story?id=43101806.

9. Warrick, *Black Flags*, 288.

10. Warrick, *Black Flags*, 288.

11. Mitchell, *Destination Jerusalem*, 70.

12. Mitchell, *Destination Jerusalem*, 71.

13. Mitchell, *Destination Jerusalem*, 71.

14. Mitchell, *Destination Jerusalem*, 73.

15. Mitchell, *Destination Jerusalem*, 76.

16. Mitchell, *Destination Jerusalem*, 76.

17. Mitchell, *Destination Jerusalem*, 77.

18. Mitchell, *Destination Jerusalem*, 82.

19. Wikipedia, s.v. "Christianity in Egypt," last modified September 2, 2018,
11:05, https://en.wikipedia.org/wiki/Christianity_in_Egypt. Please note
that Wikipedia's statement is unsourced.

20. "Africa: Egypt," The World Factbook, updated July 12, 2018, accessed July
16, 2018, https://www.cia.gov/library/publications/the-world-factbook/
geos/eg.html. The percentage is widely debated.

21. Kirsten Powers, "The Muslim Brotherhood's War on Coptic Christians,"
Daily Beast, August 22, 2013, https://www.thedailybeast.com/the-
muslim-brotherhoods-war-on-coptic-christians.

22. Johannes Makar, "How Egypt's Copts Fell Out of Love With
President Sisi," *Foreign Policy*, December 9, 2016, https://foreignpolicy.
com/2016/12/09/how-egypts-copts-fell-out-of-love-with-president-sisi/.

23. Hamza Hendawi, "Egypt: Islamists Hit Christian Churches," *San Diego
Union-Tribune*, August 17, 2013, http://www.sandiegouniontribune.com/
sdut-egypt-islamists-hit-christian-churches-2013aug17-story.html#.

24. Mitchell, *Destination Jerusalem*, 93.
25. Mitchell, *Destination Jerusalem*, 91.
26. Mitchell, *Destination Jerusalem*, 93.
27. Paul Marshall, Lela Gilbert, and Nina Shea, *Persecuted: The Global Assault on Christians* (Nashville: Thomas Nelson, 2013), 189.
28. Marshall, Gilbert, and Shea, *Persecuted*, 189.
29. "Five Years Since Maspero, Egypt's Copts Denied Permit to Remember Twenty-Seven Dead," WorldWatch Monitor, October 7, 2016, https://www.worldwatchmonitor.org/2016/10/5-years-since-maspero-egypts-copts-denied-permit-to-remember-27-dead/; "Egypt: Don't Cover Up Military Killing of Copt Protestors," Human Rights Watch, October 25, 2011, https://www.hrw.org/news/2011/10/25/egypt-dont-cover-military-killing-copt-protesters; Reem Abdellatif, "The Night Maspero Turned Into a War Zone: A Firsthand Account," Public Radio International, October 16, 2011, https://www.pri.org/stories/2011-10-16/night-maspero-turned-war-zone-firsthand-account.
30. Marshall, Gilbert, and Shea, *Persecuted*, 183–184.
31. Cam McGrath, "Egypt: 'Invisible Hand' Playing With Sectarian Fire," Inter Press Service News Agency, October 12, 2011, http://www.ipsnews.net/2011/10/egypt-invisible-handrsquo-playing-with-sectarian-fire/.
32. Associated Press, "Egypt's Army Denies Shooting Christian Protestors," CTV News, October 12, 2011, https://www.ctvnews.ca/egypt-s-army-denies-shooting-christian-protesters-1.710148.
33. Associated Press, "Egypt's Army Denies Shooting Christian Protestors."
34. Marshall, Gilbert, and Shea, *Persecuted*, 183–184.
35. Marshall, Gilbert, and Shea, *Persecuted*, 184.
36. "Egypt: New Church Law Discriminates Against Christians," Human Rights Watch, September 15, 2016, https://www.hrw.org/news/2016/09/15/egypt-new-church-law-discriminates-against-christians.
37. Mary Abdelmassih, "Egyptian Christians Clash With State Security Forces Over Church Construction," Assyrian International News Agency, November 26, 2010, http://www.aina.org/news/20101126184013.htm; Marshall, Gilbert, and Shea, *Persecuted*, 186–187.
38. Jack Shenker, "Egypt's Coptic Christians Struggle Against Institutionalized Prejudice," *The Guardian*, December 23, 2010, https://www.theguardian.com/world/2010/dec/23/egypt-coptic-christians-prejudice?intcmp=239; Abdelmassih, "Egyptian Christians Clash With State Security Forces Over Church Construction," cited in Marshall, Gilbert, and Shea, *Persecuted*, 185–187.

39. This story may be found in Marshall, Gilbert, and Shea, *Persecuted*, 191–192.

40. Kurt J. Werthmuller, "Copt's Murder a Test of Egypt's New Anti-Discrimination Law," *National Review*, October 31, 2011, https://www.nationalreview.com/corner/copts-murder-test-egypts-new-anti-discrimination-law-kurt-j-werthmuller/. The details of Ayman Nabil Labib's death accounted here are based upon Mr. Werthmuller's article.

41. Marshall, Gilbert, and Shea, *Persecuted*, 188.

42. Marshall, Gilbert, and Shea, *Persecuted*, 188.

CHAPTER 9
WHATEVER HAPPENED TO THE ARAB SPRING?

1. "The 'Arab Spring': Five Years On," Amnesty International, accessed July 16, 2018, https://www.amnesty.org/en/latest/campaigns/2016/01/arab-spring-five-years-on/.

2. "The Arab Spring: A Year of Revolution," NPR, December 17, 2011, http://www.npr.org/2011/12/17/143897126/the-arab-spring-a-year-of-revolution.

3. "Sidi Bouzid Est," City Population, updated November 11, 2017, accessed July 16, 2018, https://www.citypopulation.de/php/tunisia-admin.php?adm2id=4352.

4. Peter Beaumont, "Mohammed Bouazizi: The Dutiful Son Whose Death Changed Tunisia's Fate," *The Guardian*, January 20, 2011, https://www.theguardian.com/world/2011/jan/20/tunisian-fruit-seller-mohammed-bouazizi.

5. Rania Abouzeid, "Bouazizi: The Man Who Set Himself and Tunisia on Fire," *Time*, January 21, 2011, http://content.time.com/time/magazine/article/0,9171,2044723,00.html.

6. Abouzeid, "Bouazizi."

7. "The Arab Spring," NPR.

8. "Tunisia: The Protests Continue," In Defence of Marxism, January 11, 2011, http://www.marxist.com/tunisia-protests-continue.htm.

9. "Jasmine Revolution: Tunisian History," *Encyclopaedia Britannica*, May 2, 2018, https://www.britannica.com/event/Jasmine-Revolution; John Simpson, "Who Are the Winners and Losers From the Arab Spring?," BBC News, November 12, 2014, https://www.bbc.com/news/world-middle-east-30003865.

10. "Tunisia: President Zine al-Abidine Ben Ali Forced Out," BBC News, January 15, 2011, https://www.bbc.com/news/world-africa-12195025.

11. "The 'Spark' That Started It All," Cornell University Library, updated April 24, 2018, https://guides.library.cornell.edu/c.php?g=31688&p=200750.

12. "Arab Spring: Pro-Democracy Protests," *Encyclopaedia Britannica*, January 14, 2015, https://www.britannica.com/event/Arab-Spring.

13. "Arab Spring," *Encyclopaedia Britannica*.

14. Christopher Williams, "How Egypt Shut Down the Internet," *The Telegraph*, January 28, 2011, https://www.telegraph.co.uk/news/worldnews/africaandindianocean/egypt/8288163/How-Egypt-shut-down-the-internet.html.

15. Eric Trager, "Standing By," *New Republic*, May 23, 2011, https://newrepublic.com/article/88804/egypt-protest-violence-army-mubarak.

16. David D. Kirkpatrick, "New Turmoil in Egypt Greets Mixed Verdict for Mubarak," *New York Times*, June 2, 2012, https://www.nytimes.com/2012/06/03/world/middleeast/egypt-hosni-mubarak-life-sentence-prison.html?nytmobile=0.

17. Ruth Michaelson, "Hosni Mubarak: Egypt's Toppled Dictator Freed After Six Years in Custody," *The Guardian*, March 24, 2017, https://www.theguardian.com/world/2017/mar/24/hosni-mubarak-returns-to-cairo-home-after-six-years-in-custody.

18. "2012 Egyptian Parliamentary Elections," Carnegie Endowment for International Peace, January 22, 2015, https://carnegieendowment.org/2015/01/22/2012-egyptian-parliamentary-elections-pub-58800. The elections began in November 2011 and were completed in January 2012.

19. "Fighting Breaks Out in the Streets of Sanaa, as Saleh Refuses to Go," AsiaNews.it, May 26, 2011, http://www.asianews.it/news-en/Fighting-breaks-out-in-the-streets-of-Sanaa,-as-Saleh-refuses-to-go-21669.html.

20. Mohammed Jamjoom, "Official: Ex-Yemeni President Saleh Hospitalized," CNN, updated May 21, 2012, https://www.cnn.com/2012/05/20/world/meast/yemen-saleh-hospitalized/index.html.

21. "Yemen's Saleh Agrees to Transfer Power," Al Jazeera, November 24, 2011, https://www.aljazeera.com/news/middleeast/2011/11/2011112355040101606.html.

22. Mohammed Jamjoon, "Yemen Holds Presidential Election With One Candidate," CNN, updated February 22, 2012, https://www.cnn.com/2012/02/21/world/meast/yemen-elections/index.html.

23. "Yemen Crisis: President Hadi Flees as Houthi Rebels Advance," BBC News, March 25, 2015, https://www.bbc.com/news/world-middle-east-32048604.

24. "How the Bahraini Monarchy Crushed the Country's Arab Spring," *The Observers*, September 6, 2016, http://observers.france24.com/en/20160906-bahrain-monarchy-arab-spring-repression-revolution.
25. Frederik Richter, "Protester Killed in Bahrain 'Day of Rage,'" Reuters, February 14, 2011, https://uk.reuters.com/article/uk-bahrain-protests/protester-killed-in-bahrain-day-of-rage-witnesses-idUKTRE71D1G520110214.
26. Martin Chulov, "Bahrain Protests: Four Killed as Riot Police Storm Pearl Square," *The Guardian*, February 17, 2011, https://www.theguardian.com/world/2011/feb/17/bahrain-protests-riot-police-storm-pearl-square.
27. Martin Chulov, "Bahrain Protest: 'The Regime Must Fall, and We Will Make Sure It Does,'" *The Guardian*, February 18, 2011, https://www.theguardian.com/world/2011/feb/18/bahrain-protests-regime-fall.
28. "Gulf States Send Forces to Bahrain Following Protests," BBC News, March 14, 2011, https://www.bbc.com/news/world-middle-east-12729786.
29. "King of Bahrain Declares State of Emergency," *The Telegraph*, March 15, 2011, https://www.telegraph.co.uk/news/worldnews/middleeast/bahrain/8383310/King-of-Bahrain-declares-state-of-emergency.html.
30. Habib Toumi, "Pearl Monument in Bahrain Torn Down," *Gulf News*, March 18, 2011, https://gulfnews.com/news/gulf/bahrain/pearl-monument-in-bahrain-torn-down-1.779032.
31. "Libya: Col Gaddafi Vows to Die a 'Martyr,'" *The Telegraph*, February 22, 2011, https://www.telegraph.co.uk/news/worldnews/africaandindianocean/libya/8341133/Libya-Col-Gaddafi-vows-to-die-a-martyr.html.
32. "Highlights—Libyan TV Address by Saif al-Islam Gaddafi," Reuters, February 20, 2011, https://in.reuters.com/article/idINIndia-55032320110221.
33. Wikipedia, s.v. "Arab Spring," last modified August 30, 2018, https://en.wikipedia.org/wiki/Arab_Spring.
34. United Nations Security Council, "Security Council Approves 'No-Fly Zone' Over Libya, Authorizing 'All Necessary Measures' to Protect Civilians, by Vote of 10 in Favour with 5 Abstentions," March 17, 2011, https://www.un.org/press/en/2011/sc10200.doc.htm.
35. "Libya: US, UK, and France Attack Gaddafi Forces," BBC News, March 20, 2011, https://www.bbc.com/news/world-africa-12796972.
36. Thom Shanker and Eric Schmitt, "Seeing Limits to 'New' Kind of War in Libya," *New York Times*, October 21, 2011, https://www.nytimes.com/2011/10/22/world/africa/

nato-war-in-libya-shows-united-states-was-vital-to-toppling-qaddafi.
html.

37. Chris McGreal, Ewen MacAskill, and Richard Norton-Taylor, "Libya: Allied Air Strikes Secure Misrata for Rebels," *The Guardian*, March 23, 2011, https://www.theguardian.com/world/2011/mar/23/libya-allied-air-strikes-misrata.

38. Jamie Tarabay, "For Many Syrians, the Story of the War Began With Graffiti in Dara'a," CNN, updated March 15, 2018, https://www.cnn.com/2018/03/15/middleeast/daraa-syria-seven-years-on-intl/index.html.

39. Avi Asher-Schapiro, "The Young Men Who Started Syria's Revolution Speak About Daraa, Where It All Began," Vice News, March 15, 2016, https://news.vice.com/article/the-young-men-who-started-syrias-revolution-speak-about-daraa-where-it-all-began.

40. "Syria Protests: Homs City Sit-In 'Dispersed by Gunfire,'" BBC News, April 19, 2011, https://www.bbc.com/news/world-middle-east-13130401; "Syrian Forces Kill at Least 34 Protestors at Anti-Government Protest," *The Guardian*, June 3, 2011, https://www.theguardian.com/world/2011/jun/03/syrian-forces-kill-34-protesters.

41. Ian Black and Nour Ali, "Syria: 100 Die in Crackdown as Assad Sends In His Tanks," *The Guardian*, July 31, 2011, https://www.theguardian.com/world/2011/jul/31/syria-hama-crackdown-tanks-protests.

42. "Syrian Forces Overrun Baba Amr as Rebels Retreat," SBS News, August 26, 2013, https://www.sbs.com.au/news/syrian-forces-overrun-baba-amr-as-rebels-retreat. This "rebel bastion" would be stormed in 2013.

43. Jeffrey White and Andrew Exum, "The Free Syrian Army: A Military Assessment," Washington Institute, April 13, 2012, https://www.washingtoninstitute.org/policy-analysis/view/the-free-syrian-army-a-military-assessment.

44. Joseph Wouk, "Assad Masses Loyal Troops in Damascus After He Was Warned of a Military Coup," *A Sclerotic Goes to War*, January 31, 2012, https://warsclerotic.com/2012/01/.

45. Mousa Ladqani, "Syria: The Regime Is Shaking—Elements of Dual Power Emerge," Revolution, February 1, 2012, https://www.workersalternative.com/international/129-is.

46. Ladqani, "Syria."

47. Martin Chulov and Paul Harris, "Syria: '300 Killed' as Regime Launches Huge Attack on Besieged City of Homs," *The Guardian*, February 4, 2012, https://www.theguardian.com/world/2012/feb/05/syria-homs-hundreds-dead-barrage.

48. David Enders, "Syrian Forces Retake Zabadani as Rebels Withdraw, Refugees Say," *Miami Herald*, February 22, 2012, https://www.miamiherald.com/latest-news/article1939549.html; Scott Lucas, "Syria (and Beyond) Live Coverage: Protests Amidst the Regime's Assault?," EA WorldView, February 10, 2012, http://www.enduringamerica.com/home/2012/2/10/syria-and-beyond-live-coverage-protests-amidst-the-regimes-a.html#1546.

49. Khaled Yacoub Oweis, "Assad Holds Syria Army Despite Sunni-Alawite Divide," Reuters, April 6, 2011, https://www.reuters.com/article/us-syria-army/assad-holds-syria-army-despite-sunni-alawite-divide-idUSTRE73543X20110406.

50. "Security Council Fails to Adopt Draft Resolution Condemning Syria's Crackdown on Anti-Government Protesters, Owing to Veto by Russian Federation, China," UN Security Council, October 4, 2011, https://www.un.org/press/en/2011/sc10403.doc.htm; Marc Lynch, "The UN Fails Syria," *Foreign Policy*, February 5, 2012, https://foreignpolicy.com/2012/02/05/the-un-fails-syria/.

51. "Arab Spring," *Encyclopaedia Britannica*.

52. "Arab Spring," *Encyclopaedia Britannica*.

53. Marc Lynch, *The Arab Uprising: The Unfinished Revolutions of the New Middle East* (New York: Public Affairs, 2012), 9.

54. Joseph V. Micallef, "The Arab Spring: Six Years Later," *The Blog*, *Huffington Post*, January 29, 2017, www.huffingtonpost.com/joseph-v-micallef/the-arab-spring-six-years_b_14461896.html.

55. Micallef, "The Arab Spring."

56. Micallef, "The Arab Spring."

57. Micallef, "The Arab Spring."

58. Micallef, "The Arab Spring."

59. Micallef, "The Arab Spring."

60. Micallef, "The Arab Spring."

61. Micallef, "The Arab Spring."

62. Micallef, "The Arab Spring."

63. Micallef, "The Arab Spring."

64. Micallef, "The Arab Spring."

65. Micallef, "The Arab Spring."

CHAPTER 10
THE UNITED NATIONS VS. ISRAEL

1. Winston Churchill, "Iron Curtain" (speech, Westminster College, Fulton, MO, March 5, 1946), http://www.historyplace.com/speeches/ironcurtain.htm.
2. Charter of the United Nations, Article 1, United Nations, accessed July 18, 2018, http://www.un.org/en/sections/un-charter/chapter-i/index.html.
3. "Biography of United Nations Secretary-General Kofi Annan," United Nations, accessed July 18, 2018, http://www.un.org/ga/aids/SGBio.html.
4. Kofi Annan, report to the UN General Assembly on the Fall of Srebrenica (address, Stockholm International Forum, Stockholm, Sweden, January 26, 2004), quoted in Kofi Annan, "Address by Secretary-General Kofi Annan to the Stockholm International Forum in Stockholm, Sweden, on 26 January 2004," United Nations, accessed September 13, 2018, https://www.un.org/sg/en/content/sg/speeches/2004-01-26/address-secretary-general-kofi-annan-stockholm-international-forum.
5. "Rwanda: How the Genocide Happened," BBC News, May 17, 2011, https://www.bbc.com/news/world-africa-13431486.
6. Dore Gold, *Tower of Babble: How the United Nations Has Fueled Global Chaos* (New York: Crown Publishing, 2005), 6.
7. Gold, *Tower of Babble*, 7.
8. Gold, *Tower of Babble*, 8.
9. Gold, *Tower of Babble*, 9–10.
10. Gold, *Tower of Babble*, 12–13.
11. David Mendelsson, "British Rule," Jewish Agency for Israel, March 10, 2015, http://www.jewishagency.org/israel/content/34106.
12. United Nations Special Committee on Palestine, *Report to the General Assembly* (New York: United Nations, 1947), accessed July 18, 2018, https://unispal.un.org/DPA/DPR/unispal.nsf/0/07175DE9FA2DE5638525 68D3006E10F3.
13. "United Nations Special Committee on Palestine, 1947 (UNSCOP)," Encyclopedia.com (Encyclopedia of the Modern Middle East and North Africa), accessed July 18, 2018, https://www.encyclopedia.com/humanities/encyclopedias-almanacs-transcripts-and-maps/united-nations-special-committee-palestine-1947-unscop.
14. "Arab Higher Committee (Palestine)," Encyclopedia.com (Encyclopedia of the Modern Middle East and North Africa), accessed July 18, 2018, https://www.encyclopedia.com/humanities/encyclopedias-almanacs-transcripts-and-maps/arab-higher-committee-palestine.

15. United Nations Special Committee on Palestine, *Report to the General Assembly.*

16. United Nations General Assembly, *Resolution 181 (II): Future Government of Palestine* (New York: United Nations, 1947), https://unispal.un.org/DPA/DPR/unispal.nsf/0/7F0AF2BD897689B785256C330061D253.

17. "The Declaration of the Establishment of the State of Israel, May 14, 1948," Israel Ministry of Foreign Affairs, accessed July 18, 2018, http://www.mfa.gov.il/mfa/foreignpolicy/peace/guide/pages/declaration%20of%20establishment%20of%20state%20of%20israel.aspx.

18. Joshua Muravchik, "The UN and Israel: A History of Discrimination," *World Affairs Journal* (November/December 2013), accessed July 18, 2018, http://www.worldaffairsjournal.org/article/un-and-israel-history-discrimination.

19. Muravchik, "The UN and Israel."

20. Muravchik, "The UN and Israel."

21. Muravchik, "The UN and Israel."

22. Muravchik, "The UN and Israel."

23. Muravchik, "The UN and Israel."

24. "Myths and Facts: The United Nations," Jewish Virtual Library, accessed July 18, 2018, https://www.jewishvirtuallibrary.org/myths-and-facts-the-united-nations.

25. Muravchik, "The UN and Israel."

26. Muravchik, "The UN and Israel."

27. Colum Lynch, "Islamic Group Blocks Terror Treaty," *Washington Post*, November 10, 2001, https://www.washingtonpost.com/archive/politics/2001/11/10/islamic-group-blocks-terror-treaty/582a7d9e-06e9-48e1-a2f3-6c9dcd4e9967/?utm_term=.8bd98eb91d8b.

28. "Myths and Facts," Jewish Virtual Library.

29. "Myths and Facts," Jewish Virtual Library.

30. "Myths and Facts," Jewish Virtual Library.

31. United Nations General Assembly, *Resolution 41/162: The Situation in the Middle East* (New York: United Nations, December 5, 1986), http://www.un.org/documents/ga/res/41/a41r162.htm.

32. United Nations General Assembly, *Resolution 41/162: The Situation in the Middle East.*

33. Mitchell Bard, "United Nations: The UN Relationship With Israel," Jewish Virtual Library, accessed July 19, 2018, https://www.jewishvirtuallibrary.org/the-u-n-israel-relationship#26.

34. Bard, "United Nations."
35. Bard, "United Nations."
36. Bard, "United Nations."
37. "Myths and Facts," Jewish Virtual Library; Bernard D. Nossiter, "Iran Challenges Israel's Right to Seat at UN," *New York Times*, October 26, 1982, https://www.nytimes.com/1982/10/26/world/iran-challenges-israel-s-right-to-seat-at-un.html.
38. United Nations General Assembly, "Tenth Emergency Special Session," accessed July 18, 2018, http://www.un.org/en/ga/sessions/emergency10th.shtml.
39. "Myths and Facts Online—the United Nations," Jewish Virtual Library, accessed July 18, 2018, https://www.jewishvirtuallibrary.org/myths-and-facts-online-the-united-nations.
40. Mitchell G. Bard, *Will Israel Survive?* (New York: Palgrave Macmillan, 2007), 190.
41. Associated Press, "US Jewish Organizations Protest UN Funding of PA Banners in Gaza," *Haaretz*, August 18, 2005, https://www.haaretz.com/1.4933399.
42. Associated Press, "US Jewish Organizations Protest UN Funding of PA Banners in Gaza."
43. Associated Press, "US Jewish Organizations Protest UN Funding of PA Banners in Gaza."
44. Bard, *Will Israel Survive?*, 190.
45. Bard, *Will Israel Survive?*, 190.
46. Bard, "United Nations."
47. "Statement by the Delegation of the United States of America as Delivered by Ambassador Eileen Chamberlain Donahoe Human Rights Council 22nd Session" (Geneva: Human Rights Council, March 18, 2013), https://geneva.usmission.gov/2013/03/18/24574/.
48. United Nations General Assembly, "General Assembly Establishes New Human Rights Council by Vote of 170 in Favour to 4 Against, with 3 Abstentions," United Nations, March 15, 2006, https://www.un.org/press/en/2006/ga10449.doc.htm.
49. Bard, "United Nations"; for example, see Hillel Neuer, "UN Casts Israel as Worst Violator of Health Rights in the World," UN Watch, May 28, 2015, https://www.unwatch.org/un-casts-israel-as-worst-violator-of-health-rights-in-the-world/.
50. Bard, "United Nations."

51. United Nations Secretary-General, "Secretary-General's Message to the Third Session of the Human Rights Council [Delivered by Mrs. Louise Arbour, High Commissioner for Human Rights]," United Nations, November 29, 2006, https://www.un.org/sg/en/content/sg/statement/2006-11-29/secretary-generals-message-third-session-human-rights-council.

52. Bard, "United Nations."

53. Bard, "United Nations"; Colin Dwyer, "UN Votes Overwhelmingly to Condemn US Decision on Jerusalem," NPR, December 21, 2017, https://www.npr.org/sections/thetwo-way/2017/12/21/572565091/u-n-votes-overwhelmingly-to-condemn-trumps-jerusalem-decision.

54. May Bulman, "Ban Ki-Moon Says UN Has 'Disproportionate' Focus on Israel," *Independent*, December 18, 2016, https://www.independent.co.uk/news/world/middle-east/ban-ki-moon-united-nations-disproportionate-israel-focus-resolutions-palestinians-human-rights-danny-a7481961.html.

55. Wikipedia, s.v. "List of United Nations Resolutions Concerning Israel," last modified August 23, 2018, https://en.wikipedia.org/wiki/List_of_United_Nations_resolutions_concerning_Israel.

56. "2017 UN General Assembly Resolutions Singling Out Israel—Texts, Votes, Analysis," UN Watch, November 10, 2017, https://www.unwatch.org/2017-unga-resolutions-singling-israel/.

57. Tovah Lazaroff, "151 UN States Vote to Disavow Israeli Ties to Jerusalem," *Jerusalem Post*, December 1, 2017, https://www.jpost.com/Israel-News/UN-disavows-Israeli-ties-to-Jerusalem-515730.

58. "These 36 Countries Don't Recognize Israel," Brilliant Maps, May 2, 2015, https://brilliantmaps.com/israel-foreign-relations/.

59. "2017 UN General Assembly Resolutions Singling Out Israel—Texts, Votes, Analysis," UN Watch.

60. "The 43 Times US Has Used Veto Power Against UN Resolutions on Israel," Middle East Eye, December 18, 2017, http://www.middleeasteye.net/news/42-times-us-has-used-its-veto-power-against-un-resolutions-israel-942194703.

61. Bard, "United Nations."

62. Peter Rough, "The United Nations Should Ditch Its Anti-Israel Bias," *Hill*, June 20, 2017, http://thehill.com/blogs/pundits-blog/international/338412-the-united-nations-should-ditch-its-anti-israel-bias.

63. Rough, "The United Nations Should Ditch Its Anti-Israel Bias."

64. Rough, "The United Nations Should Ditch Its Anti-Israel Bias."

65. Rough, "The United Nations Should Ditch Its Anti-Israel Bias."

66. Rough, "The United Nations Should Ditch Its Anti-Israel Bias."
67. Rough, "The United Nations Should Ditch Its Anti-Israel Bias."
68. Rough, "The United Nations Should Ditch Its Anti-Israel Bias."

CHAPTER 11
HEZBOLLAH, HAMAS, AND THE MUSLIM BROTHERHOOD

1. "Hezbollah," *Haaretz*, accessed July 19, 2018, https://www.haaretz.com/misc/tags/TAG-hezbollah-1.5598890.
2. "Hezbollah," Counter Extremism Project, accessed July 19, 2018, https://www.counterextremism.com/threat/hezbollah.
3. "Sunnis and Shia in the Middle East," BBC News, December 19, 2013, https://www.bbc.com/news/world-middle-east-25434060.
4. Andrew Cockburn, "Iraq's Oppressed Majority," *Smithsonian*, December 2003, https://www.smithsonianmag.com/history/iraqs-oppressed-majority-95250996/.
5. "Muslim Publics Divided on Hamas and Hezbollah," Pew Research Center, December 2, 2010, http://www.pewglobal.org/2010/12/02/muslims-around-the-world-divided-on-hamas-and-hezbollah/.
6. "Hezbollah," *Encyclopaedia Britannica*, August 23, 2018, https://www.britannica.com/topic/Hezbollah.
7. Associated Press, "History of the Lebanese-Israeli Conflict," *Washington Post*, July 17, 2006, http://www.washingtonpost.com/wp-dyn/content/article/2006/07/17/AR2006071700340.html.
8. Michael Omer-Man, "This Week in History: Israel's Deadliest Terror Attack," *Jerusalem Post*, March 11, 2011, https://www.jpost.com/Features/In-Thespotlight/This-Week-in-History-Israels-deadliest-terror-attack.
9. Ron Grossman, "Commentary: The Hunt for Pancho Villa in Mexico—and the Massive Deployment of National Guard Troops," *Chicago Tribune*, May 3, 2018, http://www.chicagotribune.com/news/opinion/commentary/ct-perspec-flash-pancho-villa-mexico-border-troops-0506-20180430-story.html.
10. David K. Shipler, "Israeli Jets Strike Lebanon Positions of Syria and PLO," *New York Times*, September 14, 1982, https://www.nytimes.com/1982/09/14/world/israeli-jets-strike-lebanon-positions-of-syria-and-plo.html; Ramsay Short, "After 29 Years, Syrian Army Bids Final Farewell to Lebanon," *The Telegraph*, April 25, 2005, https://www.telegraph.co.uk/news/worldnews/middleeast/lebanon/1488649/After-29-years-Syrian-army-bids-final-farewell-to-Lebanon.html.

11. "Middle East: Lebanon," CIA World Factbook, updated August 20, 2018, https://www.cia.gov/library/publications/resources/the-world-factbook/geos/le.html.

12. Elizabeth Thompson, "South Lebanon Army," Encyclopedia.com, 2004, accessed September 13, 2018, https://www.encyclopedia.com/humanities/encyclopedias-almanacs-transcripts-and-maps/south-lebanon-army.

13. Open letter, February 16, 1985, quoted in Itamar Rabinovich and Jehuda Reinharz, eds., *Israel in the Middle East: Documents and Readings on Society, Politics, and Foreign Relations, Pre-1948 to the Present,* 2nd ed. (Waltham, MA: Brandeis University Press, 2008), 427.

14. Joseph Alagha, *The Shifts in Hizbullah's Ideology: Religious Ideology, Political Ideology, and Political Program* (Amsterdam: Amsterdam University Press, 2006), 53.

15. Hassan Ezzeddin, "In the Party of God: Are Terrorists in Lebanon Preparing for a Larger War?," interview by Jeffrey Goldberg, *New Yorker,* October 14, 2002, https://www.newyorker.com/magazine/2002/10/14/in-the-party-of-god.

16. Benjamin Weinthal, "Analysis: Hezbollah's Lethal Anti-Semitism," *Jerusalem Post,* November 12, 2012, https://www.jpost.com/International/Analysis-Hezbollahs-lethal-anti-Semitism; "Hamas MP Says Jews Recruit Prostitutes, AIDS-Infected Women, to Lure Arabs," *Times of Israel,* January 21, 2017, https://www.timesofisrael.com/hamas-mp-says-jews-recruit-prostitutes-aids-infected-women-to-lure-arabs/.

17. Robert S. Wistrich, *A Lethal Obsession: Anti-Semitism From Antiquity to the Global Jihad* (New York: Random House, 2010).

18. Blanca Madani, "Hezbollah's Global Finance Network: The Triple Frontier," *Middle East Intelligence Bulletin* 4, no. 1 (January 2002), https://web.archive.org/web/20090430111341/http://www.meib.org:80/articles/0201_l2.htm.

19. Pablo Gato and Robert Windrem, "Hezbollah Builds a Western Base: From Inside South America's Tri-Border Area, Iran-Linked Militia Targets US," NBC News, May 9, 2007, http://www.nbcnews.com/id/17874369/ns/world_news-americas/t/hezbollah-builds-western-base/#.W1Eppy2ZNEI; see also Sari Horwitz, "Cigarette Smuggling Linked to Terrorism," *Washington Post,* June 8, 2004, http://www.washingtonpost.com/wp-dyn/articles/A23384-2004Jun7.html.

20. Gato and Windrem, "Hezbollah Builds a Western Base."

21. Gato and Windrem, "Hezbollah Builds a Western Base."

22. Reuters, "Russia: Hezbollah Not a Terror Group, Their Cooperation in ISIS Fight Should Be Encouraged," *Jerusalem Post*, November 15, 2015, https://www.jpost.com/International/Russia-does-not-consider -Hezbollah-a-terrorist-group-encourages-their-cooperation-in- Syria-433175.

23. Reuters, "Russia: Hezbollah Not a Terror Group, Their Cooperation in ISIS Fight Should Be Encouraged."

24. Bart Marcois, "The Hezbollah Connection to North Korea," OpsLens, November 20, 2017, https://www.opslens.com/2017/11/20/hezbollah- connection-north-korea/.

25. Humberto Fontova, "Hezbollah Opens Base in Cuba: The Unholy Alliance in Full Motion," *Frontpage Mag*, September 5, 2011, https://www. frontpagemag.com/fpm/103964/hezbollah-opens-base-cuba-humberto -fontova.

26. JNi. Media, "Clinton E-mail Reveals Hezbollah Base in Cuba," *Jewish Press*, February 21, 2016, http://www.jewishpress.com/news/clinton-e -mail-reveals-hezbollah-base-in-cuba/2016/02/21/.

27. JNi. Media, "Clinton E-mail Reveals Hezbollah Base in Cuba."

28. "Gates Warns of Hezbollah WMD Threat," NTI, May 25, 2011, http:// www.nti.org/gsn/article/gates-warns-of-hezbollah-wmd-threat/.

29. Avi Issacharoff, "Israel Raises Hezbollah Rocket Estimate to 150,000," *Times of Israel*, November 12, 2015, https://www.timesofisrael.com/israel- raises-hezbollah-rocket-estimate-to-150000/.

30. "Profile: Hamas Palestinian Movement," BBC News, May 12, 2017, https:// www.bbc.com/news/world-middle-east-13331522.

31. "Profile: Hamas Palestinian Movement," BBC News.

32. Jeremy Bender, "These Are the Rockets Hamas Has Been Shooting at Israel," *Business Insider*, July 10, 2014, http://www.businessinsider.com/ hamas-rocket-arsenal-2014-7; Avi Issacharoff, "Hamas Has Replenished Its Rocket Arsenals, Israeli Officials Say," March 4, 2016, https://www. timesofisrael.com/hamas-has-replenished-its-rocket-arsenals-israeli- officials-say/.

33. "Hamas Hiding Rockets in Schools, Children's Playgrounds, Israel and UN Agency Say," Fox News, July 22, 2014, http://www.foxnews. com/world/2014/07/22/hamas-hiding-rockets-in-schools-children- playgrounds-israel-and-un-agency-say.html.

34. David Patrikarakos, "Hamas Is Ready for War With Israel," *Foreign Policy*, June 7, 2016, https://foreignpolicy.com/2016/06/07/hamas-is-ready- for-war-with-israel-gaza-strip/.

35. Patrikarakos, "Hamas Is Ready for War With Israel."
36. Sophia Jones, "Palestinians in Gaza Denounce Israel for Saying It Warns Civilians Before Strikes," *Huffington Post*, July 23, 2014, https://www.huffingtonpost.com/2014/07/23/israel-airstrike-warning_n_5614085.html.
37. Vladimir Sloutsker, "200 Rockets and Mortars Fired on Israel in One Day—Where Is the Outrage?," *Newsweek*, July 17, 2018, https://www.newsweek.com/200-rockets-and-mortars-fired-israel-one-day-where-outrage-1027416.
38. "Life in Rocket Town: In the Shadow of Gaza's Fury," CBN News, September 8, 2014, http://www1.cbn.com/cbnnews/insideisrael/2012/november/living-in-rocket-town-in-the-shadow-of-gazas-fury.
39. Terrence McCoy, "How Hamas Uses Its Tunnels to Kill and Capture Israeli Soldiers," *Washington Post*, July 21, 2014, https://www.washingtonpost.com/news/morning-mix/wp/2014/07/21/how-hamas-uses-its-tunnels-to-kill-and-capture-israeli-soldiers/?utm_term=.6659ffd642d8.
40. McCoy, "How Hamas Uses Its Tunnels to Kill and Capture Israeli Soldiers."
41. McCoy, "How Hamas Uses Its Tunnels to Kill and Capture Israeli Soldiers."
42. McCoy, "How Hamas Uses Its Tunnels to Kill and Capture Israeli Soldiers."
43. McCoy, "How Hamas Uses Its Tunnels to Kill and Capture Israeli Soldiers."
44. McCoy, "How Hamas Uses Its Tunnels to Kill and Capture Israeli Soldiers."
45. McCoy, "How Hamas Uses Its Tunnels to Kill and Capture Israeli Soldiers."
46. McCoy, "How Hamas Uses Its Tunnels to Kill and Capture Israeli Soldiers."
47. McCoy, "How Hamas Uses Its Tunnels to Kill and Capture Israeli Soldiers."
48. Moti Bassok, "Israel Shells Out Almost a Fifth of National Budget on Defense, Figures Show," *Haaretz*, February 14, 2013, https://www.haaretz.com/israel-news/business/.premium-report-20-of-budget-goes-to-israel-s-defense-1.5229839.
49. Lidar Gravé-Lazi, "More Than 1 in 5 Israelis Live in Poverty, Highest in Developed World," *Jerusalem Post*, December 15, 2016, https://www.jpost.com/Israel-News/

More-than-1-in-5-Israelis-live-in-poverty-highest-in-developed-world-475444.

50. Raf Sanchez and Ramat Gan, "Tens of Thousands of Israeli Holocaust Survivors Are Living in Abject Poverty," *The Telegraph*, January 27, 2016, https://www.telegraph.co.uk/news/worldnews/middleeast/israel/12122754/Tens-of-thousands-of-Israeli-Holocaust-survivors-are-living-in-abject-poverty.html.

51. Robert S. Leiken and Steven Brooke, "The Moderate Muslim Brotherhood," *Foreign Affairs*, March/April 2007, https://www.foreignaffairs.com/articles/2007-03-01/moderate-muslim-brotherhood.

52. "What Is the Muslim Brotherhood?" Al Jazeera, June 18, 2017, https://www.aljazeera.com/indepth/features/2017/06/muslim-brotherhood-explained-170608091709865.html.

53. Bryony Jones, "What Is the Muslim Brotherhood?," CNN.com, June 25, 2012, https://www.cnn.com/2012/06/24/world/africa/muslim-brotherhood-explained/index.html.

54. "Global Muslim Brotherhood," The Global Muslim Brotherhood Daily Watch, accessed July 20, 2018, https://www.globalmbwatch.com/global-muslim-brotherhood/; Leiken and Brooke, "The Moderate Muslim Brotherhood."

55. Marc Lynch, "Islamists and Their Charities," *Washington Post*, October 15, 2014, https://www.washingtonpost.com/news/monkey-cage/wp/2014/10/15/islamists-and-their-charities/?utm_term=.dd6f72707eec; Steven Brooke, "The Muslim Brotherhood's Social Outreach After the Egyptian Coup," Brookings Institution, August 2015, https://www.brookings.edu/wp-content/uploads/2016/07/Egypt_Brooke-FINALE.pdf.

56. Jonathan D. Halevi, "Where Is the Muslim Brotherhood Headed?," Jerusalem Center for Public Affairs, June 20, 2012, http://jcpa.org/the-muslim-brotherhood-a-moderate-islamic-alternative-to-al-qaeda-or-a-partner-in-global-jihad/.

57. Halevi, "Where Is the Muslim Brotherhood Headed?"

58. "Terrorism: Muslim Brotherhood," Jewish Virtual Library, accessed July 20, 2018, https://www.jewishvirtuallibrary.org/the-muslim-brotherhood.

59. Yusuf al Qaradawi, "There Is No Dialogue between Us and the Jews, Except by Sword and Rifle," MEMRI, July 27, 2004, quoted in Andrew G. Bostom, ed., *The Legacy of Islamic Antisemitism: From Sacred Text to Solemn History* (New York: Prometheus Books, 2008), 684; see also Rabbi Abraham Cooper, "Egypt's Youth Must Stand Their Ground Against Islamic Extremists," Fox News, February 25, 2011, http://www.

foxnews.com/opinion/2011/02/25/egypts-youth-stand-ground-islamic-extremists.html.

60. "Terrorism: Muslim Brotherhood," Jewish Virtual Library.

61. Ian Johnson, *A Mosque in Munich: Nazis, the CIA, and the Rise of the Muslim Brotherhood in the West* (New York: Houghton Mifflin Harcourt, 2010), 109.

62. Johnson, *A Mosque in Munich*, 111–112.

63. Irfan Husain, *Fatal Faultlines: Pakistan, Islam, and the West* (Rockville, MD: Arc Manor, 2012), 60.

64. Dr. Harold Brackman, "'Hitler Put Them in Their Place': Egypt's Muslim Brotherhood's Jihad Against Jews, Judaism, and Israel," written for the Simon Wiesenthal Center, February 2011, PDF, 12, http://www.wiesenthal.com/atf/cf/%7B54d385e6-f1b9-4e9f-8e94-890c3e6dd277%7D/HITLER-PUT-THEM-IN-THEIR-PLACE_BRACKMAN_FINAL.PDF; "Terrorism: Muslim Brotherhood," Jewish Virtual Library.

65. "Terrorism: Muslim Brotherhood," Jewish Virtual Library.

66. "Mahmūd Fahmī al-Nuqrāshī: Prime Minister of Egypt," *Encyclopaedia Britannica*, April 15, 2004, https://www.britannica.com/biography/Mahmud-Fahmi-al-Nuqrashi.

67. John Esposito, *The Islamic Threat: Myth or Reality?* (Oxford, UK: Oxford University Press, 1999), 138.

68. Paul Berman, *The Flight of the Intellectuals: The Controversy Over Islamism and the Press* (Brooklyn, NY: Melvillehouse, 2011), 33.

69. Efraim Karsh, *Islamic Imperialism: A History* (New Haven, CT: Yale University Press, 2006), 209.

70. Brackman, "Hitler Put Them in Their Place," 10.

71. Brackman, "Hitler Put Them in Their Place," 10–11; Robert S. Wistrich, *Lethal Obsession: Anti-Semitism From Antiquity to the Global Jihad* (New York: Random House, 2010), 563–544, 808–810; Matthias Kuntzel, *Jihad and Jew Hatred: Islamism, Nazism and the Roots of 9/11*, trans. Colin Meade (New York: Telos Press, 2007).

72. Brackman, "Hitler Put Them in Their Place," 13.

73. Brackman, "Hitler Put Them in Their Place," 13.

74. Brackman, "Hitler Put Them in Their Place," 4; Maurice Pearlman, *Mufti of Jerusalem: The Story of Haj Amin El Husseini* (London, Victor Gollancz, 1947), 49.

75. Brackman, "Hitler Put Them in Their Place," 14; Jeffrey Herf, *Nazi Propaganda for the Arab World* (New Haven, CT: Yale University Press, 2009), 242–244.

76. Lawrence Wright, "The Rebellion Within: An Al Qaeda Mastermind Questions Terrorism," *New Yorker*, June 2, 2008, https://www.newyorker.com/magazine/2008/06/02/the-rebellion-within.

77. "Moments in US Diplomatic History: The Cairo Fire of 1952," Association for Diplomatic Studies and Training, accessed July 20, 2018, https://adst.org/2012/09/the-cairo-fire-of-1952/.

78. Wikipedia, s.v. "Cairo Fire," last modified September 3, 2018, https://en.wikipedia.org/wiki/Cairo_fire#cite_note-Ahram_Damage-1.

79. "This Day in History—July 23, 1952: Military Seizes Power in Egypt," History, July 21, 2010, https://www.history.com/this-day-in-history/military-seizes-power-in-egypt.

80. "Gamal Abdel Nasser," *New World Encyclopedia*, last modified May 19, 2017, http://www.newworldencyclopedia.org/entry/Gamal_Abdel_Nasser; Robert St. John, "Gamal Abdel Nasser: President of Egypt," *Encyclopaedia Britannica*, November 15, 2017, https://www.britannica.com/biography/Gamal-Abdel-Nasser.

81. St. John, "Gamal Abdel Nasser."

82. Saïd K. Aburish, *Nasser: The Last Arab* (New York: St. Martin's Press, 2004), 55.

83. Mohamed Fadel Fahmy, "30 Years Later, Questions Remain Over Sadat Killing, Peace With Israel," CNN, updated October 6, 2011, https://www.cnn.com/2011/10/06/world/meast/egypt-sadat-assassination/index.html.

84. Jim Hoagl, "Sadat and Begin Get Nobel Prize as Peacemakers," *Washington Post*, October 28, 1978, https://www.washingtonpost.com/archive/politics/1978/10/28/sadat-and-begin-get-nobel-prize-as-peacemakers/64f515fb-6f1c-4dc3-8ea2-e43c15fdbe8c/?utm_term=.6c365e2b6ebd.

85. Fahmy, "30 Years Later, Questions Remain Over Sadat Killing, Peace With Israel."

86. "Egypt: Mass Attacks on Churches," Human Rights Watch, August 21, 2013, https://www.hrw.org/news/2013/08/21/egypt-mass-attacks-churches.

87. Lela Gilbert, "Saturday People, Sunday People," *Weekly Standard*, November 17, 2010, https://www.weeklystandard.com/lela-gilbert/saturday-people-sunday-people.

88. Abdellatif el-Menawy, "Have No Illusions About the Muslim Brotherhood," *Arab News*, August 28, 2017, http://www.arabnews.com/node/1151581/columns.

89. El-Menawy, "Have No Illusions About the Muslim Brotherhood."

90. El-Menawy, "Have No Illusions About the Muslim Brotherhood."

91. El-Menawy, "Have No Illusions About the Muslim Brotherhood."
92. El-Menawy, "Have No Illusions About the Muslim Brotherhood."

CHAPTER 12
TROUBLE IN IRAN

1. Andrew deGrandpre and Andrew Tilghman, "Iran Linked to Deaths of 500 US Troops in Iraq, Afghanistan," *Military Times*, July 14, 2015, https://www.militarytimes.com/news/pentagon-congress/2015/07/14/iran-linked-to-deaths-of-500-u-s-troops-in-iraq-afghanistan/.
2. DeGrandpre and Tilghman, "Iran Linked to Deaths of 500 US Troops in Iraq, Afghanistan."
3. Giulio Meotti, "The 'Protocols' Are Alive and Well World Over," Arutz Sheva, January 20, 2012, http://www.israelnationalnews.com/Articles/Article.aspx/11150.
4. Brigitte Sion, "Protocols of the Elders of Zion," My Jewish Learning, accessed July 21, 2018, https://www.myjewishlearning.com/article/protocols-of-the-elders-of-zion/.
5. Hossein Jaseb and Fredrik Dahl, "Ahmadinejad Says Israel Will 'Disappear,'" Reuters, June 2, 2008, https://www.reuters.com/article/us-iran-israel-usa/ahmadinejad-says-israel-will-disappear-idUSL0261250620080603.
6. Herb Keinon, "Steinitz to Post: Iran May Try to Fool West With 'Trust-Building' Measures," *Jerusalem Post*, September 5, 2013, https://www.jpost.com/Diplomacy-and-Politics/Steinitz-to-Post-Iran-may-try-to-fool-West-with-trust-building-measures-325285.
7. Ehsan Yarshater, "When 'Persia' Became 'Iran,'" Iran Chamber Society, July 21, 2018, http://www.iranchamber.com/geography/articles/persia_became_iran.php; Ehsan Yarshater, "Communication," *Iranian Studies* 22, no. 1 (1989), https://www.jstor.org/stable/4310640.
8. James Zogby, "The Arab and Iranian Disconnect," *Huffington Post*, November 29, 2014, https://www.huffingtonpost.com/james-zogby/the-arab-and-iranian-disconnect_b_6240264.html.
9. "Israel International Relations: International Recognition of Israel," Jewish Virtual Library, accessed July 30, 2018, https://www.jewishvirtuallibrary.org/international-recognition-of-israel.
10. Ty Joplin, "When Iran and Israel Were Friends," *Al Bawaba*, July 18, 2018, https://www.albawaba.com/news/when-iran-and-israel-were-friends-1160616.

11. "Jews in Islamic Countries: Iran," Jewish Virtual Library, accessed July 21, 2018, https://www.jewishvirtuallibrary.org/jews-of-iran#2.

12. Ethel C. Fenig, "Again, Religious Persecution in Iran," American Thinker, February 20, 2009, https://www.americanthinker.com/blog/2009/02/again_religious_persecution_in.html.

13. Joplin, "When Iran and Israel Were Friends."

14. "Mohammad Reza Shah Pahlavi," *Encyclopaedia Britannica*, July 23, 2018, https://www.britannica.com/biography/Mohammad-Reza-Shah-Pahlavi#ref279698.

15. Wikipedia, s.v. "White Revolution," last modified July 13, 2018, https://en.wikipedia.org/wiki/White_Revolution.

16. Khosrow Mostofi, Peter William Avery, and Janet Afary, "The White Revolution," *Encyclopaedia Britannica*, September 12, 2018, https://www.britannica.com/place/Iran/The-White-Revolution.

17. "The White Revolution and Its Opponents (1953–1963)," Erenow, accessed July 21, 2018, https://erenow.com/modern/iran-a-modern-history/11.php.

18. "Mohammad Reza Shah Pahlavi," *Encyclopaedia Britannica*.

19. "Mohammad Reza Shah Pahlavi," *Encyclopaedia Britannica*.

20. Jonathan C. Randal, "SAVAK Jails Stark Reminder of Shah's Rule," *Washington Post*, December 13, 1979, https://www.washingtonpost.com/archive/politics/1979/12/13/savak-jails-stark-reminder-of-shahs-rule/b2b37be2-356a-43e2-ba68-dd474e9023b0/?utm_term=.4112c8212873; Amnesty International, "Human Rights Abuses in Shahist Iran," Encyclopedia.com, November 1976, https://www.encyclopedia.com/history/legal-and-political-magazines/human-rights-abuses-shahist-iran.

21. Roya Hakakian, "How Iran Kept Its Jews," *Tablet*, December 30, 2014, https://www.tabletmag.com/jewish-news-and-politics/187519/how-iran-kept-its-jews.

22. "Jews in Islamic Countries: Iran," Jewish Virtual Library.

23. Hakakian, "How Iran Kept Its Jews."

24. Hakakian, "How Iran Kept Its Jews."

25. Orly R. Rahimiyan, "Jews of Iran: A Modern History," My Jewish Learning, accessed July 21, 2018, https://www.myjewishlearning.com/article/jews-of-iran-a-modern-history/.

26. "Jews in Islamic Countries: Iran," Jewish Virtual Library.

27. "Jews in Islamic Countries: Iran," Jewish Virtual Library.

28. "Jews in Islamic Countries: Iran," Jewish Virtual Library.

29. "Jews in Islamic Countries: Iran," Jewish Virtual Library.

30. President Barack Obama, "The Iran Deal," The White House, July 14, 2015, https://obamawhitehouse.archives.gov/blog/2015/07/14/iran-deal.

31. Jodi Rudoren, "Israel Came Close to Attacking Iran, Ex-Defense Minister Says," *New York Times*, August 21, 2015, https://www.nytimes.com/2015/08/22/world/middleeast/israel-came-close-to-attacking-iran-ex-defense-minister-says.html.

32. Herb Keinon, "PM in North: Khamenei Makes It Clear Iran Will Continue to Fund Terrorism," *Jerusalem Post*, August 19, 2015, https://www.jpost.com/Middle-East/Iran/Netanyahu-Comments-by-Iran-support-Israels-concerns-that-nuclear-deal-cash-will-fuel-terror-412457.

33. "'Israel Should Be Annihilated,' Senior Iran Aide Says," *Times of Israel*, August 25, 2015, https://www.timesofisrael.com/israel-should-be-annihilated-senior-iran-aide-says/.

34. Benjamin Netanyahu, Facebook video post, August 19, 2015, https://www.facebook.com/StandWithUs/videos/10153146895962689/.

35. Mohammad Javad Zarif, "Full Interview With Iranian Foreign Minister Mohammad Javad Zarif," interview by Ann Curry, NBC News, March 4, 2015, https://www.nbcnews.com/storyline/iran-nuclear-talks/full-interview-iranian-foreign-minister-mohammad-javad-zarif-n317516.

36. Tamar Pileggi, "Khamenei: Israel a 'Cancerous Tumor' That 'Must Be Eradicated,'" *Times of Israel*, June 4, 2018, https://www.timesofisrael.com/khamenei-israel-a-cancerous-tumor-that-must-be-eradicated/.

37. Netanyahu, *A Durable Peace*, 325.

CHAPTER 13
CATASTROPHE IN SYRIA

1. "Muslim Brotherhood," *Encyclopaedia Britannica*, September 11, 2018, https://www.britannica.com/topic/Muslim-Brotherhood; see also Jason Rodrigues, "1982: Syria's President Hafez al-Assad Crushes Rebellion in Hama," *The Guardian*, August 1, 2011, https://www.theguardian.com/theguardian/from-the-archive-blog/2011/aug/01/hama-syria-massacre-1982-archive.

2. Harriet Alexander, "John Kerry and Bashar al-Assad Dined in Damascus," *The Telegraph*, September 3, 2013, https://www.telegraph.co.uk/news/worldnews/middleeast/syria/10283045/John-Kerry-and-Bashar-al-Assad-dined-in-Damascus.html.

3. Warrick, *Black Flags*, 227–228.

4. Tracy Wilkinson and Nabih Bulos, "US Accuses Syria of Mass Executions and Burning the Bodies in a Crematorium," *Los Angeles*

Times, May 15, 2017, http://www.latimes.com/world/la-fg-syria-mass-executions-trump-20170515-story.html.

5. Wilkinson and Bulos, "US Accuses Syria of Mass Executions and Burning the Bodies in a Crematorium."

6. Nabih Bulos, "Amnesty International Accuses Syria of Hanging Thousands of Prisoners, Dumping Bodies in Mass Graves," *Los Angeles Times*, February 7, 2017, http://www.latimes.com/world/middleeast/la-fg-syria-prisons-20170207-story.html.

7. Bulos, "Amnesty International Accuses Syria of Hanging Thousands of Prisoners, Dumping Bodies in Mass Graves."

8. Priyanka Boghani, "A Staggering New Death Toll for Syria's War—470,000," PBS, February 11, 2016, https://www.pbs.org/wgbh/frontline/article/a-staggering-new-death-toll-for-syrias-war-470000/.

9. "Syrian Refugee Crisis: Facts, FAQs, and How to Help," World Vision, updated April 16, 2018, https://www.worldvision.org/refugees-news-stories/syrian-refugee-crisis-facts.

10. Ian Black, "Report on Syria Conflict Finds 11.5% of Population Killed or Injured," *The Guardian*, February 10, 2016, https://www.theguardian.com/world/2016/feb/11/report-on-syria-conflict-finds-115-of-population-killed-or-injured.

11. Rym Ghazal, "The Day That Shook Lebanon: Remembering the Killing of Hariri," The National World, February 13, 2015, https://www.thenational.ae/world/the-day-that-shook-lebanon-remembering-the-killing-of-hariri-1.68730.

12. Robert Fisk, "Rafiq Hariri Tribunal: Was the Former Lebanon PM's Assassination the Work of Syria's President Assad?," *Independent*, May 13, 2015, https://www.independent.co.uk/news/world/middle-east/rafiq-hariri-tribunal-was-the-former-lebanon-pms-assassination-the-work-of-syrias-president-assad-10245381.html.

13. Francesco Femia and Caitlin Werrell, "Syria: Climate Change, Drought and Social Unrest," The Center for Climate and Security, February 29, 2012, https://climateandsecurity.org/2012/02/29/syria-climate-change-drought-and-social-unrest/.

14. Femia and Werrell, "Syria: Climate Change, Drought and Social Unrest."

15. Louis Charbonneau, "Russia, China Veto UN Resolution Condemning Syria," Reuters, October 4, 2011, https://www.reuters.com/article/us-syria-un/russia-china-veto-u-n-resolution-condemning-syria-idUSTRE7937M220111004.

16. Richard Allen Greene, "The Free-for-All in Syria Will Make Your Head Spin," CNN News, April 11, 2018, https://www.cnn.com/2016/08/25/middleeast/syria-isis-whos-fighting-who-trnd/index.html.

17. Greene, "The Free-for-All in Syria Will Make Your Head Spin."

18. David Brunnstrom, "US Signals Open-Ended Presence in Syria, Seeks Patience on Assad's Removal," Reuters, January 17, 2018, https://www.reuters.com/article/us-mideast-crisis-syria-tillerson/u-s-signals-open-ended-presence-in-syria-seeks-patience-on-assads-removal-idUSKBN1F62R8.

19. "Israel Strikes Iranian Targets in Syria in Response to Rocket Fire," BBC News, May 10, 2018, https://www.bbc.com/news/world-middle-east-44063022.

CHAPTER 14
BETRAYAL IN EGYPT

1. Charles F. Aling, "Is the Biblical Story of Joseph Verified?," Associates for Biblical Research, accessed August 23, 2018, https://christiananswers.net/q-abr/abr-a016.html.

2. Bryant G. Wood, "The Sons of Jacob: New Evidence for the Presence of the Israelites in Egypt," Associates for Biblical Research, January 28, 2016, http://www.biblearchaeology.org/post/2016/01/28/The-Sons-of-Jacob-New-Evidence-for-the-Presence-of-the-Israelites-in-Egypt.aspx#Article.

3. Wood, "The Sons of Jacob."

4. Wood, "The Sons of Jacob," citing Manfred Bietak, *Avaris and Piramesse: Archaeological Exploration in the Eastern Nile Delta* (London: British Academy, 1996), 10.

5. Wood, "The Sons of Jacob."

6. Wood, "The Sons of Jacob," citing Bietak, *Avaris and Piramesse*, 14.

7. "Egypt Virtual Jewish History Tour," Jewish Virtual Library, accessed July 25, 2018, https://www.jewishvirtuallibrary.org/egypt-virtual-jewish-history-tour.

8. "Egypt Virtual Jewish History Tour," Jewish Virtual Library.

9. "Egypt Virtual Jewish History Tour," Jewish Virtual Library.

10. "Jews in Islamic Countries: Egypt," Jewish Virtual Library, accessed September 13, 2018, https://www.jewishvirtuallibrary.org/jews-of-egypt.

11. "Jews in Islamic Countries: Egypt," Jewish Virtual Library.

12. "Jews in Islamic Countries: Egypt," Jewish Virtual Library.

13. Matt Plen, "The Sinai Campaign," My Jewish Learning, accessed July 25, 2018, https://www.myjewishlearning.com/article/the-sinai-campaign/.

14. "Jewish Refugees from Arab Countries," Jewish Virtual Library, accessed July 25, 2018, https://www.jewishvirtuallibrary.org/jewish-refugees-from-arab-countries-2.

15. "Jews in Islamic Countries: Egypt," Jewish Virtual Library.

16. "Jews in Islamic Countries: Egypt," Jewish Virtual Library.

17. "Jews in Islamic Countries: Egypt," Jewish Virtual Library.

18. "Jews in Islamic Countries: Egypt," Jewish Virtual Library.

19. "For the First Time Since 1948, Egypt Votes for Israel at UN," Middle East Monitor, November 1, 2015, https://www.middleeastmonitor.com/20151101-for-the-first-time-since-1948-egypt-votes-for-israel-at-un/.

20. Emmanuel Parisse, "Egypt's Last Jews Aim to Keep Heritage Alive," *Times of Israel*, March 26, 2017, https://www.timesofisrael.com/egypts-last-jews-aim-to-keep-alive-heritage/.

21. "Jews in Islamic Countries: Egypt," Jewish Virtual Library.

22. "Hosni Mubarak Biography," Biography.com, April 1, 2014, https://www.biography.com/people/hosni-mubarak-37061.

23. "Egypt: Human Rights Background," Human Rights Watch, October 2001, https://www.hrw.org/legacy/backgrounder/mena/egypt-bck-1001.htm.

24. "Egyptian Revolution Cost at Least 846 Lives," CBS News, April 19, 2011, https://www.cbsnews.com/news/egyptian-revolution-cost-at-least-846-lives/.

25. "Egyptian Gov't Offers Concessions to Opposition," CBS News, February 6, 2011, https://www.cbsnews.com/news/egyptian-govt-offers-concessions-to-opposition/.

26. "Egypt's Mubarak Will Not Run for Re-Election," CBS News, February 1, 2011, https://www.cbsnews.com/news/egypts-mubarak-will-not-run-for-re-election/.

27. "Egypt Crisis: President Hosni Mubarak Resigns as Leader," BBC News, February 12, 2011, https://www.bbc.com/news/world-middle-east-12433045.

28. Global Ethics Observatory, "The Egyptian Legal System," UNESCO, accessed July 25, 2018, http://www.unesco.org/shs/ethics/geo/user/?action=Geo4Country&db=GEO4&id=9&lng=en.

29. Russell Heimlich, "Overturn Egypt-Israel Peace Agreement," Pew Research Center, May 18, 2011, http://www.pewresearch.org/fact-tank/2011/05/18/overturn-egypt-israel-peace-agreement/.

30. Ruth Sherlock, "In a Sharm el Sheikh Palace, Is Mubarak Retired or Arrested?," *National*, February 24, 2011, https://www.thenational.ae/in-a-sharm-el-sheikh-palace-is-mubarak-retired-or-arrested-1.420553.

31. Edmund Blair and Tamim Elyan, "New Brotherhood Candidate Pitched In to Egypt Race," Reuters, April 21, 2012, https://www.reuters.com/article/us-egypt-presidency-islamist-idUSBRE83K0AE20120421; Mostafa Ali, "Mohamed Morsi," Ahram Online, May 6, 2012, http://english.ahram.org.eg/NewsContent/36/124/40539/Presidential-elections-/Meet-the-candidates/Mohamed-Morsi.aspx.

32. Robert Satloff and Eric Trager, "Egypt's 9/11 Conspiracy Rhetoric," *Washington Post*, September 11, 2012, https://www.google.com/url?sa=t&rct=j&q=&esrc=s&source=web&cd=1&ved=2ahUKEwjG8vGmjr3cAhWFzlMKHcfWDBUQFjAAegQIABAB&url=https%3A%2F%2Fwww.washingtonpost.com%2Fopinions%2Fgetting-egypts-morsi-to-give-up-911-conspiracy-rhetoric%2F2012%2F09%2F11%2F4ca304ea-fb97-11e1-8adc-499661afe377_story.html&usg=AOvVaw3Q3omesglRy8t3cpLHFZ2I.

33. Ron Friedman, "Egypt's Morsi, in 2010 Interviews Posted Online, Called Zionists 'Bloodsuckers' and Descendants of Pigs, Urged to Sever All Ties With Israel," *Times of Israel*, January 4, 2013, https://www.timesofisrael.com/egypts-morsi-in-2010-statements-posted-online-called-zionists-bloodsuckers-and-descendants-of-pigs-urged-to-sever-all-ties-with-israel/.

34. Friedman, "Egypt's Morsi."

35. "Morsi: 'Zionists' Taken Out of Context," News 24 Archives, January 16, 2013, https://www.news24.com/Africa/News/Morsi-Zionists-taken-out-of-context-20130116.

36. Shaimaa Fayed, "Thousands Protest in Egypt Against Israeli Attacks on Gaza," Reuters, November 16, 2012, https://www.reuters.com/article/us-palestinians-israel-egypt/thousands-protest-in-egypt-against-israeli-attacks-on-gaza-idUSBRE8AF1D720121116.

37. Reuters, "Mohamed Morsi's Decree 'Temporary,' Presidency Says," *Huffington Post*, November 25, 2012, https://www.huffingtonpost.com/entry/mohamed-morsi-decree_n_2188065.

38. "Egypt: Who Holds the Power?," BBC News, July 3, 2013, https://www.bbc.com/news/world-middle-east-18779934.

39. Associated Press, "Egypt's Coptic Christian Pope Says Country's Constitution Is Discriminatory," Fox News, February 5, 2013, http://www.foxnews.com/world/2013/02/05/egypt-coptic-christian-pope-criticizes-country-constitution.html.

40. Basil El-Dabh, "ElBaradei: Constitution Will Go Into the 'Dustbin of History,'" *Daily News Egypt*, November 30, 2012, https://dailynewsegypt.com/2012/11/30/elbaradei-constitution-will-go-into-the-dustbin-of-history/.

41. Ibrahim Eissa, as quoted in Yasmine El Rashidi, "Egypt: The Rule of the Brotherhood," *New York Review*, February 7, 2013, https://www.nybooks.com/articles/2013/02/07/egypt-rule-brotherhood/.

42. Patrick Kingsley, "Protesters Across Egypt Call for Mohamed Morsi to Go," *The Guardian*, June 30, 2013, https://www.theguardian.com/world/2013/jun/30/mohamed-morsi-egypt-protests.

43. Kingsley, "Protesters Across Egypt Call for Mohamed Morsi to Go."

44. Kingsley, "Protesters Across Egypt Call for Mohamed Morsi to Go."

45. Kingsley, "Protesters Across Egypt Call for Mohamed Morsi to Go."

46. Kingsley, "Protesters Across Egypt Call for Mohamed Morsi to Go."

47. Reuters, "Mohamed Morsi Death Sentence Overturned," *The Guardian*, November 15, 2016, https://www.theguardian.com/world/2016/nov/15/mohamed-morsi-death-sentence-overturned.

48. Peter Hessler, "Egypt's Failed Revolution," *New Yorker*, January 2, 2017, https://www.newyorker.com/magazine/2017/01/02/egypts-failed-revolution.

49. Ro Yeger, "Poll Shows Egyptians View Israel as Most Hostile State," *Jerusalem Post*, September 29, 2015, https://www.jpost.com/Arab-Israeli-Conflict/Poll-shows-Egyptians-view-Israel-as-most-hostile-state-419403.

50. "Netanyahu Praises Sisi's Call to Expand Egypt-Israel Peace to Other Arab States," *Jerusalem Post*, September 27, 2015, https://www.jpost.com/Arab-Israeli-Conflict/Netanyahu-praises-Sisis-call-to-expand-Egypt-Israel-peace-to-other-Arab-states-419242.

51. Yeger, "Poll Shows Egyptians View Israel as Most Hostile State."

52. Wikipedia, s.v. "List of Arab Countries by Population," last modified July 1, 2018, https://en.wikipedia.org/wiki/List_of_Arab_countries_by_population.

53. "World's Muslim Population," ThoughtCo, June 18, 2017, https://www.thoughtco.com/worlds-muslim-population-2004480.

54. Wikipedia, "List of Arab Countries by Population."

55. Dominic Dudley, "The 10 Strongest Military Forces in the Middle East," *Forbes*, February 26, 2018, https://www.forbes.com/sites/dominicdudley/2018/02/26/ten-strongest-military-forces-middle-east/#5f4583b816a2. Iran and Turkey also have large militaries, but they are not part of the Arab world; see "Is Iran an Arab Country?," *Slate*,

October 3, 2001, http://www.slate.com/articles/news_and_politics/explainer/2001/10/is_iran_an_arab_country.html.

56. Raphael Ahren and Alexander Fulbright, "Netanyahu Meets With Egypt's Sissi in First Public Talks," *Times of Israel*, September 19, 2017, https://www.timesofisrael.com/netanyahu-meets-with-egypts-sissi-in-first-public-talks/.

57. Ahren and Fulbright, "Netanyahu Meets With Egypt's Sissi in First Public Talks."

58. Khalil al-Anani, "What Happened to Egypt's Muslim Brotherhood?," Al Jazeera, February 15, 2017, https://www.aljazeera.com/indepth/opinion/2017/02/happened-egypt-muslim-brotherhood-170212130839987.html.

59. Abeer Aloush, "Should Washington Accept the Rise of Political Islam in Egypt?," *Globe Post*, June 27, 2018, https://theglobepost.com/2018/06/24/muslim-brotherhood-egypt-us/.

60. Ewelina U. Ochab, "Persecution of Christians in Egypt," *Forbes*, April 10, 2017, https://www.forbes.com/sites/ewelinaochab/2017/04/10/persecution-of-christians-in-egypt/#7edfa3c115ea.

61. Ochab, "Persecution of Christians in Egypt."

62. Ochab, "Persecution of Christians in Egypt."

63. Ochab, "Persecution of Christians in Egypt."

64. Ochab, "Persecution of Christians in Egypt."

CHAPTER 15
JORDAN: FRIEND OR FOE?

1. "Israel to Build Smart Fence on Jordan Border," *Times of Israel*, September 6, 2015, https://www.timesofisrael.com/israel-to-build-smart-fence-on-jordan-border/.

2. "Thousands Protest in Jordan," Al Jazeera, January 28, 2011, https://www.aljazeera.com/news/middleeast/2011/01/2011128125157509196.html.

3. David Rohde, "The Arab Spring Is Just Getting Started," Reuters, July 19, 2013, http://blogs.reuters.com/david-rohde/2013/07/19/the-arab-spring-is-just-getting-started/.

4. Ben Brumfield and Arwa Damon, "Jordanian Protesters Make Rare Move: Speak Out Against King Abdullah," CNN, November 15, 2012, https://www.cnn.com/2012/11/14/world/meast/jordan-gas-prices/index.html.

5. H. Valrulkar, "Reform in Jordan: Comprehensive Change or Nominal Amendments?," MEMRI, July 22, 2011, https://www.cnn.com/2012/11/14/world/meast/jordan-gas-prices/index.html.

6. "Jordan Country Reclassification: Questions and Answers," World Bank, July 6, 2017, https://www.worldbank.org/en/country/jordan/brief/qa-jordan-country-reclassification.

7. "Culture and Religion," Embassy of the Hashemite Kingdom of Jordan, Washington, DC, accessed July 26, 2018, http://www.jordanembassyus.org/page/culture-and-religion.

8. "Culture and Religion," Embassy of the Hashemite Kingdom of Jordan, Washington, DC. Reported figures vary; the Jordanian government cites a 6 percent Christian population.

9. "The country was a center of refuge for Christians who fled persecution in Jerusalem and Rome during the first century AD." "WWL 2018: Church History and Facts—Jordan," PDF, accessed July 26, 2018, https://tinyurl.com/y7h6yqnbE.

10. "Jordan, Egypt Have 'Special' Relationship With Israel, Says Jordanian King," *Times of Israel*, April 11, 2017, https://www.timesofisrael.com/jordan-egypt-have-special-relationship-with-israel-says-jordanian-king/.

11. Lally Weymouth, "King Abdullah: Compromise With Russia on Crimea to Get Its Help in Syria," *Washington Post*, April 6, 2017, https://www.washingtonpost.com/opinions/king-abdullah-compromise-with-russia-on-crimea-to-get-its-help-in-syria/2017/04/06/b985b894-1a61-11e7-bcc2-7d1a0973e7b2_story.html.

12. "42nd Descendant of the Prophet (PBUH)," His Royal Highness Crown Prince Al Hussein Bin Abdullah II, accessed November 6, 2018, http://www.alhussein.jo/en/family-tree.

13. "42nd Descendant of the Prophet (PBUH)," His Royal Highness Crown Prince Al Hussein Bin Abdullah II; "Introduction," KingHussein.gov, accessed July 26, 2018, http://www.kinghussein.gov.jo/hash_intro.html.

14. "Introduction," KingHussein.gov; see also Charles Bybelezer, "The Jekyll and Hyde Israeli-Jordan Relationship," *Jerusalem Post*, June 19, 2008, https://www.jpost.com/Arab-Israeli-Conflict/The-Jekyll-and-Hyde-Israel-Jordan-Relationship-560355.

15. Benjamin Pogrund, "The Balfour Declaration Promised Lebanon and Jordan to the Jews, Too," *Haaretz*, October 25, 2017, https://www.haaretz.com/opinion/.premium-balfour-promised-lebanon-and-jordan-to-the-jews-too-1.5460342.

16. "Expulsion of Jews From Jordan," Jewish Virtual Library, accessed July 26, 2018, https://www.jewishvirtuallibrary.org/expulsion-of-jews-from-jordan.

17. Helen Chapin Metz, ed., *Jordan: A Country Study* (Washington: GPO for the Library of Congress, 1989), chap. "Ottoman Rule," http://countrystudies.us/jordan/6.htm.

18. Roger Spooner, "The McMahon Promise to Hussein," Balfour Project, January 26, 2015, http://www.balfourproject.org/the-mcmahon-promise/.

19. Firas Alkhateeb, "The Arab Revolt of World War One," Lost Islamic History, August 4, 2014, http://lostislamichistory.com/the-arab-revolt-of-world-war-one/.

20. "Sykes-Picot Agreement," *Encyclopaedia Britannica*, May 31, 2016, https://www.britannica.com/event/Sykes-Picot-Agreement.

21. "Sykes-Picot Agreement," *Encyclopaedia Britannica*.

22. David A. Graham, "How Did the 'Secret' Sykes-Picot Agreement Become Public?," *The Atlantic*, May 16, 2016, https://www.theatlantic.com/international/archive/2016/05/sykes-picot-centennial/482904/.

23. Aaron S. Klieman, *Foundations of British Policy in the Arab World: The Cairo Conference of 1921* (Baltimore: Johns Hopkins, 1970), 228–234; "Transjordan: Initial Contacts With the British," British Empire, accessed July 27, 2018, https://www.britishempire.co.uk/maproom/transjordan.htm.

24. Richard Meinertzhagen, *Middle East Diary, 1917–1956* (London: Thomas Yoseloff, 1960), 99–100.

25. Meinertzhagen, *Middle East Diary, 1917–1956*, 99–100.

26. Arnold as quoted in William B. Ziff, *The Rape of Palestine* (Eastford, CT: Martino Fine Books, 2010), 79.

27. "Irgun Zvai Leumi: Jewish Right-Wing Underground Movement," *Encyclopaedia Britannica*, March 2, 2012, https://www.britannica.com/topic/Irgun-Zvai-Leumi; "Stern Gang: Zionist Extremist Organization," *Encyclopaedia Britannica*, March 1, 2017, https://www.britannica.com/topic/Stern-Gang.

28. "Irgun Tz'va'i Le'umi (Etzel): Background and Overview (1931–1948)," Jewish Virtual Library, accessed August 28, 2018, https://www.jewishvirtuallibrary.org/background-and-overview-of-the-irgun-etzel.

29. "Haganah: Zionist Military Organization," *Encyclopaedia Britannica*, July 18, 2016, https://www.britannica.com/topic/Haganah.

30. "The Irgun: The Bombing of the King David Hotel (July 22 1946)," Jewish Virtual Library, accessed July 27, 2018, https://www.jewishvirtuallibrary. org/bombing-of-the-king-david-hotel.

31. "Stern Gang," *Encyclopaedia Britannica*.

32. Sasson Safor, *Zionism and the Foundations of Israeli Diplomacy* (Cambridge, UK; Cambridge University Press, 2007), 253–254.

33. "British White Paper Restricts Jewish Immigration and Land Purchase," Center for Israel Education, accessed July 27, 2018, https://israeled.org/ white-paper/.

34. "The Yishuv's Response to Hitler and the British," My Jewish Learning, accessed July 27, 2018, https://www.myjewishlearning.com/article/the-yishuv-responds/.

35. Benjamin Netanyahu, *A Place Among the Nations: Israel and the World* (New York: Bantam Books, 1993), 69.

36. Abram L. Sachar, *The Redemption of the Unwanted: From the Liberation of the Death Camps to the Founding of Israel* (New York: St. Martin's Press, 1983), 231.

37. "Stateless Again: Palestinian-Origin Jordanians Deprived of Their Nationality," Human Rights Watch, February 1, 2010, https://www.hrw. org/report/2010/02/01/stateless-again/palestinian-origin-jordanians-deprived-their-nationality.

38. Netanyahu, *A Place Among the Nations*, 343.

39. Netanyahu, *A Place Among the Nations*, 344.

CHAPTER 16
UPHEAVAL IN TURKEY

1. Aria Bendix, "Turkey Dismisses Thousands of Police, Civil Servants, and Academics," *The Atlantic*, July 14, 2017, https://www.theatlantic. com/news/archive/2017/07/turkey-dismisses-thousands-of-police-civil-servants-and-academics/533754/.

2. "Turkey: Government Targeting Academics," Human Rights Watch, May 14, 2018, https://www.hrw.org/news/2018/05/14/turkey-government-targeting-academics.

3. Daren Butler and Tuvan Gumrukcu, "Defiant Erdogan Attacks EU, Backs Restoring Death Penalty," Reuters, July 16, 2017, https://www. reuters.com/article/us-turkey-security-anniversary-idUSKBN1A10E7.

4. Amy LaPorte, Ivan Watson, and Gul Tuysuz, "Who Is Fethullah Gulen, the Man Blamed for Coup Attempt in Turkey?," CNN, July 16, 2016, https://www.cnn.com/2016/07/16/middleeast/fethullah-gulen-profile/

index.html; Fabio Vicini, "Fethullah Gülen's Educational Philosophy," Gulen Movement, accessed July 27, 2018, http://www.gulenmovement. com/fethullah-gulens-educational-philosophy.html.

5. La Porte, Watson, and Tuysuz, "Who is Fethullah Gulen, the Man Blamed for Coup Attempt in Turkey?"

6. Jillian D'Amours, "Analysis: Dissecting Turkey's Gulen-Erdogan Relationship," Middle East Eye, July 25, 2016, http://www. middleeasteye.net/news/analysis-dissecting-turkeys-gulen-erdogan-relationship-528239159.

7. Jack Moore, "Turkey's Recep Tayyip Erdogan 'Disillusioned' With Barack Obama Over Syria and Gulen," *Newsweek*, November 21, 2016, https://www.newsweek.com/erdogan-says-he-disillusioned-obama-over-syria-and-gulen-523218.

8. Mark Landler, "Obama Denies US Involvement in Coup Attempt in Turkey," *New York Times*, July 22, 2016, https://www.nytimes. com/2016/07/23/us/politics/obama-denies-us-coup-turkey.html.

9. "Turkey's Most Wanted Man," Euronews, May 8, 2016, http://www. euronews.com/2016/08/05/turkey-s-most-wanted-man.

10. David L. Phillips, "Was Turkey's Coup for Real?," *Huffington Post*, July 17, 2017, https://www.huffingtonpost.com/entry/was-turkeys-coup-for-real_us_596cbc9ee4b06a2c8edb4815.

11. Phillips, "Was Turkey's Coup for Real?" This report suggests that bombs were not necessarily dropped from the air but exploded from within the structures.

12. Maayan Jaffe-Hoffman, "Fethullah Gülen and the Jews: A Different Angle," *Jerusalem Post*, July 10, 2016, https://www.jpost.com/Opinion/Fethullah-G%C3%BClen-and-the-Jews-A-different-angle-459953.

13. Henri Barkey, "One Year Later, the Turkish Coup Attempt Remains Shrouded in Mystery," *Washington Post*, July 14, 2017, https://www. washingtonpost.com/news/democracy-post/wp/2017/07/14/one-year-later-the-turkish-coup-attempt-remains-shrouded-in-mystery/.

14. Barkey, "One Year Later, the Turkish Coup Attempt Remains Shrouded in Mystery."

15. Stanley Weiss, "It's Time to Kick Erdogan's Turkey Out of NATO," *Huffington Post*, February 23, 2016, https://www.huffingtonpost.com/stanley-weiss/its-time-to-kick-erdogans_b_9300670.html.

16. Weiss, "It's Time to Kick Erdogan's Turkey Out of NATO."

17. Weiss, "It's Time to Kick Erdogan's Turkey Out of NATO."

18. Weiss, "It's Time to Kick Erdogan's Turkey Out of NATO."

19. Weiss, "It's Time to Kick Erdogan's Turkey Out of NATO." All the bullet points listed are from Weiss' article.

20. Keren Setton, "News Analysis: Rocky Israel-Turkey Ties Hit New Low, but Full-Blown Crisis Could Be Prevented," China-Europe, May 17, 2018, http://www.xinhuanet.com/english/2018-05/17/c_137186839.htm.

21. "Water in Israel: Israel-Turkey Water Cooperation," Jewish Virtual Library, updated July 2015, https://jewishvirtuallibrary.org/israel-turkey-water-cooperation.

22. Umut Uzer, "Turkish-Israeli Relations: Their Rise and Fall," *Middle East Policy Council* 20, no. 1 (Spring 2013), https://www.mepc.org/turkish-israeli-relations-their-rise-and-fall.

23. Jonathan Gorvett, "Turkey's Outreach Hints at Ottoman Revival," *Asia Times*, February 18, 2018, http://www.atimes.com/article/hold-sunday-put-check-turkey-reaches/.

24. "Israel to Erdogan: The Days of the Ottoman Empire Are Over," Turkish Minute, July 26, 2017, https://www.turkishminute.com/2017/07/26/israel-to-erdogan-the-days-of-the-ottoman-empire-are-over/.

25. Lizzie Dearden, "Turkish President Erdogan: 'I Can't Say If Israel or Hitler Is More Barbarous,'" *Independent*, November 22, 2016, https://www.independent.co.uk/news/world/middle-east/erdogan-turkish-president-israel-hitler-more-barbarous-gaza-interview-palestinians-decide-holocaust-a7431311.html.

26. Mark Lowen, "Turkey's Declining Christian Population," BBC News, November 28, 2014, https://www.bbc.com/news/av/world-europe-30241181/turkey-s-declining-christian-population.

27. Anne-Christine Hoff, "Turkey Turns on Its Christians," *Middle East Quarterly* 25, no. 3 (June 1, 2018), accessed July 27, 2018, https://www.meforum.org/articles/2018/turkey-turns-on-its-christians.

28. Aykan Erdemir, "Catholic Church in Turkey Attacked—Again," *The Globalist*, March 11, 2018, https://www.theglobalist.com/turkey-religious-minorities-christians-hate-crimes/; Robert Jones, "Turkey's Tradition of Murdering Christians," Gatestone Institute, July 31, 2016, https://www.gatestoneinstitute.org/8577/turkey-christians-murders.

29. Nick Gutteridge, "Islamist Turkey Seizes ALL Christian Churches in City and Declares Them 'State Property,'" *Express*, April 22, 2016, https://www.express.co.uk/news/world/663089/Islamist-Turkey-Erdogan-seize-Christian-churches-Diyarbakir-persecution-state-property.

30. Gutteridge, "Islamist Turkey Seizes ALL Christian Churches in City and Declares Them 'State Property.'"

31. Gutteridge, "Islamist Turkey Seizes ALL Christian Churches in City and Declares Them 'State Property.'"
32. Tom O'Connor, "Turkey Tries to Scare Voters With Warning About Jews Ahead of Kurdish Referendum," *Newsweek*, September 15, 2017, https://www.newsweek.com/turkey-fake-news-jews-promote-hate-kurds-iraq-666130.
33. O'Connor, "Turkey Tries to Scare Voters With Warning About Jews Ahead of Kurdish Referendum."
34. O'Connor, "Turkey Tries to Scare Voters With Warning About Jews Ahead of Kurdish Referendum."
35. Gabriele Barbati, "25 Years After Worst Chemical-Weapon Massacre in History, Saddam Hussein's Attack on Halabja in Iraq, the City Is Reborn," *International Business Times*, March 15, 2013, https://www.ibtimes.com/25-years-after-worst-chemical-weapon-massacre-history-saddam-husseins-attack-halabja-iraq-city.
36. "The History of Kurdistan: Why Britain Owes a Debt to the Kurdish People," *The Telegraph*, September 21, 2017, https://www.telegraph.co.uk/news/world/kurdistan-independence-referendum/history-of-britain-and-the-kurdish-people/.
37. Mitchell, *ISIS, Iran and Israel*, 49–50.
38. "Mavi Marmara: Why Did Israel Stop the Gaza Flotilla?," BBC News, June 27, 2016, https://www.bbc.com/news/10203726.
39. "Mavi Marmara," BBC News.
40. Wikipedia, s.v. "Gaza Flotilla Raid," updated October 4, 2018, 05:23, https://en.wikipedia.org/wiki/Gaza_flotilla_raid.
41. Patrick Keddie, "Remembering the Mavi Marmara Victims," Al Jazeera, July 21, 2016, https://www.aljazeera.com/news/2016/06/remembering-mavi-marmara-victims-160630105303709.html.
42. Keddie, "Remembering the Mavi Marmara Victims."
43. Barak Ravid, "Turkey PM Erdogan: World Must Punish Israel for Its 'Massacre' on Gaza Aid Flotilla," *Haaretz*, June 1, 2010, https://www.haaretz.com/1.5127988.
44. Julian Borger and Constanze Letsch, "Turkey Expels Israel's Ambassador Over Refusal to Apologise for Gaza Flotilla Raid," *The Guardian*, September 2, 2011, https://www.theguardian.com/world/2011/sep/02/turkey-israel-ambassador-mavi-marmara.
45. Herb Keinon, "Netanyahu Apologizes to Turkey Over Gaza Flotilla," *Jerusalem Post*, March 22, 2013, https://www.jpost.com/International/Obama-Netanyahu-Erdogan-speak-by-phone-307423.

46. Marc Pitzke, "The Lone Survivor of the 'Struma,'" *Spiegel Online*, May 23, 2013, http://www.spiegel.de/international/world/interview-with-lone-survivor-of-torpedoed-jewish-refugee-ship-struma-a-901490-2.html.

47. "Immigration to Israel: 'Struma' Illegal Immigration Ship (December 1941–February 1942)," Jewish Virtual Library, accessed August 23, 2018, https://www.jewishvirtuallibrary.org/quot-struma-quot-illegal-immigration-ship.

48. "Romania," *Holocaust Encyclopedia*, United States Holocaust Memorial Museum, accessed July 28, 2018, https://www.ushmm.org/wlc/en/article.php?ModuleId=10005472.

49. Jennifer Rosenberg, "The Struma," Thought Co, updated February 5, 2018, https://www.thoughtco.com/jewish-refugees-ship-struma-1779679; see also Peters, *From Time Immemorial*, 369.

50. Pitzke, "The Lone Survivor of the 'Struma.'"

51. Peters, *From Time Immemorial*, 369.

52. Peters, *From Time Immemorial*, 368–369.

53. Peters, *From Time Immemorial*, 368.

54. Peters, *From Time Immemorial*, 368.

55. Peters, *From Time Immemorial*, 368.

56. Rosenberg, "The Struma"; see also Peters, *From Time Immemorial*, 368–370.

57. Peters, *From Time Immemorial*, 370.

58. "Turkey," World Jewish Congress, accessed July 28, 2018, http://www.worldjewishcongress.org/en/about/communities/TR.

59. "Turkey," Jewish Virtual Library, accessed August 23, 2018, https://www.jewishvirtuallibrary.org/turkey.

60. "Turkish Historical Jewish Community," Geni, accessed July 28, 2018, https://www.geni.com/projects/Turkish-Historical-Jewish-Community/18613.

61. "Turkey," World Jewish Congress.

62. "Turkish Historical Jewish Community," Geni.

63. "Turkey," World Jewish Congress.

64. "Cave Church of St. Peter, Antioch," Sacred Destinations, accessed July 28, 2018, http://www.sacred-destinations.com/turkey/antioch-cave-church-of-peter.

CHAPTER 17
RUSSIA'S PLANS FOR THE MIDDLE EAST

1. "Pogroms," History.com, January 25, 2018, https://www.history.com/topics/pogroms.
2. Sion, "Protocols of the Elders of Zion."
3. Oleg Yegorov, "Why Did the USSR Help to Create Israel, but Then Became Its Foe," *Russia Beyond*, December 15, 2017, https://www.rbth.com/history/327040-ussr-and-israel-from-friends-to-foes.
4. Alan Taylor, "The Soviet War in Afghanistan, 1979–1989," *The Atlantic*, August 4, 2014, https://www.theatlantic.com/photo/2014/08/the-soviet-war-in-afghanistan-1979-1989/100786/; Bill Keller, "Home From Afghanistan; Russia's Divisive War," *New York Times*, February 14, 1988, https://www.nytimes.com/1988/02/.../home-from-afghanistan-russia-s-divisive-war.html.
5. Noor Ahmad Khalidi, "Afghanistan: Demographic Consequences of War, 1978–1987," *Central Asian Survey* 10, no. 3 (1991): 101, https://www.tandfonline.com/doi/abs/10.1080/02634939108400750.
6. Natasha Bertrand, "An 'Infantile Argument': Experts Pour Cold Water on Russia's 'Fanciful' Explanation for Syrian Gas Attack," *Business Insider*, April 5, 2017, https://www.businessinsider.com/russia-explanation-for-syria-chemical-weapons-attack-2017-4.
7. Bertrand, "An 'Infantile Argument.'"
8. Bertrand, "An 'Infantile Argument.'"
9. Jeremy Herb, "US Intelligence Report: 1,400 Killed in Syria Chemical Attack," *Hill*, August 30, 2013, http://thehill.com/policy/defense/319667-us-intelligence-report-1400-killed-in-syria-chemical-attack.
10. Bertrand, "An 'Infantile Argument.'"
11. John F. Walvoord, "10. The King of the North," Bible.org, January 1, 2008, https://bible.org/seriespage/10-king-north.
12. "Where Are We on the End Times Timetable?" CBN News, January 1, 2016, http://www1.cbn.com/cbnnews/insideisrael/2015/November/Where-Are-We-on-the-End-Times-Timetable, as quoted in Mitchell, *ISIS, Iran and Israel*, 168–169.

CHAPTER 18
RECOGNITION AT LAST

1. Olivia B. Waxman, "The 1995 Law Behind President Trump's Plan to Move the US Embassy in Israel to Jerusalem," *Time*, December 5, 2017, http://time.com/5049019/jerusalem-embassy-history/.

2. Colin Dwyer and Scott Neuman, "How the World Is Reacting to Trump Recognizing Jerusalem as Israel's Capital," NPR, December 6, 2017, https://www.npr.org/sections/thetwo-way/2017/12/06/568748383/how-is-the-world-reacting-to-u-s-plan-to-recognize-jerusalem-as-israeli-capital.

3. Dwyer and Neuman, "How the World Is Reacting to Trump Recognizing Jerusalem as Israel's Capital."

4. Dwyer and Neuman, "How the World Is Reacting to Trump Recognizing Jerusalem as Israel's Capital."

5. Oren Dorell and Kim Hjelmgaard, "Palestinian Leader: Trump's Jerusalem Decision a 'Withdrawal' of Peace Process," *USA Today*, December 6, 2017, https://www.usatoday.com/story/news/world/2017/12/06/trumps-jerusalem-decision-alarms-world-leaders/926109001/.

6. Dorell and Hjelmgaard, "Palestinian Leader: Trump's Jerusalem Decision a 'Withdrawal' of Peace Process."

7. Dwyer and Neuman, "How the World Is Reacting to Trump Recognizing Jerusalem as Israel's Capital."

8. Dwyer and Neuman, "How the World Is Reacting to Trump Recognizing Jerusalem as Israel's Capital."

9. "World Reacts to US Israel Embassy Relocation Plan," Al Jazeera, December 6, 2017, https://www.aljazeera.com/news/2017/12/world-reacts-israel-embassy-relocation-plan-171205175133734.html.

10. "World Reacts to US Israel Embassy Relocation Plan," Al Jazeera.

11. "Full Text: US Vice President Mike Pence's Speech at Israel's Knesset," *Haaretz*, January 22, 2018, https://www.haaretz.com/israel-news/full-text-u-s-vice-president-mike-pence-s-speech-at-the-knesset-1.5751264.

12. "S.1322—Jerusalem Embassy Act of 1995," Congress.gov, accessed July 28, 2018, https://www.congress.gov/bill/104th-congress/senate-bill/1322/all-actions?overview=closed&q=%7B%22roll-call-vote%22%3A%22all%22%7D.

13. William Safire, "Essay; Move the Embassy," *New York Times*, July 1, 1996, https://www.nytimes.com/1996/07/01/opinion/essay-move-the-embassy.html.

14. Safire, "Essay; Move the Embassy."

15. Eli Kavon, "The Balfour Betrayal: How the British Empire Failed Zionism," *Jerusalem Post*, November 2, 2013, https://www.jpost.com/Opinion/Op-Ed-Contributors/The-Balfour-betrayal-How-the-British-Empire-failed-Zionism-330440.

16. John Kifner, "Hussein Surrenders Claims on West Bank to the PLO; US Peace Plan in Jeopardy; Internal Tensions," *New York Times*, August 1, 1988, https://www.nytimes.com/1988/08/01/world/hussein-surrenders-claims-west-bank-plo-us-peace-plan-jeopardy-internal-tensions.html; see also Wikipedia, s.v. "Jordanian Annexation of the West Bank," last modified August 3, 2018, https://en.wikipedia.org/wiki/Jordanian_annexation_of_the_West_Bank.

17. "Paraguay Becomes 6th Nation to Say It Will Move Israeli Embassy to Jerusalem," Missions Box, May 3, 2018, https://missionsbox.org/news/paraguay-becomes-6th-nation-to-say-it-will-move-israeli-embassy-to-jerusalem/.

18. Eric H. Cline, *Jerusalem Besieged: From Ancient Canaan to Modern Israel* (Ann Arbor, MI: University of Michigan Press, 2005), 2.

19. "December 1, 1947: The Grand Mufti of Jerusalem," Center for Online Judaic Studies, accessed July 28, 2018, http://cojs.org/december-1-1947-grand-mufti-jerusalem/.

20. "Israeli War of Independence: The Battle for Jerusalem (1947–1948)," Jewish Virtual Library, accessed August 23, 2018, https://www.jewishvirtuallibrary.org/the-battle-for-jerusalem-1947-1948.

21. "Demographics of Israel: Population of Jerusalem (1844–Present)," Jewish Virtual Library, accessed July 28, 2018, https://www.jewishvirtuallibrary.org/population-of-jerusalem-1844-2009.

22. "Demographics of Israel: Population of Jerusalem (1844–Present)," Jewish Virtual Library.

23. Dennis Prager, "Those Who Curse the Jews and Those Who Bless Them," *Dennis Prager Show*, July 31, 2002, http://www.dennisprager.com/those-who-curse-the-jews-and-those-who-bless-them/.

24. Koenig, *Eye to Eye.*

25. Koenig, *Eye to Eye*, 78–79.

26. Koenig, *Eye to Eye*, 79–80.

27. Koenig, *Eye to Eye*, 87–89.

28. Koenig, *Eye to Eye*, 110–111.

29. Koenig, *Eye to Eye*, 116–117.

30. Koenig, *Eye to Eye*, 202.

CHAPTER 19
WHERE DO WE GO FROM HERE?

1. Bill Federer, "Edmund Burke Born January 12, 1729," January 12, 2015, http://selfeducatedamerican.com/2015/01/12/edmund-burke-born-january-12-1729/.

2. Mr. Lincoln may have said these words in the Illinois legislature. "Abraham Lincoln Quotes," Goodreads, accessed November 6, 2018, https://www.goodreads.com/quotes/4870-my-concern-is-not-whether-god-is-on-our-side.

ABOUT THE AUTHOR

JONATHAN BERNIS IS a Jewish Believer in Jesus who has been a leader in Messianic Jewish ministry for more than thirty years. He serves as president and CEO of Jewish Voice Ministries International (JVMI).

JVMI exists to transform lives and see all Israel saved. Their mission is to proclaim the gospel, grow the Messianic Jewish community, and engage the church concerning Israel and the Jewish people.

Jonathan hosts JVMI's syndicated television program, *Jewish Voice with Jonathan Bernis*, which airs on Christian networks and by satellite throughout the world. It is available via live streaming on the internet.

JVMI conducts humanitarian/medical outreaches to some of the most impoverished Jewish communities on earth, including regular outreaches in Ethiopia, Zimbabwe, and other points of need. The ministry's outreaches also include large-scale international festivals of Jewish music and dance in major cities of the world with large Jewish populations.

In addition to its Phoenix headquarters, JVMI has an office in Jerusalem, where JVMI staff work with sixty ministry partners throughout Israel.

Jonathan is the author of several books, including *Unlocking the Prophetic Mysteries of Israel* and his best-selling Rabbi series (*A Rabbi Looks at the Afterlife*, *A Rabbi Looks at the Last Days*, *A Rabbi Looks at Jesus of Nazareth*, and more). Jonathan and his wife, Elisangela, live in Phoenix with their two daughters.